THEY CALL ME
SUPERMENSCH

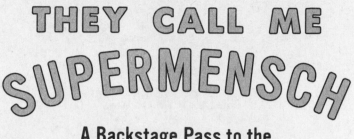

THEY CALL ME SUPERMENSCH

A Backstage Pass to the Amazing Worlds of Film, Food, and Rock 'n' Roll

SHEP GORDON

AN ANTHONY BOURDAIN BOOK

ecco

HarperCollins books may be purchased for educational,
business, or sales promotional use. For information, please e-mail the
Special Markets Department at SPsales@harpercollins.com.

A hardcover edition of this book was published in 2016 by Ecco,
an imprint of HarperCollins Publishers.

FIRST ECCO PAPERBACK EDITION PUBLISHED 2017.

Designed by Ashley Tucker

Library of Congress Cataloging-in-Publication Data has been applied for.

ISBN 978-0-06-235596-6

17 18 19 20 21   OV/LSC   10 9 8 7 6 5 4 3 2 1

THEY CALL ME SUPERMENSCH

May the poor find wealth
Those weak with sorrow find joy.
May the forlorn find new hope,
Constant happiness and prosperity.

May the frightened cease to be afraid,
And those bound be free.
May the weak find power
And may their hearts join in friendship.

—*His Holiness the Dalai Lama*

INTRODUCTION

ONE NIGHT IN 1968 I WAS DRIVING IN LOS ANGELES, looking for a place to stay, after just quitting the job that had brought me from New York to California. I saw a hotel vacancy sign, pulled into the semicircular driveway, and parked. The Landmark Motor Hotel at 7047 Franklin Avenue was built in the 1950s and looked it. Very Southern California Modern—a long strip of concrete, steel, and glass, with two tiers of rooms whose doors opened out onto balconies. Palm trees and typical L.A. shrubbery stood around it.

I went up three or four steps and through the glass doors of the lobby. From the lobby I could see into the central courtyard and the swimming pool, with more rooms surrounding it. The man behind the desk was small, slender, well manicured, with a thin mustache. He looked like a character actor from a James Cagney movie—which it turned out he had been. His name was Charles Latour, but I'd learn that no one ever used his first name. Everyone addressed him as Mr. Latour. He and Mrs. Latour were the managers. He was very nice and gave me a good rate on the only unit available, a two-bedroom suite, number 224. I didn't have a bank account, just the cash in my pocket, but that was enough to get me the room for three or four weeks.

Mr. Latour walked me into the courtyard, around the pool, and up to the second-floor balcony. Number 224 was a corner unit. The living room had a sofa and a couple of chairs in that fifties plastic style that was never comfortable. You always felt you were going to slide off them onto the floor. Past that was a dining table and chairs, and a small kitchen. Bedrooms were left and right, with a bathroom in the middle.

I settled into the place and took a hit of acid. On one hand I was really scared to be in Los Angeles. I was in my early twenties and a continent away from my family and friends. The job I had headed to California for had ended in less than a day. I had enough money to survive for maybe a month, and no prospects beyond that. My mother had always accused me of being irresponsible. I seemed to be proving her right.

On the other hand, I was ecstatic. I was on my own in Hollywood, California, high as a kite on acid. For the first time in my life I had nobody to tell me what to do. I was simultaneously scared to death and thinking, Wow, man, look at you!

Around midnight I stepped out onto the balcony. The courtyard was hazy with that kind of misty fog that rolls into L.A. some nights, and lit from inside by the blue pool lights. I was standing there, awash in my confusion of fear and elation, when from somewhere in that blue haze, down by the pool, I heard a girl scream. I could barely make out some figures down there. For some reason, whenever someone is in trouble, in any way, my instinct is always to be the guy on the white horse who saves them. I hurried down the stairs and into the haze. Ahead of me vague figures tumbled around beside the pool near the diving board. My brain went right to rape. I'm not sure why. Rape had never been any part of my life.

I said something like, "Hey, man, you can't do that," and went to separate them.

That's when the girl punched me in the mouth.

"We're fucking," she said. "Would you please leave us alone?"

Boy was I embarrassed. I made a hasty retreat back up to my room, feeling much more like a schmuck than a hero. The ecstatic side of my mood vanished, and it took a while to get to sleep.

The next afternoon I woke up to a beautiful day of Southern California sunshine. I went down to the pool, where some young people my age were lounging around in the shade. The girl among them asked, "Are you the guy who interrupted us last night?" She told everyone the story and they all started laughing.

Then she introduced herself. She was Janis Joplin. Lounging on pool chairs around her were Jimi Hendrix; Lester and Willie Chambers of the Chambers Brothers, who had the hit song "Time Has Come Today"; Bobby Neuwirth, Bob Dylan's road manager; and Paul Rothchild of Elektra Records, who produced albums by Janis, the Doors, and others.

Completely by chance, without knowing a thing about it, I had put myself in the hotel where a lot of music people stayed when they came to L.A. I had no idea at that moment, but the rest of my life had just begun.

||||||||||||||||||

In January 2012, it ended.

Twice.

I was on an operating table at the time, unaware of the drama as I flatlined twice and the doctors revived me. I didn't know about my deaths until I woke up in a hospital bed a couple of days later, feeling really peaceful and at ease. When they told me, it occurred to me that if I hadn't woken up, I would be okay with that.

Now, I was on intravenous painkillers, which I'm sure contributed to my blissful state. Still, I have never forgotten that feeling, like death was really easy. It wasn't that I wanted to die. I wasn't suicidal. But if I had died, I could accept that. I was sixty-six years old. I had lived a relatively long and very successful life, with many incredible adventures since that night I stumbled on the Landmark. I had gotten to know and be friends with a lot of amazing people. I had cooked for the Dalai Lama! I got to experience love! I considered myself very, very lucky. If it had all ended while I was blissfully unaware, so be it.

I couldn't hold on to that sense of peace forever, though. In fact, by the next day I was beginning to feel pretty low and sorry for myself. I had almost died! I was alone in a blank white hospital room, with no wife and family around me. And it was Friday the thirteenth. I could look out the window at beautiful trees, but I couldn't touch them, and didn't know if I ever would again.

The phone rang. It was Mike Myers.

"Ready to say yes now?"

He was referring to the documentary he wanted to make about me, an idea I had been resisting for years by then. I was touched and flattered that he thought anyone would want to watch a movie about a guy they probably had never heard of. I mean, a lot of people in show business knew who I was. I probably have more celebrity friends than most of my celebrity friends. Guess I'm part groupie. But I had never sought fame and celebrity for myself. My job as a manager had always been to make other people famous. My own satisfaction came from being very good at that, and from helping my clients get what they wanted. When the band Alice Cooper, my very first clients, were inducted into the Rock and Roll Hall of Fame in 2011 at the Waldorf-Astoria in Manhattan, we were elated. It had been a long, often bizarre journey since we met in Los Angeles in 1968. I was so happy for them, and proud of myself. But I left the ceremony right after and was back in my hotel room ten minutes later. I high-fived myself in the mirror and went to sleep. It was my job, not my life.

I have learned that fame has no intrinsic value. And I have seen what harm fame did to many of my friends and clients. The more fame they got, the more damage it seemed to do them. Why would I want that?

But now I said yes to Mike. Maybe it was ego, maybe it was the painkillers, but whatever the reason, I'm really glad I agreed. Because in making *Supermensch*, Mike got me to start seeing my life in a new way. I had always thought of my life as a series of random events, all luck and circumstance, like the way I met Janice and Jimi. Soon after that I started managing Alice Cooper as a cover for selling my rock friends drugs. Within a few years Alice was one of the biggest rock acts in the world, and I started branching out to manage other types of performers.

I first went to Maui because I was trying to quit smoking. I didn't quit, but I bought a house, and have lived in Paradise ever since. In the 1970s I started producing and distributing independent films as a favor to a friend. Having dinner during the Cannes Film Festival, I met the world-renowned chef Roger Vergé. That led me on another journey, managing the careers of many of the greatest chefs in the world. More important, Vergé showed me how to live a happy and fulfilled life in service to others. I saw it again when I met His Holiness the Dalai Lama. I met him through Sharon Stone—whom I met at Cannes.

My whole life has seemed to go that haphazard way. I get up in the morning, start down one path, and it leads to another, and another. I always knew that I was living a very lucky life, but it wasn't until Mike made *Supermensch* that I started seeing that there might be a way to connect the dots. Mike helped me realize that maybe there's something to my life's journey, some lessons I've learned along the way, that would be useful to other people.

Since *Supermensch* had its world premiere at the Toronto Film Festival in September 2013, I've been overwhelmed by the response. All kinds of people, from all over the world, seem to be touched in some positive way by the movie. Everywhere I go, strangers stop me on the street to thank me for it. They have sent me letters and emails and left hundreds of comments on Facebook and Twitter, like:

"I was blown away by his generous, giving spirit."

"Shep should run the planet."

"We should all approach business the way this great man has."

Of course, some of the people I hear from are struggling writers, actors, or musicians who want me to manage or advise them. I guess the movie makes it seem like I have the magic touch and can make anybody a star. I've heard from women who want to meet my friends or have my baby. People send me gifts, too. A vintner in Napa Valley shipped me some bottles of a very, very precious wine with a note: "I love your approach to business and to life. If there is anything I can do to be of assistance to you in Napa or northern Cal, just let me know." Somebody else sent me a check for a thousand dollars to donate to the charity of my choice.

I've also heard from titans of industry and well-known entertainers who've seen the movie, were deeply affected, and want to meet me or just talk on the phone. I got really curious to know what it was they were seeing and hearing in the movie, so I accepted some of the invitations. I was hoping they would show me a pattern in my life I wasn't aware of.

This search led me once again to say yes to something I had said no to many times. At a Brooklyn book signing by my friend chef Roy Choi, Anthony Bourdain (there I go being a groupie again) came over to me and said he wanted to do my memoir as one of the line of books, including Roy's, that he was putting out through Ecco. "I want to look behind the curtain and see what makes a supermensch," he said. I thought about it for a day, and decided maybe doing a book would help me understand why my life has unfurled the way it has. I called him and said yes, and the journey began.

As I wrote this book I looked for some common threads linking the events in my apparently accidental life. One of the things people seem to respond most strongly to in the movie is the perception that I've managed to become successful in the cutthroat worlds of the music and movie businesses while staying a nice guy, and apparently a happy one. It's not something we're used to seeing. In business, and especially in the music and movie businesses, you're supposed to get ahead by being the alpha dog who barks the loudest, bites the deepest, and doesn't care who he screws over.

I'm not that guy. I've always taken a very different approach. Writing this book got me thinking about what that is, some guiding principles I've lived and done business by.

Two simple words came up over and over again: *Thank you.* I wake up in the morning and say thank you. I say it again when I go to sleep at night, and countless times in between. I've been doing it for decades, and it always makes me feel good. To me, life is a miracle. It's a miracle that I'm here, no matter what kind of day I'm having. It's a miracle that I have this extraordinarily complex body that can feel both pleasure and pain. It's a miracle that I have this amazingly complex brain that's capable of both joy and sadness. When I'm feeling lonely or sad or confused, it's a miracle I'm even here *to* feel lonely or sad or confused. I'm so happy that I *can* feel sad.

We have so many things to be thankful for. Pick a few each day. Your health, your friends, your weather, your dog, your breathing, your seeing, your walking. Lots to choose from. Try it.

Something else that makes me happy: *Do something nice for someone today.* Something you didn't have to do, maybe for someone you don't know. I find that making others happy makes me happy. Simple, but very effective.

Then there's a big principle behind the way I have always tried to conduct business: *Create win-win situations.* I call it doing compassionate business. It doesn't have to be winners and losers. It can be winners and winners.

Along with that goes my idea of the coupon. When somebody does me a favor, I feel I am obligated to return that favor. I say they have a coupon with me. They can redeem that coupon anytime, in any way, and I will honor it. That's win-win, too.

I have tried never to hurt people or draw blood. If I did, it was by accident, and I certainly didn't gloat about it. I try to live by a mantra: *Don't get mad. Getting mad only hurts. Use that energy to accomplish your goal.*

And then there's this: *Create history, don't wait for it to happen.* Visualize your goal, then create the road that will take you there.

I realize how lucky I have been to have mentors who illuminated a path for me. I had always thought of it as random, but maybe it isn't. That's way too big a question for me, but it did get me to examine my life for those common threads. I hope that in reading this you will find some simple tools that will help make your journey through life happier and more meaningful. At the very least you can get a peek into a life well lived (I think), and hear some great stories.

One note: The events and experiences detailed in this book are all true and have been faithfully rendered as I remember them, to the best of my ability. Some of it happened a long time ago, and I wasn't taking notes thinking I'd write this book someday. The conversations come from my recollection of them, but I can't claim they represent word-for-word documentation. Rather, I tell them in a way that I think evokes the real feeling and meaning of what was said, and in keeping with the true essence of the events.

1
||||

I WAS BORN ON OCTOBER 18, 1945, in Jackson Heights, Queens. We lived in an apartment there until I was in the third grade. I had one brother, Edward, three years older than me. My father, Benjamin, and mother, Pauline, were first-generation Americans, the children of immigrants. My mother's mother, Fanny Frank, lived seven or eight blocks away. She and a lot of her sisters had come over from Poland, and I grew up knowing their large family. My mom's brother Benny lived with Fanny.

My earliest recollections are of walking from our apartment to my grandmother's when I was five or six, holding my father's hand or my uncle Benny's. Jackson Heights was very Russian and Eastern European Jewish, plus some Italian. Everyone lived in brick apartment buildings like ours, twenty-five units, fifty, a hundred. It was a nice neighborhood, clean and safe, just like in the old TV serials. All the neighbors knew each other and helped each other out. When someone new moved into the building everybody brought them housewarming gifts. It was all people just like us on the street, lots of babies in carriages and kids playing. The older people, my grandmother's generation, spoke the languages of back home, which I didn't understand.

In my memory I look up at my dad as we walk through the neighborhood. He's middle-aged, six feet tall, brown hair going gray and thin on top, wearing thick glasses that made his eyes look a bit squinty. I don't think he ever looked in a mirror. Clothing meant nothing to him. But he kept himself in good shape, and although he never talked about it, he was athletic. He had some trophies he'd won playing handball, and he was a good golfer. I always felt he was a handsome man. After he passed away, I went through a box of his things and found a card he and a few of his friends had printed up when they were young men in the 1930s. It said, "Bachelors available for parties." That makes me laugh every time I see it. He and my mother made a striking couple. She was five foot seven and beautiful, with jet-black hair.

He was a bookkeeper all his life. At first he worked at a brewery called Feigenspan's in Brooklyn, then as the office manager at a place called Herman's Handkerchiefs and Scarves in midtown Manhattan. He never talked about his work. He didn't talk much at all. He had a beautiful smile, though, and could laugh himself to tears. I don't know if *timid* is the right word to use, but he certainly was not an aggressive man. He never pushed himself forward. He never even drove a car, which was really unusual for a man in those days. I only saw him angry once. He was not a sad man, not depressed in any way, just quiet.

My grandmother's apartment was on the second floor, at the end of a hallway. It had a metal door with a buzzer and a little round viewer so the person inside could see who was there. When that door opened you could see through her foyer and down a hall straight into her kitchen, which was right out of *Happy Days*. It was very small, with just barely room for her to turn around. A Formica table with benches stood on the linoleum floor. She had a primitive white icebox with a chrome handle, and a four-burner gas stove. And she had knickknacks all around, snow globes and little porcelain animals.

Every time we opened the door and looked down the hall into the kitchen, she was in there, my little grandmother, maybe four foot eight, always in the kitchen either squeezing oranges or flipping latkes. As long as she was alive, whenever you opened her door the view was the same. When I was in college in Buffalo and drove to New York I always stopped at her place first, and there she was in the kitchen, same as always, squeezing the oranges or flipping the latkes. The first thing I did, every time I visited, from when I was a kid onward, was to sit down at her kitchen table and eat. And *then* we would say hello. Our relationship was built on an amazing amount of love, but also food.

I always joke when I'm cooking in my house that I'm channeling my grandmother. When people show up here, there's chicken soup on the stove. It's her recipe. I changed one thing. I use chicken stock instead of water and cook it down. Chicken, carrot, celery, onion. Dill is the only herb she used, except every once in a while she would put in a piece of garlic. So I do the same.

My grandmother's apartment was a very nice one-bedroom. Her bedroom was in the back. My uncle Benny slept on a foldout sofa bed in the living room. He never married, and lived with my grandmother until she passed away. He was a short man, maybe five foot eight, bald, with a great big beautiful hooked nose. I was very close to him. I don't remember this, but I'm told he used to help me with my ingrown toenails, which still bother me. He'd sit for hours and hours pushing the skin back. He was that kind of guy, a beautiful man, very kind and gentle.

What I do remember about Benny is that he always seemed to be drifting off to sleep. He'd nod at the table, he'd nod watching TV. Many years later I found out why. Benny worked in the vehicle transport business. Giant cargo ships unloaded thousands of cars at the docks in Newark, New Jersey. Transporters picked them up and delivered them to various locations. They might load a dozen cars onto a big truck, or a driver might pick up a single car and drive it somewhere. Benny was one of those. Each driver carried his own license plate, which he put on the car when he picked it up, and removed on delivery.

One day I was sitting in my office with the very successful jazz producer Joel Dorn, who said in passing, "How's License Plate Benny?"

I said, "Who's License Plate Benny?"

"Don't you have an Uncle Benny who delivers cars? Well, he's a very famous poker player around town. They call him License Plate Benny. Plays every night."

For the first time I understood why Benny nodded off all the time.

When I was in the third grade we moved out to a new suburb, Oceanside, farther out on Long Island, very near the seaside town of Long Beach. Oceanside was famous for having the second Nathan's hot dog stand (after the first one, in Coney Island). It's still there, on Long Beach Road, which runs through Oceanside straight out to the boardwalk. When I was in high school a group of us went to Nathan's for lunch almost every day. I was caddying at a golf course, two bags at a time for eighteen dollars a round, and spent all the money on Nathan's hot dogs, fried clams, and clam chowder. My mouth is watering as I'm writing this.

||||||||||||||||||||

Oceanside grew up about the same time that Levittown did, that 1950s moment when suburbs flourished, and it looked very similar, like Ozzie and Harriet's neighborhood. On our street, Henrietta

Avenue, maybe twenty houses faced each other on a block, all exactly the same split-level design. They were really nice houses, with big yards in front and back, maybe a half or three-quarters of an acre. Through our front door you walked into the living room, which my mother furnished very much of that era, with plastic slipcovers on everything because that furniture was never to be sat on. It was just for show. That led into the dining room, also rarely used, only for formal occasions. We did almost all our eating in the kitchen, which was not unlike my grandmother's, with a round table and benches and some chairs. Downstairs was the den, where the TV was. The utility room was right off the den, and then there was the garage. One flight up from the kitchen were two bedrooms. I had one, my brother had the other. Our own bedrooms—that was huge! Up another flight was the master bedroom for my parents.

For all of us who had moved out from the city, Oceanside was an entirely new world. For the first time in our lives we had landscape, we had pets, we had trees and grass and air. It was another very nice, very friendly community. Everybody knew everybody else on the block. I took to it right away. I always had little jobs in the neighborhood, like delivering newspapers on my bicycle, and helping the man with the neighborhood dairy route deliver eggs and butter. I'd never go a block without waving to somebody. Very Beaver Cleaver.

But the move to Oceanside came with one major drawback, and its name was Skippy. My brother wanted to be a veterinarian. Not long after we moved to Oceanside my mother let him get a dog, because now we had a backyard. My mother gave my brother anything he wanted. Of the two of us, he was definitely her favorite. (Or at least I thought so until I was sixty-five. That's when my brother told me he always thought *I* was her favorite.

Maybe she didn't have a favorite.) Edward was the firstborn, and he was everything a Jewish mother at that time wanted in a son: responsible, focused, very good with money, with a career picked out and a plan of how to get there. Everything about him said he'd be the successful one.

To my mother, I was the irresponsible son. I didn't have a career plotted out from when I was a kid. And for some reason I was always losing things, which drove her crazy. I'd get a baseball glove for my birthday and lose it the next day. I've come to recognize a trait in me, that as soon as I get something I want I don't much care about it anymore—like that night at the Hall of Fame ceremony. My mother got so fed up with me losing my things, one year when I got ten dollars for my birthday she made me give it to Edward. As cruel and unfair as that sounds, I've come to understand it. He was the opposite of me—extremely thrifty. *Extremely.* She knew that at least he'd use that money, not lose it like I would. He bought a parakeet with it, which really made me crazy. Because of Skippy I hated animals by then.

When Skippy showed up, life radically changed for me. Skippy was a miserable mutt, his fur black and white splotches, and all teeth. During the day he was chained up out back. At night he was moved to the utility room. He barked twenty-four hours a day. He hated me, and I hated him back. But then, Skippy hated everyone except Edward. Skippy's sole purpose in life was to bite people. He must have nipped at me fifty times. I can still show you the scars. There was a girl in our neighborhood, Robin, who had polio. He attacked her and, as I recall it, she had to have thirty stitches. I may be exaggerating that, but he definitely bit her. Everyone in the neighborhood became aware of Skippy, and stayed away. I couldn't have friends over because their parents wouldn't allow it. Even our relatives wouldn't come over. If Skippy broke free, someone was going to get nipped at.

One of my chores was to get food out of the freezer, which was in the garage. To get to the garage, I had to go through the utility room, where Skippy was locked up. I developed a strategy. I'd open the door just wide enough to toss some food into the room, hoping to distract the dog long enough for me to run through to the garage door. Sometimes it worked, but sometimes it didn't.

In a bizarre way my life came to revolve around that dog. Because he was in the house, I spent as much time as I possibly could out of the house. I couldn't wait to get to school. After school I played basketball until I had to go home at dark. When I got home I grabbed my dinner, ran up to my room, and ate alone up there. I stayed in there until morning, a prisoner in my own home. I'm sure I must have eaten *some* meals with my family down in the kitchen after Skippy arrived, but I swear I don't remember any.

This went on until I got my driver's license. I don't think I realized how strange it all was until other people pointed it out. When a cousin from Israel came to visit, he lasted one day hiding with me in my room before he said, "This is crazy. Come on, we're getting out of here." He got me started learning the trombone so at least I'd have something to do in my room.

I can't say that I was unhappy. I wasn't angry, either. I was just very confused about it. I'd ask my mom, "What would make you pick this dog over me?"

She wouldn't say, "It's because you're a jerk." She'd say, "Your brother really loves animals. He really wants to be a veterinarian. This is important to him."

I asked my dad, "How can you let Mom give the dog freedom in the house and not us?"

He said, "Would you like me to leave and leave you alone with her? What else can I do? She's not going to change."

He hated conflict. I suppose that by hiding in my room all the time I was dealing with the issue the way he would, by avoiding it.

The only time I felt safe out of my room was watching TV shows like *Sgt. Bilko* and old Marx Brothers movies down in the den with my dad. If my father was there I felt safe to come downstairs, even though the dog was behind the door in the utility room barking endlessly through the shows. There were two couches in the den, very fifties, with heavy fabric and thin cushions. The big TV console stood on legs against a wall, and the utility room door with the dog behind it was right beside it, so that when you were watching TV it was always in your view. There was a lamp, and otherwise the room was very spare.

But it didn't feel barren, because my father was there. I'd put my head on my father's lap and watch TV with him. Anytime we coughed or laughed—if we were lucky enough to catch a Marx Brothers movie we laughed our heads off—Skippy started barking and scratching at that door, like all he wanted to do was leap out and bite your throat. But I felt so safe with my dad. I loved him so much, and I could feel how much he loved me. His love for me was pure. He never asked me to do anything for him. He was my protector, my haven, and my friend.

One of my favorite times as a kid came maybe once a month, when he and I would go play golf. It started when I was twelve or thirteen and was on the junior high school golf team. I wasn't good, but I could play well enough to go with him. My father devoted himself entirely to supporting his family. This was the one thing he did for himself. He loved being on the golf course. He just glowed out there.

Our journey there was beautiful, although strange. It started when he woke me up at three in the morning. He'd wake me very gently, with a big smile on his face. "Come on, let's go." And I'd moan and complain, although after the first few years I really was looking forward to it. I'd get dressed in my room, he'd get dressed in his. Even in summer it was a little chilly out at three in the morning, so I'd put on layers of clothes. I'd hear him coming down the stairs and follow him. Down in the kitchen we'd have some hot chocolate or something. Never a real breakfast. We'd eat later. Then we would walk a quarter of a mile, with our clubs, on the dark and quiet streets, to the bus stop.

The golf course was at Bethpage State Park, maybe an hour's bus ride farther out on Long Island. The bus was usually fairly empty at that hour. For me those are some of the greatest moments of my life, because I got to share them with my dad, knowing that he was going to be happy. We were going to a place where no one—not the dog, not my mother—was going to bother us.

We'd reach the golf course just before light, sign up, and then go out to the benches there. We'd each find a bench to stretch out on and nap for an hour or two until tee time. Or I'd nap in his arms. And then we'd go out and play eighteen holes. We were always paired with two other golfers to make a foursome. We had the greatest time. We'd have lunch out there and then ride a bus home before dark. Golf has remained a very big part of my life ever since. I have a box of my dad's handkerchiefs. Whenever I play golf, or do anything exciting or fun, I carry one of those handkerchiefs with me. I feel like he's with me, and that makes me feel *really* good.

Looking back on it, I wonder why I never asked my dad why my mother didn't drive us or pick us up. Not once. I mean, he paid for the car, he paid for the gas, he paid for the house. I never asked him, "How could she let you take the bus?"

Another regular journey we made was into Manhattan, to Herman's Handkerchiefs and Scarves. They made linen handkerchiefs and scarves for women. It was a fairly big operation. I'd say my father had eight people in his accounting department. Every other Saturday or so, though the office was closed, he took the Long Island Rail Road into the city to get some work done. If I didn't have something I had to do for school, I went with him.

We'd leave the house around 8 A.M. Sometimes my mother even took us to the Oceanside LIRR station, about a ten-minute drive. Just being on a train with my dad was a huge deal to me. The cars were pretty new, with wide plastic seats, and there was a cafe car where you could get an egg sandwich. My dad always bought a *New York Post* for the trip in. So happy to be with him, I just sat next to him as he read. And I could feel how proud he was that he had his boy with him.

The train took us into Penn Station, and from there we walked a few blocks to Herman's. While my dad worked I'd do homework or read a book. The office was pretty dreary, a big room with no windows, eight or so desks piled with paperwork, under fluorescent lighting. No air moving, no natural light, a real *shmata* operation. I had never experienced anything like it. It felt like a jail to me. I was sorry that my dad had to go there every day. I could see that nothing about the work excited him. He was working to support us, not because he liked it. It was my first inkling of how the adult work world could be imprisoning. He never talked about it. Never once in our whole lives did he ever say one word about his work.

These trips were my first look at a real job, as opposed to delivering papers. I have great respect for my dad for going into that cheerless, windowless office every day, and for anyone else who works any kind of nine-to-five job. But the sad way that place made me feel gave me, I think, my first inklings that maybe I wasn't going to be suited for that kind of regular work. So I'm grateful to my dad for taking me there. My life might not have been the fantastic journey it has been without this early exposure to the real work world.

The moment I waited for was when he said it was time to break for lunch. It was a high point of my life until I went to college, when we walked out of that drab place onto the streets of midtown Manhattan on a Saturday afternoon and went to a delicatessen for lunch. We sometimes went to famous ones like the Stage Deli and the Carnegie Deli, but for the most part we went to one whose name I can't remember. I do remember that it was very narrow, with a row of maybe eight tables. In the middle of the room was a big wooden barrel of pickles. "A pickle for a nickel." They had new and old pickles in there, but all you could see on the surface was the brine, with seeds floating in it. You reached in there with tongs, picked a pickle, and dropped it in a plastic bag.

My dad let me order any sandwich I wanted. That was a big deal. When we went out to dinner as a family, you couldn't order what you wanted. My mother made us order what was cheap. The sandwich I loved the most was brisket, chopped liver, and Swiss cheese with Russian dressing on rye bread. Oh my God was that good. I treasured every bite. I can still taste it. My grandmother's cooking I had never really thought of as food in some strange way. It was just part of the fabric of my life. The Saturdays at the deli were the first time I got really excited about going to have a meal.

My dad and I would sit at a table by ourselves. It was the closest he ever came to talking about himself, but it wasn't much. I'd ask him a question like, "Did your dad take you for sandwiches when you were a kid?" And he'd say, "Well, not really." I couldn't get anything out of him about his family. I never met his dad.

We were not allowed to talk about his dad. The name was never brought up in the house. My dad's parents had a very ugly divorce, and I believe his father remarried, though to this day I truly don't know much. I think my father went behind his mother's back once to speak to him.

My father's mother, Rebecca Gordon, was the opposite of my mother's mother. She was a large lady, maybe five foot nine, and broad. She had come over from a place on the Russian-Polish border. She was very refined, read and wrote well, and she never cooked. She had two sons, my father and his younger brother Al. She and I had a special relationship, and I love her very much. She's buried in the same cemetery in New Jersey as my mom, dad, Uncle Benny, my other grandmother, and my grandfather. I go there once a year and give her and the whole family as much love as I can.

Where my father never spoke about his family, my mother couldn't *stop* talking about them. She had a real attitude against them from as early as I can remember. They were never invited or included in our family affairs. My mother told me that because my father was the older brother, he had to support the family after the divorce. He worked in the daytime and went to night school at the Community College of New York to get his accounting degree. He wrote for and I think edited the school newspaper, while sending his brother through school and supporting his mother. He went right to work after getting his degree, and never had the money or the opportunity to get a CPA. So he remained a bookkeeper instead of an accountant, which meant he never made more than ten thousand dollars a year in his life.

His brother Al went on to open a dress factory and become a multimillionaire. Yet he never, according to my mother, gave my father a dime—never paid him back for his education, never helped him out. It would have been so easy for him to say, "Go back and get your CPA." Or, "Come work for me." He never did, and that's why my mother disliked him. According to my mother, the last straw, the event that got Al and his family banned from our home, occurred one night when I was really sick—so sick that I was in my parents' bed rather than my own. I have no memory of this. My mother said that Al and his wife, Mildred, came over and brought me one of those Chinese magic boxes where you put a penny in, shut it, and when you open it the penny has disappeared. Supposedly they gave it to me, then came back upstairs and took the penny out. That's how cheap they were, my mother said. And from that night on they didn't come back, whether by their choice or her request I'll never know.

In fairness to them, my mother had a story like that for everybody. I never felt comfortable asking my father about it. It's something he would never, ever discuss. I've never felt comfortable asking Al's kids about it, either, because why would I at this point? Why would I want them to think badly of their dad? So I never learned the facts, but that's the cloud I was raised under, made up of my mother's anger, greed, and envy. Not a pretty picture. My father never showed the slightest anger or envy toward his brother. He just sat there quietly. But the fact that we weren't rich like Al and his family rankled my mother fiercely.

||||||||||||||||||||

I had such a strange childhood that by my mid-fifties I was convinced I had made it all up. A few years ago I reconnected with my cousin Patti. Cousin Patti was one of the few relatives on my father's side I got to know. She lived not too far from us on Long Island. Patti is the cutest thing you have ever seen, under five feet tall with the happiest face, like a little girl. She surfed and boogie-boarded into her eighties. She's a pistol. She's about twenty years older than me. Her daughter and I were born around the same time, and Patti remembers us as infants being wheeled around together in our baby carriages. Once a year all the cousins would get together at a hotel in the Catskills, which is where I got friendly with her. When I was in the eighth or ninth grade Patti had a summer job at a waterskiing school not far from Oceanside. She started coming by the house in the mornings to pick me up and take me there for the day. Not to learn to ski, just to get away from my mother and Skippy. I had lunch with her, sat in the boat, read a book. It was just great to be out of the house for a day.

When Mike was working on *Supermensch,* they got in touch with Patti to interview her. She was around ninety and still a dynamo.

"I think I made my whole childhood up," I said to her. "Did you ever come to the house?"

She said, "I couldn't come to the house. You had that *dog*. Don't you remember, I tried to adopt you. Your mother never spoke to me after that."

I had never heard that before. She actually spoke to my mother about adopting me, which of course meant my mother banished her from our home.

So I didn't make it up. My childhood really was strange enough that Cousin Patti tried to adopt me to rescue me from it. Patti earned a giant coupon from me for doing this, which I keep paying back happily. In the summer of 2015 I lectured at the University of Hawaii School of Law about ethics in the music business (an oxymoron?) to get three VIP passes to a Grateful Dead concert in Chicago for Patti's granddaughter, a Deadhead. The Dead's lawyer and manager was on the panel. Patti's grandson Mikey, whom I love so much, lived with me in Maui for a year and recently got married at my house. Patti still has lots of coupons with me.

I didn't brood about my life as a kid. That's not how I am. It's only been fairly recently that I've looked back and recognized ways that my childhood and family had an impact on the adult I became. For one thing, spending all that time in my room meant that I learned how to be alone, and how to think. I didn't have a TV in there, or a telephone. We didn't have computer games in those days. I had my thoughts, my books, and my imagination. I learned solitude. I can get lonely, same as anyone, but my ability to sit alone quietly for hours at a time, thinking, visualizing, would play a huge role in my successes as an adult. I also think that my mother's attitude toward me as the son who was not destined for success must have in some way driven me to be successful. I think in some ways I tried to prove her wrong, or prove myself to her.

I think that because my father was so quiet and reserved, and allowed my mother to so dominate our lives, I spent a number of years instinctively seeking out mentors and surrogate father figures to fill some void I must have felt. But as it turned out, my two greatest and most influential mentors would be men who reminded me of him. My father spent his whole life in service to others—first his mother and brother, then his wife and kids. He never had money or power, but he was happy, proud to be a provider. In their own ways, my later mentors did the same. And in my own way, imitating them all, so would I.

Thank you, thank you.

|||||||||||||||||||

When I got to be fourteen or fifteen, Long Beach became my main escape. My parents gave me permission to hitchhike. In those days you could still hitchhike fairly safely. Our street, Henrietta

Avenue, ran right to Long Beach Road, which ran straight to the boardwalk, about fifteen minutes away. It was a very easy hitch, because it was a very high-traffic road. It usually took two rides. The first ride was generally up to this big intersection with a stoplight. They'd turn off there, and I'd thumb a second ride the rest of the way to the beach. The drivers were almost always strangers, which made it my first time out alone in the world, meeting strangers, without a safety net, without my dad by my side. It was a little scary. A car would stop, there'd be some stranger behind the wheel. Ninety-nine times out of a hundred I'd get in. Every once in a while I'd get a weird vibe and say, "Oh sorry, I left something at home," and not get in. The road to Long Beach ran straight through the neighborhood of Island Park, which was very Italian and full of mobsters and gangsters. Every now and again there'd be a mafia killing or a big arrest in Island Park, and my mom wouldn't let me hitchhike for a couple of weeks.

Long Beach is a narrow barrier island, reached by a couple of bridges across a channel just off the south shore of Long Island. It was a mix of residential and resorts. I started getting summer jobs at the beach clubs there. One was Malibu Beach Club, another the Colony Beach Club, another El Patio, but they were all very much the same, all strung along a road running down the center of the island called Lido Boulevard. They all had the same basic footprint. An impressive driveway and entrance, where young, good-looking guys took your car and put it in the large parking lot. You'd go into a lobby that was fairly fancy, with gin games going on everywhere, old Jewish guys with pinkie rings, and elderly blondes in high heels. Lots of young, beautiful girls, too. There'd always be a snack bar or a restaurant, always a pool with a lot of cabanas around it, and then a beach with beach chairs and striped umbrellas.

If you've seen the Matt Dillon movie *The Flamingo Kid*, you know exactly what my life was like then. It was even shot at Long Beach. When I got to whichever club I was working at I went straight to a locker room and changed into whatever outfit the job required. In one job I worked as a beach boy. I ran out to set up chairs, fetched people drinks, took the chairs back inside when they left. I worked at a snack bar, which was interesting because it was my first experience with peer pressure to do something I didn't agree with. Some of the guys working there were older, heavily tattooed, dangerous characters. When we made hamburger patties, they'd laugh and press them in their armpits, or do other disgusting things. Just to be cool. I couldn't rat on them, because they'd beat the hell out of me. I knew I should give them up, but I didn't. I think it was the first real moral dilemma I ever confronted. Wow, how am I going to conduct my life? Am I really going to stand by and watch this happen? Which I did. I cooked those hamburgers and served them to people. It wasn't so much that what these guys did was unsanitary, because these snack bars were so dirty anyway. What confused and upset me was that one human being would want to do this to another, just for a laugh. It still gets me to this day. When I see a TV show where they're laughing because someone fell down the steps, I still can't figure what it is in human nature that can make that funny.

The most interesting job of all was as a cabana boy. The cabana boy opens up the cabana for the customers, sets them up with towels, brings them their food and drink orders, and cleans up afterward. You're basically their house servant for the afternoon, only it's a cabana. Observing those people was a real education for me. There was always one hot gin or poker game going on in one of the cabanas, and there was always an alpha male who was the leader, and everyone knew he was the guy. He had the biggest pinkie ring, and the darkest tan, and the hottest wife, and won the most hands. I'd never been exposed to that sort of social behavior before, how hierarchies work, how society chooses its leaders.

It was a very good time for me. I had all the things I couldn't get at home. I finally had my own individual, independent life, away from all the neighbors who knew everything about me, away from my mother and always being compared unfavorably to my brother. I was free to come and go, and I had a social life at the clubs. I could be whoever I wanted to be. I didn't have to be Shep Gordon from Oceanside living in a house where I couldn't leave my room. I started experimenting. There was a doo-wop group called Shep and the Limelites at the time, who had a big hit with the song "Daddy's Home." For a while, to the girls at the clubs I was Shep of the Limelites. I never actually *said* I was. I'd just go around humming the song, and my name was Shep, so they leaped to that conclusion. I didn't dissuade them. I even signed autographs. Until they found out the Limelites were black.

But it was great while it lasted, and maybe it was necessary. Because I was very, very interested in all those pretty girls, but at fourteen and fifteen I was also very, very shy and totally inexperienced. It wasn't the last time I'd use a ruse or a pretext to be with girls. Because I've been with many gorgeous women as an adult, with movie stars and fashion models, I have this reputation as a world-class ladies' man. You can see it in the documentary, my male friends talking about me and all my beautiful women. The truth is I don't think of myself that way at all. I have never felt that I was good-looking. I have always felt shy and self-conscious around pretty women. Their beauty overwhelms me. Certainly this was true when I was young. I was still a virgin when I went to college.

But I always had eyes for pretty girls. There was this one cute little blonde at one of the clubs where I worked, Leslie Feldstein. Her dad was the alpha male at that club. I really wanted to be with her, and the other guys all said, "Ask her out on a date." I didn't have a car and had never been on a date before. But I asked if her she wanted to go on one, and she said yes.

"What do you want to do?" I asked, hoping she'd have some idea, because I didn't.

"I don't know," she said.

"Well," I said, "my high school is playing a basketball game I want to go to."

"Okay," she said. "How are we going to get there?"

"Um, do you hitchhike?"

"No. Let me ask my dad if he'll take us."

He agreed. So now the big alpha male is going to chauffeur me on my first date. I gave her my address. On the night of the game, this enormous, shiny car with big tail fins, a DeSoto or Chrysler, one of those types, pulled up outside my house on Henrietta Avenue. I got in the back with Leslie; her dad sat up front, chauffeuring. The seats of the car were covered in clear plastic, just like the furniture in my living room, only under the plastic was all covers of *MAD* magazine. I loved *MAD*. I think I said something stupid like, "Wow, do you collect *MAD* magazines? So do I!"

Leslie said, "My dad is the editor."

And he was. Al Feldstein, editor of *MAD* for nearly thirty years, drove me on my first date. He was really nice about it, too. After the game he took us to a Jahn's ice cream parlor. Jahn's was a local chain famous for its huge Kitchen Sink Sundae, an actual tub of dozens of scoops of ice cream in all the flavors, which served eight. He ordered one of those for the three of us. That was the only time I ever had one.

That was also the only time I ever went on a date with Leslie. Guess I didn't do so well.

I loved those summers at Long Beach. I played a lot of Fascination on the boardwalk, where you rolled a rubber ball into holes and tried to set off a pattern of lights, sort of like in bingo, to win a prize. I got very good at it. I ate a lot of Izzy's knishes. I got high for the first time at Long Beach, too, sniffing glue out of a paper bag under the boardwalk. I can still smell and taste it. Disgusting. But that's what we did then. We thought it was cool. We observed those high-rolling gamblers with their gold watches and dark, dark tans and wanted to be like them. During senior year my friend Dennis Greenstein and I used to sneak off to the racetrack at night. I used pillows and blankets to make it look like I was in bed, then slipped out of the house around nine o'clock and walked thirty minutes to his house, which was in an area identical to mine. He met me outside. We would roll his mother's black Valiant down their driveway and then down the quiet street until we felt we were far enough away, then he'd start it up and drive us to Roosevelt or Yonkers Raceway. They'd let you in free for the last race, around ten thirty. We rarely had any money to bet. We just watched and felt like big shots.

Thirty years later I went to Dennis's parents' house for the holidays. I said to his mother, "Mrs. Greenstein, I have to make a confession."

She said, "Really? What about?"

I said, "Well, there were nights when you thought Dennis was sleeping—"

And she said, "Oh, you mean the nights you rolled the car out of the driveway?"

Jewish moms. You had to be awfully slick to put one over on them.

|||||||||||||||||||

While I was developing a life of my own, Edward was living his, and we barely interacted at all. Our bedrooms were right next to each other, but my door was always shut. He had his friends over all the time, usually in his room, and I was not allowed to go in there. We had no real interests in common. I liked sports, and he couldn't have cared less about that. He loved animals, and because of Skippy I hated animals. I was growing into a big kid, and he was always slight and skinny.

Edward was very, very close to my mother and my mother's mother. Very close. It was probably my grandmother who influenced him to be so thrifty. She'd grown up poor in the old country, and she never got over squeezing every penny. Edward became obsessed with thrift, saving every penny, never wasting an opportunity to make another penny. He had us all cutting out coupons every weekend. When I was out playing basketball, he was out collecting bottles for the deposit. It's the way he is to this day. He has never veered an inch from who he is. It took me a long time, but I have come to respect that about him. There's certainly nothing phony about him. He makes no excuses. He is who he is.

When we were kids Edward was on his path, laser-focused on becoming a veterinarian, which he did. After we left our parents' home, he went off in his direction and I went in mine. We barely saw each other for the next twenty, thirty, forty years. Our lives were just so different. He was very successful, made a lot of money, and raised a loving family. And he still collects bottles and clips coupons.

I haven't clipped a coupon since I left home. I have completely the opposite relationship to money. But I must have absorbed something from Edward, because the idea of the coupon is very important to the way I live and do business.

2

I GRADUATED FROM HIGH SCHOOL IN 1963. One night toward the end of that summer, my mother drove my dad and me into Manhattan, to the big, gloomy Port Authority bus terminal on Forty-Second Street just off Times Square. I was going to catch a midnight Greyhound bus to Buffalo.

The University of Buffalo had just switched from a private school to being incorporated into the State University of New York (SUNY) system, which meant you could take the exam for what was called a state Regents scholarship. The test wasn't hard. If you were a middle-class Jewish kid who had paid any attention in high school, you could get one of these scholarships, which easily paid for tuition at Buffalo. So that year there was a huge exodus from New York to Buffalo of Jewish kids on Regents scholarships, Buffalo being the farthest away you could get from your parents and still be in the state.

The Port Authority ran 24/7 and was never empty, but it was fairly quiet at that time of night, just some knots of travelers waiting around on hard benches under fluorescent lights. It has since been fixed up, but in 1963 it was just a huge bus terminal, pretty grim, no amenities. If there was a coffee machine it probably didn't work. I didn't care. I was thrilled to be there. I was getting away from home, getting out on my own.

I didn't want to be seen there with my parents. I wasn't a kid anymore. I was making believe I wasn't with them when I saw a guy my age sitting on the floor in a corner of the waiting area. Something about him intrigued me right away. He was a handsome guy, with thick, straight brown hair, which I didn't have. He looked cool, which I didn't think I was. I went and sat on the floor near him, and we discovered we were both trying to get away from our parents, and both taking that midnight bus to Buffalo. His name was Joe Greenberg. We sat on the bus together, an eight-hour ride, and by the time we got to Buffalo we were good friends.

When we got to Buffalo that morning we weren't housed in dormitories but in off-campus apartments, a complex called the Allenhurst Apartments. It was about three-quarters of a mile from campus, in a neighborhood that was similar to Oceanside, in that it was all symmetrical and identical, but instead of single-family homes it was a garden apartment complex, all built around central courtyards, with maybe a dozen two-bedroom duplex garden apartments on each courtyard. It was all relatively new and very nice. My assigned roommate was a Jewish kid from Troy, New York, with whom I became very friendly.

It felt like it was the first day of my life. The journey was about to begin. I had no idea where I was going, no real aspirations. I thought I might become a lawyer, because it seemed that every Jewish kid did that. But I wasn't committed to it. Eventually I settled on sociology, but I didn't really know what I wanted to do with that. The truth is, if I had any aspirations it was to become a millionaire beachcomber, as quickly as I could. I knew that working in a windowless office like my dad's was not what I wanted.

I was willing to work my ass off, but I wanted it to be fun and rewarding work.

I was free for the first time in my life. I could do whatever I wanted. I think this is when I began to develop a personality. I don't think I really had one before then. Maybe I did to other people, but not to myself.

For all of us freshmen, it was the greatest thing in our lives to be so far away from our parents, in our own apartments, on our own for the first time. We could shop for our own food and cook it, which most of us had never done. Or we could get pizzas delivered, which we did a lot. There was a laundromat on the corner where we did our own laundry, another first for me. There were girls there doing their laundry, so we washed our clothes often. I had to manage my money. The scholarship paid for rent and tuition; I think my parents gave me a hundred dollars a month. It was the first time I had to think about how to pay for everything else. More important to me, it was the first time I really had a social group, all of us living in those apartments. I had lived a solitary life until then, except when I was at school.

The day after we arrived we took the bus to school for the first time. I had never seen anything as beautiful as the University of Buffalo campus. And very cool as well, guys my age driving up in their own cars, girls all around. The bus dropped us off in front of Norton Union, the student union building, which had the look of a small public library. Very wide and impressive steps went up to the entrance level, and lots of kids sat on the steps and watched who was coming and going. Upperclassmen on the steps made wisecracks about the new girls, a lot of whom came with their parents for orientation. One upperclassman was a guy I later became very friendly with, Barry Weinstein, nicknamed the Rat. I would soon learn that everybody had a nickname. (Mine was EZ, because my middle name is Ezra.) This beautiful freshman girl came walking up with her parents that first day, and he ran over and pinched her ass. In front of her parents. And made kissy noises at her and ran off. All the other older guys laughed. I had never seen behavior like that in my life. I was so out of my wheelhouse.

I stuck with Joe those first days. He always had a mischievous twinkle in his eye, and the girls all loved him. I clung to him. Joe and I and the other new guys we were quickly bonding with got settled in and registered for classes. But I can't say that going to class was ever a big part of my experience at Buffalo. In fact, it was the smallest part. Buffalo wanted to be the Berkeley of the east. It was all very laid-back and hippie and nontraditional. I remember going to a class on "Everything, Nothing, and Something Else," taught by Marty Kriegel, who was then a guest lecturer, and who went on to be a professor, and is still a great friend. After we graduated, I would come back to Buffalo and drop in on his then three formal courses with those same names. Marty's a year younger than I am, and a genius. He became a lawyer, has taught at universities around the world, and has written briefs for the Supreme Court. Along the way he also went to medical school and studied both Western and Eastern medicine. I think he has degrees in a half dozen different areas. There were no desks in Marty's classroom. In all three courses we sat on the floor around a record player. For "Everything" you brought a record and we all listened to it. For "Something Else" you brought as many records as you wanted. And for "Nothing" you brought nothing and we all just sat there. It may have been a Zen lesson. I think.

People who weren't around for the sixties don't believe me when I describe Marty's classes. When *Supermensch* came out, A&E bought the TV rights. I had dinner with Abbe Raven, who was president, CEO, and chairman of A&E. She and her husband told me that when they went to Buffalo they also took Marty's courses. So at least *they* believe me.

No one took school too seriously. I bet I didn't attend ten classes in four years. There was also a lot of cheating, tests handed around beforehand so you could pass without ever attending.

For me, what I mostly got out of college wasn't my education, but the large group of great friends I made there. In fact, when I look back I see it was the last time I really made friends just because I liked them and wanted to be friends with them. Almost every friend I have from after then is someone I had some kind of business relationship with before we became friends. Or we were neighbors first and became friends. Always some bridge, some pretext. In Buffalo it was just a pool of kids from which you picked the ones you liked. You didn't need or want anything from them. I've stayed very close with thirty-five or more friends I made then, fifty-odd years ago.

President Kennedy was assassinated that fall. It was so shocking. Everybody in Allenhurst met in the middle of the street, held each other in a big circle, and cried. It was a transformative moment. I think that's when most of us got radicalized. I don't think any of us had thought of anything other than our dicks up until then. For a lot of us, that was a moment when we realized we were living in a world where actions mattered, thoughts mattered, and holy shit they're going to leave this planet to us. We'd better do something. It was the first step of a journey that led to burning our draft cards, demonstrating against the war, protesting the screwed-up world of our parents. It also sent us on a path toward pot and psychedelics and all the ways we explored alternatives to the mindset that we felt had created that fucked-up world.

Before then, I had not done any drugs, unless you count

sniffing that glue once under the boardwalk. I did drink, but I didn't like to get really drunk and hungover. Luckily, I inherited my dad's capacity to hold his liquor. He could drink a bottle of cognac and stay in control, and I found I was like him. I could drink a bottle of vodka, two bottles even, and get a buzz, but not get blind drunk. So I was always the designated driver, even though we didn't use that term then. It would be the same when we were all taking LSD; I was always the one who was able to drive.

The first time I smoked pot, Joey and I were in an apartment shared by guys named Jerry Singer and Alan Stein; Alan, Jerry, and I are good friends to this day. We shared a joint, and I remember thinking, This isn't doing anything. Then, out of nowhere, the sound of an approaching train filled the room. I was terrified. It sounded like it was going to crash straight through a wall. There was in fact a train going by somewhere outside, and the pot made it sound much louder and closer than it was. Once the other guys calmed me down, I realized I was really enjoying this experience, this heightened sense of my surroundings. Joey and I smoked again a week or so later, and I liked it even more.

After my freshman year I was a regular, lifelong pot smoker. When we were home that year for summer vacation, Jerry pulled up at my house on a motorcycle with his pot dealer. We went to the Oceanside Nathan's, where everybody hung out, and I bought some grass from the guy.

It struck me as a good way to make some money, so I started dealing in my sophomore year. Dealing pot led to some pretty amazing and scary adventures. Like the two times I personally smuggled pot across the border from Mexico. I drove down to Laredo, Texas, in my Mustang convertible, my first really good and cool car. I had bought it with my life savings, going all the way back to bar mitzvah money. Laredo is right on the Mexico-U.S. border, the Rio Grande River. I parked the Mustang there and went into a bar, where I met my connection. I don't remember his name now—I had met him when he was passing through Buffalo, and we set the deal up. He introduced me to his Mexican counterpart. Then the Mexican guy and I went through the border checkpoint on foot, separately, and walked over the bridge that crossed the river to the Mexican side, which is the city of Nuevo Laredo. We met up again at some little bar over on that side. I'm a Jewish college kid from Long Island, and I'm in a bar in Mexico, alone with strangers, about to become a drug trafficker. I was scared to death. We met another guy in the bar. He gave me a big bag of pot, and I gave him the cash I had brought.

We left the bar, got into a pickup truck, and drove out of town. There were big ranches on the banks of the river just outside Nuevo Laredo. We drove to one of them, where we met the rancher. Then they brought out a horse, and explained to me that once it got dark I was going to ride this horse across the Rio Grande back into the States with my bag of weed. I had never been on a horse in my life. They said, "That's all right. The horse knows what to do. He's done this plenty of times."

When night fell they got me up on it, strapped the bag of pot to it, slapped the horse on the rump, and waved good-bye. The Rio Grande was very narrow and very shallow. The horse never had to swim, he just walked across. When we got to the other side I got down and took the pot. The horse turned and headed back across the river.

That was that. I walked back to the Mustang and drove home.

Since it had all gone so smoothly, I went back the following year. This time I took a guy with me named Bruce. (Bruce, if you read this, aloha and I'm sorry!). I had told him how easy it was, and he needed cash, so he came along. It all went the way it had the first time. We walked over to Nuevo Laredo, bought the pot, and rode horses back that night into Texas. Then, as we were walking toward the Mustang, we saw that it was surrounded by police. Every cell in my body rang alarm bells. We hung back, trying to act normal, and watched them mill around for two, maybe three hours. Finally they left. They'd been there on some other mission, nothing to do with us and our car.

Bruce and I were ecstatic with relief. We collected the car and drove off. Bruce was in the backseat with the bags of pot, maybe four pounds of it. He had just opened one bag to inspect the goods when blinding headlights lit us up. All my alarms clanged again. I was absolutely sure we were going to prison. But it was some sort of border patrol, on the watch for illegal immigrants. They had no interest in a couple of American college boys and waved us through. Bruce and I drove on, laughing hysterically. Twice we had thought we were goners, and twice we'd skated.

We drove back to Buffalo without any more incidents. At this point I lived on Main Street in Buffalo, behind an optometrist and a Kentucky Fried Chicken. We carried the bags in and examined our booty, and found that the pot bricks were stuck together with sugar water to add weight. It was something unscrupulous dealers sometimes did. I put the bricks in the oven to bake the sugar water out, and the apartment filled up with a nice smell of warm pot. It was cozy.

Then there was a knock on the door. A cop was standing there. For the third time this trip I almost passed out with fright. But he only wanted me to move the Mustang because I'd parked it illegally. So for the third time I evaded catastrophe. Somebody up there was looking out for me for sure. I never made that trip again.

We also ran a weekly poker game to make money, and because it was a hell of a lot of fun. This had started before the second pot trip, when Joey and I were living with roommates in a big four-bedroom place on Beard Avenue, which runs parallel to Main Street. It was a typical upstate New York brick house, solid, old, wood floors, a fireplace in the family room, on a block of similar houses, all private homes. The poker game had a 5 percent rake. The rake is the commission the house takes out of the winner's earnings. For that we provided a safe place where we wouldn't get raided or robbed; food and drink; and sometimes a woman. At first the players were mostly college kids, then some people from the city started showing up. We started to make serious money, which, after paying the rent and bills, we took to the track and lost. Our day became pot and gambling 24/7. Forget school and classes.

After a few months we got a message that the local Hells Angels were going to bust our game. We never learned why. We were rushing for a fraternity, Sigma Alpha Mu, called "Sammy," and we got all the Sammy members to come to the house with baseball bats and such. The Angels never came, but it scared us enough to stop the game. Then a couple of townies who had played with us convinced us to start it up again. One was named Wally Jagoda, nicknamed "Walloon," and the other was Arthur Corrigan, aka "Black Arthur" Corrigan, aka "Kargoon." Arthur's family was well known and well connected in Buffalo, so he became our protection. With Arthur in the game we'd be left alone.

Arthur had a wooden leg. If a new player showed up and started winning big, at some point Arthur would unstrap the leg, slap it on the table, and say, "I raise you one leg." The guy wouldn't win another hand all night, he was so rattled.

One night a guy named Burr Vogel showed up and started winning hand after hand. He was a great poker player. So at some point Arthur put his leg on the table.

"I raise you one leg."

Cool as anything, Burr says, "I call, and raise you one eye."

He had a glass eye!

Fifty-odd years later, those two are still playing poker. Black Arthur lives in Vegas now. They all meet there once a year. A guy we called Coffee Boy, because he was the kid who got coffee and sandwiches for the players, became an executive at Coca-Cola Enterprises. He has his own plane and flies everybody to Vegas for three or four days of gambling.

iiiiiiiiiiiiiiiiiii

A stunt we pulled in Buffalo gave me my first insights into how easy it is to create publicity and press out of nothing, although at the time I just thought of it as a hilarious joke. When we were all still living in the Allenhurst Apartments, we were studying for the Botany 101 final exam. We crammed for the exam by staying up all night on Black Beauties, which were big, black, really strong Dexedrine pills. After being up a few days and nights in a row we were pretty delirious. At one point my friend Artie Schein started laughing at something in the textbook about the reproductive organ of *Marchantia polymorpha,* also known as the common liverwort. Its sex organ was called a thallus. For some reason that struck us as very funny, and we began riffing on the Thallus of Marchantia, like Marchantia was a country and the Thallus was its ruler.

This gave us the idea for the prank, which we put in motion over the next few days. Somebody got hold of some United Nations stationery and typed a letter from His Majesty the Thallus of Marchantia to the president of the university saying that he wanted to come visit the campus. We followed it up with a telegram sent from a Western Union office in New York City. The university took it seriously. Somebody at the school contacted local radio stations and the *Buffalo Evening News,* who contacted the mayor's office. No one checked us on our facts—including the part where we'd said that Marchantia was "an island in Arabia." Those words actually appeared in the *News.* The paper also said that the mayor of Buffalo would greet his majesty on the tarmac when his flight arrived.

We pooled our cash to send Artie to New York, where he'd change into an "Arabian" outfit and fly back to Buffalo. Then I got the brilliant idea of contacting the local B'nai B'rith. Were they aware that the city of Buffalo was rolling out the red carpet for the Thallus of Marchantia, well known for his anti-Semitic beliefs? Shouldn't somebody protest?

It worked like a charm. In the mid-1960s, protests happened every day. The afternoon that the Thallus's American Airlines flight from New York landed at Greater Buffalo International Airport, a crowd the *News* estimated at between six hundred and two thousand protesters—mostly our fellow students, who had no idea it was all a hoax—was running riot through the place. They broke a plate glass window, overturned the furniture in the waiting areas, then spilled out onto the tarmac, where the mayor and a detachment of police waited for the Thallus to step down out of the plane. One student brought a bugle. He played a cavalry charge, and the whole crowd went stampeding toward the plane. A contingent of maybe one hundred people from B'nai B'rith was there to protest as well.

Finally, Artie stepped out of the plane and waved to the crowd from the top of the mobile stairway. He was tripping on acid, and wearing a winter coat, a white bedsheet, and a towel wrapped around his head in a makeshift kaffiyeh. It was not terribly convincing—especially when you saw that the towel had HOTEL SAINT GEORGE printed on it. It was from the pool at a Brooklyn Heights hotel. But the crowd was too worked up by this point to notice. They went berserk, surrounding the plane, shouting, chanting, waving placards. "THALLUS GO HOME. PEOPLE ARE STARVING IN MARCHANTIA." "THALLUS GO BACK TO YOUR PALACE." "MALICE FOR THE THALLUS."

Artie wobbled down the stairs. Cops led him through the mob—but not into the mayor's waiting limo. They shoved him into the back of a patrol car, and sped away.

That was the first sign that we'd been found out. Driving away from the airport, we heard local radio news declaring the whole thing a college prank. The cops drove Artie straight to jail. He was charged with disorderly conduct and fined fifty dollars. The dean of students suspended Artie indefinitely, but only after posting his bail and putting him up for the night. Artie was convicted but later got it overturned, and the student body coughed up six hundred dollars for the airport damages.

I didn't know it then, but I had learned an invaluable lesson that I'd apply many times in my show business career: how to create history, not just wait for it to happen.

||||||||||||||||||||

My mother and father moved out of Oceanside while I was at Buffalo. Before I left, my father had had a heart attack or two; now they were coming more often. In those days doctors didn't know much of anything to do for heart attacks except to give you nitroglycerin capsules; when you suffered chest pains you placed one under your tongue and supposedly it relieved the symptoms.

If you were an old Jew from New York, the other thing you could do for it was retire and get away from the cold weather by moving to Florida, which they did, selling the Oceanside house. I think they got eighteen thousand dollars for it.

At first they lived in a hotel on Collins Avenue at the north end of Miami Beach. It had a name like the Seaview or the Seacrest, maybe four stories tall, right across from the water. They had a little studio apartment with a kitchenette. It wasn't a lot, but it got my dad away from the cold winters, which were hard on his heart. At one point I took a psychological leave of absence from school—it was the easiest way to get out of the draft, I thought—and drove down to stay with them. The place was so small I slept in a closet. But that was fine, and I got to spend some real quality time with my dad.

Joe Greenberg and I stayed friends all the way through school. Joe was handsome, cool, and a little bit of a scoundrel. So of course the girls found him irresistible. Every woman he wanted to fall in love with him did. I was the opposite. I was convinced I was not attractive or cool or interesting to girls, which made me terribly shy and inhibited with them. I loved women and was as horny as any college boy, but being with women never came easy to me. I hardly dated, barely kissed a girl, and my inexperience made me even more gun-shy.

At the end of senior year I found I was three credits short of a diploma and could not graduate on time. Marty Kriegel's close friend David was teaching a summer course. I made a deal with him to get those credits without going to class. Instead I went to Acapulco. It was the first summer I had ever gone on a real summer vacation.

I loved Acapulco. Ever since my great summers at Long Beach I have always been drawn to warm weather, blue skies, and beaches.

The hot spot was Carlos'n Charlie's, a Mexican restaurant that has grown into a chain with something like fifty locations now throughout the Americas. The emphasis was all on fun—fun food, fun drinks, fun atmosphere. I met a guy there named Rubio. I had a bag of peyote, so he was very nice to me. He explained to me that Acapulco was full of gigolos who serviced the tourist women. They mostly slept on the beach and didn't accept cash from the women, only clothes, jewelry, and meals—especially meals at Carlos'n Charlie's.

I decided to become a gigolo. I was probably the worst gigolo in history. No one invited me to dinner or gave me jewelry. I ran out of money pretty quickly. I still had some of the peyote, so I'd swim out to a raft in front of the Hilton and take some of that. One afternoon a really nice girl swam out to the raft. Susan told me she was a teacher from Brooklyn. I told her I was starving. She took me to a Big Boy for a hamburger. She did that every day for the rest of the summer. Very nice girl. Five or six years later, when I was managing Alice Cooper, the guitarist Glen Buxton introduced us to his new girlfriend. It was Susan. I'd never gotten her number and hadn't been in touch since she was buying me those hamburgers. We were rehearsing at the Fillmore East in Manhattan. I went out and bought fifty hamburgers and brought them back for Susan. It was the least I could do.

When I returned to Buffalo at the end of the summer, David said, "I can't give you a grade. You never came to class."

"You know I never go to class," I said.

He said, "I can't help it. I have to fail you."

"I can't tell my parents I failed because I was in Acapulco instead of here," I said. "They'll kill me."

He wouldn't budge. I called Marty, and he said, "Meet me at his office."

We sat together across the desk from David, who said, "Marty, what can I do? He didn't even attend a class. How can I pass him? It's not right."

And Marty said, "*Sprechen sie Deutsch?*"

David went pale. After a moment he sighed. "Okay, I'll give you a D."

"Make it a B," Marty said.

David said, "Will you settle for a C?"

"Take it, Marty!" I said.

When we left the office, I asked Marty what that was about. He had arranged for David to pass his required German course for his Ph.D., even though David did not in fact *sprechen* any *Deutsch*. He owed Marty. With that little bit of extortion I graduated and got my diploma in February 1968—and learned my first coupon lesson.

||||||||||||||||||

I headed back to New York. So did Joey. After four years as roommates and best friends we fell a little out of touch for a while as each of us tried to figure out what he was going to do now. I still didn't know. I'd heard about the New School for Social Research, in Greenwich Village. A cousin of mine owned a clothing factory in Manhattan's shmata district called Divine Garments. I thought maybe he'd give me a day job and I'd go to night school and try to figure myself out. I took an apartment on Sixth Avenue in the Village, a sixth-floor walk-up that I shared with the guy who had sold me my first pot back at Nathan's.

Divine Garments was a strange place. They made backless suits and dresses for corpses to wear in open-casket funerals. I spent a lot of time around people who were grieving for lost loved ones. I was very appreciative for the job, but I can't say I liked it, and I sure couldn't see myself spending the rest of my life toiling away in the Garment District. Night school wasn't working for me, either. I couldn't be a student anymore. Then some recruiters from California's juvenile probation system came to the New School. I thought maybe I should get on my white horse, go to California, and save some kids. I had my degree in sociology, and it sounded like they could really use the help. Governor Ronald Reagan had declared war against hippies like me. Also, a girl I had a bit of a crush on had moved to San Francisco, and a friend of mine, Richie Lawrence, had moved to Los Angeles to be a TV producer. California was the hippie Mecca, the place a lot of young people were flocking. I felt like it was calling me, too. I'd go to San Francisco and wear some flowers in my hair, as the song said. So I applied for a job as a probation officer at the Los Padrinos Juvenile Hall in Downey, south of L.A., and was accepted.

I went first to San Francisco, where the girl now had a boyfriend. I stayed in a commune there for four or five nights and found communal life was not for me. So much for flowers in my hair. From there I hitchhiked to L.A., where I slept on Richie's floor in his studio apartment in Hollywood. For a while I sold the *Los Angeles Free Press* on Sunset Boulevard and ate the fantastic white-bread hamburger sandwiches from Greenblatt's Deli. I'd also go to Griffith Park for the free lunch the hippies handed out every day.

My parents had given me a few bucks, which I used to buy the old car I drove down to Los Padrinos Juvenile Hall one morning to start my new job. Los Padrinos was a way station for juveniles being processed for court or for transfers in the California Youth Authority system. I didn't have a clue what that meant. In my mind I pictured it like something out of the old movie *Boys Town*. The kids would be basically good boys who'd only gotten in trouble with the law because they were poor, and I'd be the kindly Spencer Tracy father figure who helps them straighten out. But Spencer Tracy wasn't tripping on acid when he showed up for work the first day, with long hippie hair and a Pancho Villa mustache. I did have the presence of mind to hide the strip of blotter acid I had brought with me from New York in the trunk of the car. Reagan was governor, which meant that I was working for him, and Reagan hated hippies, druggies, college students, and just about anyone else who wasn't clean-cut and straight-arrow.

I was at Los Padrinos so briefly that I honestly have almost no recollection of the place except that it looked and felt pretty much like any other grim penal institution. The uniformed guards were all tough, crew-cut cop types who took an instant dislike to me. They gave me a perfunctory orientation, a locker, and a uniform. Then a couple of them led me out to a fenced-in field where I was supposed to supervise a softball game. One of them said to me, "Don't worry. All you gotta do is watch 'em."

The kids were all tough-looking, mostly Hispanic. Everything about their body language and their cold stares told me they could not have cared less who I was or what I thought I was doing there, but I felt a need to explain and ingratiate myself with them. I said something along the lines of, "Listen, guys, this is the luckiest day of your lives. Look at me. I'm not like those other guards. I'm here to help. All I want is for you guys to do good and be happy and get out of here and have a productive life. I'm going to do everything I can to help you get through this. I know what it's like to be trapped in a room." I didn't mention I'd been trapped in a room by a mutt named Skippy.

They just stared. No reaction at all. I wasn't even sure they understood English.

"Okay, fellas. Let's just play ball."

That's what they wanted to hear. They fanned out in two teams and started to play. For a few minutes they were just like any teenagers on a ball field, and I relaxed a little. Maybe this wasn't going to be so bad.

Then they stopped playing. And started to make a circle around me and move in, those hard looks still on their faces. It was like something out of *West Side Story,* only these kids weren't Broadway dancers playing gang members, they were the real deal. One of them shoved me from behind. Then another punched me in the face. Then a kid whacked me on the shins with a bat. None of the blows were really hard. They weren't actually beating me up, which they could easily have done. They were just testing me, showing me what was what. Still, it was pretty frightening. I looked around, over their heads and their cold stares, and discovered that those other guards had left me out there alone. I'm sure they knew what I was in for. I'm sure they liked it.

I started yelling for help, and gradually they sauntered out to the field and broke it up. There was an eerie calm to the way they and the kids all went through the motions. No one was much bothered, except for me.

"What the fuck?" I asked one of the guards.

He shrugged. "Happens every day here. This is what we do."

"I guess you guys don't want me here."

He snickered. "Good guess, Barbara."

Barbara? The contempt everyone in this place felt for me—the guards, the kids—hit me like a train. Whatever I had been thinking this job was going to be like, this wasn't it. I went inside, took off the uniform, walked out to my old car, and drove away. I hadn't lasted four hours.

3

I DROVE UP THE FREEWAY THAT NIGHT and took the exit marked "Hollywood," because that was where Richie's place was. But it was late and I didn't know if I could test our friendship by sleeping on his couch anymore. I had some cash on me and decided it would be better to stay in a motel. I drove along busy, six-lane Highland Avenue until I saw a motel vacancy sign. It looked like a fleabag, which I figured meant I could afford it, but the rooms were too expensive. I continued along Highland until I got to a place where the right lane was right turn only, onto Franklin Avenue. The lights and all the action seemed to be back on Highland, but I kept going.

A few blocks farther along I saw another vacancy sign. It was the Landmark Motor Hotel. That was the night Janis punched me. The next day I was hanging at the pool with her, Jimi, and the others, and my new life's journey began.

I should note here that as clear as my memory of meeting Janis and the others at the Landmark is to me, my partner Joe has a very different recollection of the sequence of events—a story I'm sure he'll tell sometime. Alice always says that if you remember the sixties and seventies, you weren't there. I am the perfect example.

Things I remember couldn't have happened, and things I can't remember have been proven to me to have happened. Joe, Alice, and I agree on the most important points, though.

The Chambers Brothers and Paul Rothchild spent the most time at the Landmark. The Chambers Brothers had a house in Watts where their mother lived, but kept a room two doors down from mine. Paul lived at the hotel permanently, and Jim Morrison often came to visit. Janis had a room downstairs, Room 105, and came and went as she toured around. Sadly, that was the room where she would die of an overdose in 1970. Jimi was in and out. Creedence Clearwater Revival regularly stayed there when they came to record. All the English groups who came to L.A. on tour or to record stayed there, unless they had a lot of money, in which case they stayed at the Continental Hyatt in West Hollywood, better known as the Continental Riot House for the wild times Led Zeppelin, Rolling Stones, and other bands had there. But not many had any money at that time, so they stayed at the Landmark.

It was a different time. Rock music wasn't the corporate industry it would become in the 1970s. The artists weren't the giants they became. They weren't Mount Rushmore. They were just a bunch of young people struggling to make it. They were a great group of friends and in some ways a family to me. They'd all gather down by the pool in the afternoons, talk shop, and sometimes they'd jam and sing. The leader of the jams, if he was there, was always Arthur Lee of Love. He would give out the harmonies, say, "Why don't you come in [with vocals] here?" They all looked to him to guide them. That was interesting, because to the public, the rest of them were all much bigger stars, but among themselves they all really respected Arthur.

With all those rockers at the hotel, it was a Mecca for groupies.

You could sit at the pool and see these girls come into the hotel and work their way around the balconies, moving from Hendrix's room to Morrison's room to Bobby Neuwirth's and so on. Occasionally I'd get to be with one myself, just by being there. The first groupie I was with, I was so naïve I thought, Wow, this girl really likes me. And then she was two doors down the next night. Oh, maybe she didn't like me that much. But at least I was no longer a virgin.

There were all types of groupies. A lot of them kept lists of the guys they scored, and had competitions. In a class by themselves were the GTO's, Girls Together Outrageously. They were at the Landmark all the time. Seven pretty, insane young girls who all called themselves Miss Something—Miss Christine, Miss Pamela (Pamela Des Barres, who wrote a couple of widely read books about the groupie life), Miss Sparky, Miss Mercy, Miss Lucy, Miss Sandra, and Miss Cynderella. They originally called themselves the Laurel Canyon Ballet Company. Frank Zappa suggested the name GTO's when he turned them into a singing group and produced their first and only album, *Permanent Damage*. They made themselves indispensable around the hotel. They would do anything anybody needed: buy clothes, run errands, cook meals. They used to cook me meals, and it was colors you never saw before in nature: weirdly green-and-yellow food, purple-and-blackish stuff—unbelievable. But they were very sweet, and they did anything you needed, just to help.

One day we were all down at the pool and looked up to see a clothesline full of ladies' underwear hanging in the sun outside a room near mine. Was it some new groupie phenomenon? No—the Ice Capades had come to town and the skaters were staying at the hotel. That was one of the most exciting things that ever happened there for Willie and Lester Chambers and me.

|||||||||||||||||||||

I started doing business with the musicians at the Landmark within a few days of getting there, but it wasn't music business. I had brought quite a bit of acid with me that was left over from my days of dealing it back at college. LSD came in such tiny doses that you could fit thousands of hits on a sheet of blotter paper or in a vial.

I found Jimi by the pool and asked him, "Anybody here take acid?"

"I do. If it's really good I might tell my friends."

It was really good. I started selling it to people at the hotel to support myself. Then I got some hash, which I traded for a type of excellent grass called Icepack, which came in extremely compressed, very hard one-kilo bricks. You could build a house with them. Joe came out to join me; we were roommates again, and partners. Within a couple of months we had built a very profitable business dealing. We bought a shiny black 1954 Cadillac limo, which the Chambers Brothers' cousins slept in at night for a year or so, because there wasn't enough bed space in their room. The Chambers Brothers were the ones who went out of their way to befriend us and make us feel comfortable. I can't say I had a real relationship with, for example, Jimi or Janis, but the Chambers Brothers and I became family. We're still good friends to this day; Lester's kids come to visit and have dinner when they're in Hawaii.

It was because of the Chambers Brothers—and the drugs— that we got started in the business of managing acts. One day Joe and I were hanging at the pool with Lester, Willie, and Jimi. Lester asked us, "What are you going to say if the police come around and ask where you got the money for that limo?"

I said, "What do you mean? Who's going to ask?" In Oceanside cops never came to the door asking where you got the money to buy your house.

"Where I come from in Watts," Lester explained, "if you have a new watch you better be able to tell the cop on the beat where you bought it. Otherwise you're going to have eyes on you. You don't want eyes on you considering the business you're in. You need a cover. You guys are Jewish, right?" When we said yes, he said, "Well, then you should be managers."

We said, "Yeah, we should be managers!"

We had a great friend from college, Roger Rubenstein, who managed the Left Banke ("Walk Away Renée") in New York. We asked Roger if he'd let us say we represented the Left Banke in California.

One day Joe and I walked into a clothing store on Santa Monica Boulevard. We were pretending to be the Left Banke's managers. We met a girl who worked there, named Cindy, who said, "Oh, I have a brother in a band. You should meet them."

At just about the same time, someone at the Landmark, maybe Jimi, said to Lester, "Don't you have that band of freaks from Phoenix living in your basement in Watts? Why don't you tell them you found these two Jewish guys who manage the Left Banke and they'd like to represent them?"

Lester said he'd bring them over.

We had just gotten a new shipment of grass, and everybody came up to our place to try it. At one point I answered a knock on the door, and the five guys in this band were standing out there. When they tell this part of their story, they always laugh and say that the room was so thick with pot smoke they couldn't see anyone. But as the smoke cleared there were Janis, Jimi, and Jim Morrison on the couch. Alice Cooper were a "band of freaks" all right. They all had really long hair—one of them down to his ass—and though they were all wearing dungarees, they also sported giant earrings and fingernails painted all different colors, like nothing I'd ever seen in my life.

They were Alice Cooper: guitarist Glen Buxton, guitarist and keyboardist Mike Bruce, bassist Dennis Dunaway, singer Vince Furnier, and drummer Neal Smith—Cindy's brother! They had started out together in high school in Phoenix, Arizona, calling themselves the Earwigs and lip-synching to Beatles records, "and we were awful," Alice writes in his book *Alice Cooper, Golf Monster*. "Simply awful." Then they learned how to play and became the Spiders, a typical mid-1960s rock band, except that they were already starting to play around with stage props, a big black spiderweb. They made a couple of singles that were local hits, then came to Los Angeles in 1967 to try to make it there. They were all around nineteen, twenty, a couple of years younger than me, and what they discovered when they got to L.A. was that every other rock band west of the Mississippi had the same idea. L.A. was crowded with bands, and there were only so many places to play. Since their music at that point was pretty much the same psychedelia every other band was playing, they needed to stand out in other ways. So they came up with their new band name, Alice Cooper. Since all the other bands wore jeans and hippie clothes, they started wearing their weird outfits. Vince Furnier wasn't identified as "Alice Cooper" yet; the whole band was Alice at that point. But he was on his way. He wore runny makeup inspired by movies like *Whatever Happened to Baby Jane?* And they started developing an increasingly bizarre stage act inspired by horror movies and the art of Salvador Dali, whom they had discovered in high school art class. Vince would use anything for a prop. He says that what they were doing was "stylistically a cross between an out-of-control freight train and a horrible car crash." Nobody in mellow, hippie L.A. rock was doing anything like it.

What made all that even odder was that Vince came from a very conservative Christian household. His grandfather and father were ministers in the Church of Jesus Christ, an offshoot of Mormonism. As a kid, Vince divided his time between church, school, and watching TV, where he first saw and started imitating Elvis Presley and then Mick Jagger. The family moved around when Vince was a kid. He grew up in Detroit until he was ten, then in L.A., then in Phoenix.

In L.A., Alice Cooper definitely stood out from the pack, but they still weren't going over well at all with the hippies. The Chambers Brothers, some of the nicest people you could ever meet, took pity on them and let them stay in their basement in Watts while they struggled to get gigs.

And now Lester and Willie found them "a manager." To me Alice Cooper seemed like the perfect band to manage, because from what I could see they had absolutely no chance of ever making it, so I wouldn't have to do any work.

They stayed maybe half an hour that day. I took them into my bedroom and gave them a big handful of grass, not knowing then that despite their weird look they were all pretty straight kids who didn't smoke pot or do other drugs . . . yet. We agreed that I was their manager. It was that simple. Vince later told an interviewer, "Shep and I met on a lie. I said I was a singer, he said he was a manager."

Then I saw them play. It was at Bob Gibson's Cheetah Ballroom on a pier in Venice Beach. I thought they were awful, just dreadful. Vince remembers them starting the show with the corny theme song from *The Patty Duke Show,* instantly alienating their hip, hippie audience. Musically it was scattered rock and roll, not my style at all, and visually it was really strange. Vince wore a striped metallic shirt and had dyed blond streaks in his hair. They used theatrical stage props, which *nobody* else in rock did then. One was a free-standing door that Vince stood behind and stuck his head through the window to sing the whiny song "Nobody Likes Me." He was right. He was really drunk and antagonistic to the audience, and they were shouting at him things like, "You suck, Alice Cooper!" He said, "Why don't you all go home?" And they did. The place emptied out.

One of the few people left by the end of the set was Frank Zappa. Zappa was revered among rock fans as the renegade genius who created the Mothers of Invention. His music mixed rock and jazz with avant-garde electronic and orchestral compositions, plus heavy doses of up-yours satire. With his business partners Herb Cohen and Neil Reshen he ran his own independent production company, and the Bizarre and Straight record labels. He was the king of the freaks, so naturally Alice Cooper worshipped him. Just before I met them they had gone up to Frank's log cabin home in Laurel Canyon to audition for him. He'd told them to come at seven. They showed up at 7 A.M. and Miss Christine let them into the basement. They set up their equipment and started playing, loud enough to shake the walls. The way Vince remembers it, Zappa ran down the stairs, naked and sleepy-looking, and yelled at them to stop making all that noise so early in the morning.

"You told us to be here at seven," they replied.

"I meant seven P.M.!"

They agreed to stop, but only if he'd come see them play an actual show.

When I went backstage after their set, not knowing what to say to the band because their music was so bad, Zappa was back there talking to them. When he left, I asked Vince what that was about.

"He wants to sign us to his record company," he said. "And he wants his manager to manage us. We said okay. We didn't tell him that we found you. We're supposed to go in this week and sign the contract."

I probably should have been angry with them, but this whole business was so new to me that I didn't know that. So I just said, "No problem. I'll go tell them."

One morning that week I called the office of Herb Cohen, Zappa's manager and partner, and told the receptionist I'd be dropping by. Then I got in the limo and drove to my first meeting. And I do mean my first meeting. I had never been to a business meeting in my life and had no idea what was supposed to happen. I parked in the underground garage of a typical glass and steel L.A. office building on Wilshire Boulevard a few blocks west of Fairfax. I took an elevator up to the third floor. The door that had HERB COHEN MANAGEMENT on it also said Bizarre Records, Straight Records, and several other things. I walked into the reception area, which was like a dentist's waiting room—a few chairs, a few magazines, no love or care put into it at all.

I'd been sitting there maybe five minutes when this guy came out a door. He was a bearded, burly man, maybe five ten, 220 pounds of solid muscle, really tough-looking. He looked more like a bouncer than a manager, but it was him, Herb Cohen.

"Come in here," he growled.

I followed him into his office, he closed the door, and with no preamble, no layup of any kind, Herb Cohen started verbally lashing into me, raging, playing the heavy, nasty in a way no one had ever been to me in my life.

"Who the fuck do you think you are?" he shouted. "I fuckin' manage this group. The fuckin' balls on you. I'll ruin them. I'll ruin you!" And so on.

I told him I was sorry about the mix-up, that I was excited for them to have this opportunity, things like that. It didn't calm him down at all. In fact, he actually picked up a chair, lifted it over his head, and started coming at me with it, screaming at the top of his lungs. "*YOU FUCKIN FUCK FUCK . . .*"

At that moment the door burst open and the GTO's rushed in. They had heard him screaming and come to save me. It was like a miracle. I didn't know at the time that he managed them. They formed a circle around me and walked me out of the office.

I drove back to the Landmark and thought, What the fuck just happened? That's when Lester explained to me that I'd had a pretty standard business meeting with Herbie Cohen. He was a tough New York Jew, a horrible guy, an intimidator. He acted like that with everybody and I shouldn't take it seriously.

I had nothing to lose. Managing the band wasn't my livelihood, it was my cover. So I wasn't intimidated as much as I was angry. Who the hell did this guy think he was?

Eventually Herb moved on to other acts and I guess forgot about us because our earnings were so insignificant. Joe and I remained the band's managers, and Straight Records still wanted to put out their album. One good thing that came out of it was that Cohen's number two, Joe Gannon, started working with us as production manager. Joe Gannon was the real deal, with a lot of experience from being on the road with acts that ranged from the Kingston Trio to Bill Cosby. He became an integral member of our organization and a very good friend.

Joe Greenberg and I started trying to book the band some shows. I knew nothing about booking shows. The first one we got them, I think, was at Fort Huachuca, an army base in Arizona. The guy who booked us was a real Sergeant Bilko type who ran the entertainment side of the PX. He promoted the show as

"Alice Cooper, Stripper-Singer." He hired sexy girls in hot pants to sell tickets to the soldiers on their payday. When Vince and his band of long-haired weirdos took the stage, this crowd of red-blooded American GIs who were expecting a strip act were *very* disappointed. They booed and threw bottles and food at them until they drove them off the stage.

Still, as so often happens in my life, something really good came out of this. Joel Siegel, later the movie reviewer on ABC, was the PR man at the base. When he came to New York he contacted me and we began a great friendship. For many years we met at a Jewish deli once a week for breakfast. In the 2000s, when he knew he was dying of colon cancer, he wrote a book for his son, *Lessons for Dylan*. It's one of the proudest things in my life that in this book he gave Dylan my grandmother's recipe for chicken soup. So thank you, thank you, Fort Huachuca.

We asked Lester if he could help get us some real shows. The Chambers Brothers were scheduled to play the first Newport Pop Festival, at the Orange County Fair Grounds on the first weekend in August 1968. The bill included Jefferson Airplane, the Grateful Dead, Sonny & Cher, the Byrds, the Animals, Tiny Tim, Steppenwolf, Canned Heat, and several other top acts. Somehow Lester got us on there. But when we drove up to the main gate and told the guard "Alice Cooper," he didn't see us on his list and wouldn't let us in. Fuck. In the age before cell phones, we had no way to reach anyone. As we drove away I looked at the bands listed on the fairgrounds' sign and saw the James Cotton Blues Band. It gave me an idea. We drove around to another gate and I said to the guard, "Joseph Cotton Blues Band." I meant to say *James* Cotton, but it came out wrong. Luckily the guard must have never heard of Joseph Cotton, and he didn't know that James Cotton was black, either, so he waved us in. The festival drew an immense crowd of 140,000, the largest pop concert ever at that point. It was great exposure.

In this early period Joe was more aggressive and successful at booking gigs than I was. It was Joe who got us booked at Bill Graham's Fillmore in San Francisco, which was the premier venue for rock bands at the time. All the top acts played there. If a smaller band like us did well at the Fillmore, venues all around the country would start booking you, and you were on your way up the ladder to being a top act yourself.

"I'm going to get us in there," Joe said. I didn't think that was possible, but Joey was determined. He hitchhiked up to San Francisco, took some acid, and sat in the waiting room for days before getting an audience with Graham. Graham had never heard of Alice Cooper, of course, and apparently assumed that she was one of the hippie folksingers who went over well in San Francisco. We made no effort to disabuse him of this notion. Miraculously, we got on a bill opening for Ike & Tina Turner and It's a Beautiful Day. When Alice Cooper arrived on the night of the show it was like a band of freaks from outer space invaded Graham's holy temple of rock. Alice wore a jacket of dead rats; the rest of the band was in glitter spandex and high-heeled boots. Nobody in San Francisco had ever seen anything like them—nobody in the world had. Joe said the band was into their second song, I think, when Graham stuck his head out of his office, saw them onstage, and flew into a rage. Bill had a history of that. He was the epitome of the tough Jew, who'd come to America without a penny and worked his way up. He had a really short fuse and a tendency to get physical when provoked.

When it came time to do the album with Zappa, neither the band nor I knew a thing about that process. I was in way over my head. At eight on the appointed morning we showed up at the Whitney

Recording Studio in Glendale. We were amazed by the place, very impressive, home of a famous pipe organ. Frank's younger brother Bobby met us. At nine Frank walked in and said, "Bobby's going to record you. I'll come back at five and pick up the tapes."

The band ran through their songs a few times that day. We all thought it was a rehearsal for the actual recording. Frank showed up at the end of the day, picked up the tapes, and said, "That's it. The album's done."

We all said, "Really? Wow. Okay." We had an entirely different idea of how you made an album, but since we had no clue we just figured this must be how it was normally done. The GTO's told us that was how they did it. Wild Man Fischer, another act on the label, did it that way, too. What did we know?

When the album, *Pretties for You,* came out in 1969, the rock critics killed it. Lester Bangs called it "totally disposable" and a waste of vinyl. I was quickly learning a mantra of show business: "Every rejection brings you closer to acceptance." We must have been getting close!

iiiiiiiiiiiiiiiii

In 1969 I added another act to our roster—briefly.

One afternoon I was hanging around the pool with Lester, Willie, and Jimi. They said they might have another group for me to manage.

"Got a card?" Lester asked.

I said, "A card?"

"A business card. You got to have a second act to be a real business. You need some cards to help get you some acts. It's important for clients to know you got a real business. What are you going to call your company?"

"No idea."

In those days, when they closed their shows with "Time Has Come Today," the Chambers Brothers always flashed the peace-sign V. Besides being the bass player, Willie was a good artist. So Lester said, "Willie, you think you can draw the peace sign for Shep's business cards?" Willie drew a hand with two fingers making the V.

The business still needed a name. I went to the front desk and asked Mr. Latour if he had a dictionary. I don't know why I expected him to, but he reached under the desk and pulled out a big Webster's. I opened it to the A's and went down the list to the first word with a *v* in it—*alive*. And that's how we became Alive Enterprises. We got cards printed up with Willie's V-sign drawing in the middle of the word *Alive*.

Then they introduced me to this band—Pink Floyd. They were mildly successful but nowhere near the giant act they'd later be. They had toured their way across the country and were now in effect stranded in L.A. They were usually second on the bill, maybe headlining once in a while, getting maybe $2,500 a night. They were getting ready to go back to London and wanted one more show before they left.

Their road manager, Steve O'Rourke, said to me, "Okay, man. If you can get us a decent gig on the way back to England, we'll let you represent us over here."

I asked Lester, "What's a gig?" Shows you how new I still was at this managing thing.

He said, "It's a *job*. I'll help you out." Pink Floyd had played once the previous year at a club in Chicago, the Kinetic Playground. Anybody who played the Fillmore in San Francisco also played the Kinetic Playground. It was in a former dance hall and roller rink on Clark Street, with state-of-the-art psychedelic light shows, very counterculture, perfect for Pink Floyd. When I called the owner, Aaron Russo, he immediately agreed to book the band. This was on a Tuesday or Wednesday, and he wanted them for that Friday. He'd pay seventy-five hundred dollars, which was a huge amount back then.

When I told O'Rourke he was stunned. "This Friday? Seventy-five hundred dollars? We've *never* made seventy-five hundred. You're our U.S. manager!"

If I had known anything about the business I'd have known there was something fishy here, but I didn't know anything about the business. I asked Lester about the gig and he told me, "Make sure you get half the money wired up front." I didn't know how to go about that, so Pink Floyd went to Chicago without anything up front. When they got there, they called and left me a message that there'd been a fire in the club. Russo had shut it down, canceled their gig, and wasn't paying the fee. Everybody but me seemed to know that Russo had his own place torched for the insurance money. But he couldn't afford to burn good relationships with artists' agents by booking too many acts and not paying them all. So he had booked only four acts for that week: Iron Butterfly, King Crimson, Poco, and Pink Floyd. The fire happened after Iron Butterfly's first show, the remaining dates were canceled, and Russo was refusing to pay the other bands' fees.

So Russo wouldn't pay Steve and Steve wouldn't pay me, and Steve fired me to boot. I'd worked with Pink Floyd for maybe nine days. And I could really have used the money Steve was refusing to pay me, so I was pissed. But I learned a very important lesson. Jerry Wexler of Atlantic Records, a brilliant man who became a dear friend, would later put it to me this way:

"The three most important things a manager does are, number one, get the money. Number two, always remember to get the money. Number three, never forget to always remember to get the money."

4

BY 1969 THE COPS WERE MAKING MORE AND MORE DRUG BUSTS at the Landmark. It was time to get out of that business. We'd had a good run, made good money and great friends. Quitting that meant this music business would be my only business.

I sat Alice and the band down and said, "If you want to do this seriously, let's do it. And not quit until we're all millionaires."

We shook hands, and I've been Alice's manager ever since. Just on that handshake, never a written contract between us from that day to this.

We were getting gigs, but not enough to live on. I realized that we had to do something radical. It seemed to me that part of the appeal of the big rock acts, the ones who were on the level that we wanted to get to, was that parents hated them. Elvis in his day, the Stones in ours—because parents hated them, the kids loved them. Alice was already pretty good at making rock audiences hate him, but that wasn't enough. I had to think of ways to make their *parents* hate him. Elvis had ridden the hatred and revulsion of his audience's parents to the top of the world. I was convinced that his legendary manager, Colonel Tom Parker, had done everything in his power to fan that hatred, because it made for fantastic global publicity. For instance, one of the best-known stories in rock-and-roll history was about how the cameramen for Ed Sullivan's TV show were ordered not to show "Elvis the Pelvis" below the waist, because his gyrating hips were too sexy for family audiences. Everybody I knew thought that this censorship was a terrible violation of Elvis's rights as a performer, and that Colonel Parker should have refused to let him go on under those restrictions. I thought that was dead wrong. I would have bet you any amount of money that the Colonel *insisted* that Elvis not be shown below the waist. The week after the show, every newspaper in the country ran stories about Elvis's invisible pelvis. No one in America could *not* think about Elvis's pelvis. It was brilliant publicity—and look where it got him.

I wanted us to generate the same hateful press for Alice. Then the kids would love him. No other rock band was working that angle at the time. They were all making hippie peace-and-love music. I thought that the more outrageous, obnoxious, and offensive Alice could be, the more we'd stand out.

My first idea was a ridiculous stunt. There was a small club in a former storefront on Sunset Boulevard called Thee Experience, owned by a very sweet couple, Marshall and Marsha Brevitz. Marshall was the exact replica of Larry in the Three Stooges. The stage was on the right as you walked in, and the space only held twenty-five or thirty small tables. Although it was small, it had a lot of cachet. All the biggest rock acts liked to play and jam there. My relationship with the Brevitzes was that three or four nights a week before the club opened I'd go by and drop off fifty dollars in change for their cash registers. At the end of the night I'd swing by again and they'd give me back the fifty. So when I explained my stunt idea to Marshall and asked if we could stage it at the club, he agreed.

The stunt involved the band wearing outrageous new outfits. The guys were used to wearing odd clothes onstage. The GTO's had found a bunch of sparkly old Rockettes and Ice Capades type outfits at a thrift store in L.A. and gave them to the band to wear.

Cindy, Neal Smith's sister from the clothing store, was a seamstress. I had her cut and stitch up the new outfits for the stunt. We got to the club early, before it would usually open, and the band went into the bathroom to change into these outfits. They came out wearing pants and shirts of transparent plastic. Not thin plastic like Saran Wrap, but thick and heavy, like see-through tarpaulin. And they were completely naked underneath.

They started to play a set. There weren't more than ten or fifteen people in the audience, mostly friends we'd brought to help us with the stunt. I went to the pay phone to get phase two going. The phone was on the wall by the bathrooms, which were down a hallway, through the kitchen, and down another little hallway, so you couldn't see the stage. I called the police and said, "My child is in this club and the band is onstage naked. This is horrible. How could they allow this to happen?" They said they were sending a squad car and that I should stay on the line until it arrived. I stood there a while. I could hear the band playing but not see them. Eventually I heard a siren outside, hung up, and made my way back out to the main room.

My plan was that the band would get arrested for indecent exposure, which would get a lot of press, and parents would hate us. But there was one thing I hadn't counted on. It was hot up there onstage under the lights, and those thick plastic outfits had completely fogged over. You couldn't see the band was naked at all. The police came in, looked around, scratched their heads, and left.

After the show I said to the band, "You know, we've just hit that classic moment where we can't even get arrested in this town. It's definitely time to leave Los Angeles." We agreed that the band would stay on the road until the first city where they got a standing ovation, and that's where we'd settle.

That was the start of a long, hard road trip for Alice Cooper, into the spring of 1970. They played a lot of places in a lot of cities all around the Southwest and Midwest. They barely made enough money to put gas in the van. Forget food and lodging: they slept in the van and starved. As I remember it, Joe took them on the road. I didn't meet up with them until about a month into the tour, in Cincinnati, where they got their first steady engagement, playing a place called the Black Dome for maybe six weeks. A guy named Ron Volz ran the shows. When I asked him if he knew a cheap or preferably free place for us to crash, he told us all the fraternity houses were empty for the summer. "I can show you one, but you have to get out when the frat boys come back." We all lived in this frat house for weeks. Then one afternoon we looked out the windows and the frat boys, real jocks, had returned. We ran out, some of us jumping out windows, and got out of there quick. Ron was staying with us, so when we hit the road again he came along. He worked with us for the next thirty years. He's in Hollywood now.

From Cincinnati we drove to Detroit. Vince still had relatives there, so it seemed like a destination. For our first couple of weeks we bounced around from one fleabag motel to another, and I bounced a lot of rubber checks on them. I never felt good about that; I was doing it out of necessity. Later, when we started making money, I gave all those places good checks to cover the bad ones, with my apologies. Karma is important.

Our standing ovation happened at a rock festival in Saginaw, Michigan, where Alice Cooper played last. The crowd got to their feet. We were stunned and delighted. Then a couple of the Hells Angels the festival had hired for security walked onto the stage while the band was playing and wanted them to stop. I remember one of them pointing some kind of weapon at Vince, Vince tossing him a pink toy bunny rabbit he used as a prop, and the Angel ripping and slicing it up. That was the cue to get off the stage. Still, we'd gotten the audience standing, so when we got to our cars we said, "This is it. We're moving to Michigan." It was only later that we learned the crowd had stood because there were more Angels in the back, using their bikes to get the crowd up and out.

By then we'd already moved into a house in Pontiac, the Detroit suburb. This is when things really started to come together. We all lived together under the same roof, so they could rehearse whenever they wanted. When they did, people started gathering at the fence to listen. We noticed there was something a little odd about them, and realized we lived next door to an insane asylum. The funny thing was, they looked at us like *we* were the crazies. We figured it was a sign we were doing something right.

The rock scene in Detroit was much wilder and more vibrant than on the West Coast. Detroit bands like the MC5 ("Kick Out the Jams") and the Stooges rocked *hard*, they played loud and fast and angry and don't-give-a-fuck, and the Motor City kids loved it that way. They were some wild shows. People responded much better to Alice Cooper than the folks had in laid-back L.A.

It was at this point that I said to Vince and Dennis, "We have to develop this Alice character. Let's do something new that nobody's ever seen before, and let's stick with it." We got very innovative about putting on theatrical performances that didn't cost a lot—because we didn't have a lot to spend. We still wanted that standing ovation, and started thinking up ways to get it. One simple strategy worked every time. Alice skewered a bunch of dollar bills on a sword and waved it over the audience. The people in the front would start jumping up and reaching for it, so everybody behind them got up, too. It had nothing particular to do with the song, but it had the desired effect of getting everyone up and cheering and having fun. Looking for a way to close the show, I started bringing feather pillows. We slit them open, and Alice waved them over the crowd, filling the place with feathers. Whenever we could we used CO_2 tanks to blow the feathers all over the hall. It looked fantastic in the stage lights. A good friend, the New York promoter Ron Delsener, told me that for years after we played at Town Hall in Manhattan, feathers continued to drift down from the ceiling during other acts' performances there. Sorry about that.

I took the feathers idea to a whole new level at the Toronto Rock and Roll Revival festival. The bill featured Chuck Berry, Jerry Lee Lewis, Little Richard, Gene Vincent, Bo Diddley, Junior Walker, the Doors—and John Lennon and Yoko Ono with the Plastic Ono Band, John's first live performance since the Beatles broke up. It was televised in prime time. I had gotten a call from the festival organizer, who said he'd pay me 30 percent of the proceeds to help them organize it. I said I wouldn't charge them a fee, but they had to put Alice on the bill between John Lennon and the Doors in prime time. It was a fantastic opportunity for our little-known band to share the stage with all those greats in front of a festival audience of sixty thousand, on TV. It was an early foray into the tactic I call "guilt by association." If you want to be famous, get next to somebody who already is famous. Millions of kids would be watching this show to see the Doors and John Lennon. In between, they'd see Alice Cooper, and just assume they were famous, too. I would play that card successfully many times over the years.

We went all out to make an impression at the festival. Alice kicked a football into the crowd, chopped a watermelon with a hatchet, and tossed feathers everywhere. In the midst of all that, he remembers, he looked down and an actual chicken was strutting across the stage. He knew nobody in the audience had come to a rock festival with their chicken. It could only have been me. And it was. It was a feral chicken that happened to be roaming around backstage. I just thought, We've been doing the feathers, why not a whole chicken? So I let it loose on the stage. Alice bent down, grabbed it, and tossed it out over the heads of the audience. He didn't know chickens can't fly. It dropped like a meteor into the crowd. For a second they seemed stunned. And they went wild. It was astounding. This was the height of the peace-love hippie era. But Alice had gotten them so worked up into a frenzy that they ripped that chicken apart, just tore it to pieces, and threw it back at him—wings, legs, the head, all bloody. I had to turn my head. I faint when I see blood.

The press we got for that was phenomenal. Stories ran in all the newspapers about this bizarre new act, Alice Cooper, who ripped the head off a chicken and drank its blood. You can't buy that kind of publicity for a million bucks. One day Alice Cooper was unknown. The next they were sitting for press conferences, fielding questions about why they killed the chicken. Alice's answer gave perspective to the issue. "On the way in from the airport," he said, "I drove by four Colonel Sanders fried chicken places. Is anyone asking him about killing all those chickens? I'm sorry. I thought it could fly. All I did was throw it."

It was the same for me. I thought chickens could fly. Oops. I can say that we never threw another chicken. We didn't need to. That incident ignited the booster rocket we needed to blast off toward notoriety and success.

It was around that time that a very good publicist, Pat Kingsley, suggested to me that having the whole band identified as Alice Cooper and doing press conferences together wasn't going to work. It was confusing. She said we should pick one spokesman. I met with the band, and we decided it should be Vince. He was a natural with the press, friendly, funny, easygoing. He always had a smile and a good quip for them. The rest of the guys were musicians. They wanted to talk musical theory. Vince instinctively knew what the press wanted to hear and fed them their lines.

From then on Vince began to be identified as Alice Cooper, and the rest of the guys were Alice Cooper's band. Over the next few years, as Alice grew into one of the biggest rock stars in the world, the rest of the guys fell increasingly into his shadow, and it rankled them more and more. Understandably so. But we all went into it with our eyes wide open. We were very, very clear about it and shook hands on it. I told them all, "We agree that we're going to do this thing until each of us has a million dollars in the bank. We're going to stick with it and either fall on our faces or come out millionaires." And to do that we had to make Vince Alice. We were still just kids. The idea of us all becoming millionaires was the wildest fantasy. But we all agreed to try, and we all agreed that turning Vince into Alice was a key piece of the puzzle.

5
ıııııı

SINCE MOVING TO CALIFORNIA I hadn't been in touch much with my parents. I had written to them occasionally—remember, no email yet—telling them that I was managing a rock band named Alice Cooper, a guy, not a girl. I don't think it did much to change their expectations that I was going to be a complete failure. Now I swung us a gig in New York—and not just in New York, but at Madison Square Garden. It was in the Felt Forum, the smaller space next to the arena, but still. I had gotten us on a bill with an all-girl group called Enchanted Forest, because their agent, Bob Ringe, was a guy I knew from high school. I was so proud to have a group at the Garden that I asked my parents to come. They drove up from Florida for this big night. Well, I walked into the Felt Forum, and there were fewer than a hundred people in the audience, two of them being my parents. They were civilized about it and polite when they met Alice, but I could see it in their eyes: I was still a failure. It was not a great moment.

Onward and upward.

While I was in Toronto working on the festival, I had gone to dinner with David Briggs, a record producer who lived there. I told him about the failure of Alice's first album, and he said, "I'm in the middle of producing one now with Neil Young. We've been at it about two months."

I said, "Two months? We did ours in a day."

"Come on."

"No, really." I told him about our one day in the studio.

"You're out of your minds!" he cried. "That's not how you make albums. They take months."

I brought Alice up to Toronto to meet David. It was a real education for both of us. We asked David if he'd produce Alice's next album and he agreed. Somehow we convinced Zappa and Herb Cohen to let us do it with him—but they put him on an extremely limited budget. Still, it covered more than a month in the studio. Now the band really experienced the process of making a record the right way, how a producer helps to construct songs, take them apart, and put them back together correctly—all the things Zappa did not do. It didn't really work on this second LP, *Easy Action*. David didn't much like the music—he called it "psychedelic shit"—and the band hadn't really gotten their songwriting down. When it came out in 1969 the critics were harsh again; *Rolling Stone* summed it up as "nothing that interesting here. The freaky music is sort of freaky, but the pretty stuff sounds like something Walt Disney had the good sense to leave in the can."

Still, the process of making it was a good education for the band and me. We realized that in terms of commercial success a producer can be almost more important than the artist. A good producer figures out how to frame a song to make it work. This was a giant revelation to us. We knew we needed to find a producer like that. This is when my management skills started to develop, I think.

"Let's not reinvent the wheel," I said. "Who makes the best records?"

"The Beatles."

"Forget that. Who else makes great-sounding records?"

We all hit on the Guess Who, the Canadian band whose "American Woman" was just then topping the charts. They also had big hits with "No Time" and "These Eyes." They were a band without a giant following, yet making amazing hit records. That seemed like a good model for us.

It was a huge realization for us that you could go to a producer like you went to a dentist and get him to fix your music. This Guess Who producer sounded like the best dentist around. He was Jack Richardson, at a Toronto studio called Nimbus 9. We tried to get to him, but he didn't return our calls or answer our letters. So we went to Nimbus 9 and hung around in the lobby. We still didn't meet Richardson, but a young guy named Bob Ezrin, who worked with Richardson, agreed to come to New York and hear the band. We had a gig at Steve Paul's The Scene on West Forty-Sixth Street, one of the hottest rock clubs in New York at the time. Hendrix, the Doors, the Chambers Brothers, Traffic, Johnny Winter, everybody played there, and when they weren't playing a gig they hung out and put together late-night jams. All the media in the city went there, the Warhol crowd, everyone who was anyone hip or cool. It was a very big opportunity for a struggling band with two failed records to its name. The only reason we got it was that a good friend of mine in the city was a mobster who ran a protection racket. The Scene was one of the clubs they "protected." He got us the gig.

Bob Ezrin came. We found out later that Richardson had hired him the very day that we met him; that he had never produced an album; and that Richardson had sent him out to the Nimbus 9 lobby that day saying, "There's no way in the world I'm going to produce this band. They're horrible. Go out there and get rid of them." Instead, he caught a great show at the Scene. The hip New York audience loved everything about Alice Cooper that the Los Angeles audiences had hated. Bob went back to Toronto determined to convince Richardson to produce the next album.

I flew to L.A. to tell Herb Cohen and Zappa about it.

"Absolutely not," they said. "Wrong guy. He makes pop music. We don't do pop music. We don't want a hit record."

"What do you mean you don't want a hit record? Isn't that what this is all about?"

"Not at Straight," they said. "That's not what we do." It would ruin the label's edgy, rebellious, noncommercial image.

I explained the situation to the band. "We can't continue without a hit record," I said. "What do you want to do?"

They wanted a hit. They wanted Richardson. It was my job to strategize how to make that happen despite Cohen and Zappa's opposition.

I had by then formed a couple of relationships with executives at Warner Bros. Records, Straight's distributor. One of them was Clyde Bakemo. I told Clyde we had gotten Jack Richardson to produce the next LP, but Herb wouldn't give us the money because he and Zappa didn't want us to have a hit.

"Are they crazy? They don't want a hit? What are we working so hard for?"

"If you can just give me the money for four tracks," I said, "somehow I'll get Richardson to do them."

Clyde found the money—I believe it came from a Doobie Brothers' recording budget. Which is funny, because I'm really good friends with Doobies Pat Simmons and Michael McDonald. It wasn't a whole lot of money—I think it was thirty or forty thousand. The thought was if we could cut four good tracks and Clyde played them for Herbie, then Herbie would allow it. In other words, Clyde thought it was an artistic problem. I later decided that was not the problem, as I'll explain.

As it turned out, Richardson did not produce the tracks. Bob Ezrin did. He was excited about the band's potential after seeing that show in New York. He met us at the gigantic RCA recording studio in Chicago. We had never been to anything like it. This was the big time. And the process with Bob was nothing like our previous experiences recording. The band worked with Bob for a month and a half before cutting the tracks, breaking each song down and building it back up, inspecting every detail, every line of the lyrics, and every lead solo. They constructed each song like you build a beautiful house.

"I'm Eighteen" came out of this process. Bob had worked particularly hard with them on it. It started out a long, rambling jam. Bob got them to toss away the excess and hone it down to a tight three-minute anthem we all thought was a potential hit. I now thought that instead of just playing Herbie the tapes, wouldn't it be more convincing to get "I'm Eighteen" some radio play? I was showing my ignorance about how the business worked. But I was trying to learn. I was reading *Billboard* voraciously, reading everything I could get my hands on to educate myself. One of the things I discovered was that there were certain "breakout" radio stations that led the way in putting songs on the air. If they played a record, others followed. The two biggest breakout stations in North America were WIXY in Cleveland and CKLW in Windsor, Ontario. Working on the Toronto festival, I had met CKLW's program director, Rosalie Trombley. Canada had just passed a content law stipulating that all Canadian TV and radio had to play a certain amount of Canadian product. Although we'd cut the tracks in Michigan, we had a Canadian producer, so we qualified. Alice's road manager, Leo Fenn, engineered putting "I'm Eighteen" in

Rosalie's hands. (Leo was the father of the actress Sherilyn Fenn. We babysat her when she was little.) Leo knew Rosalie's young son. I don't remember if we had a test pressing made or just a tape or what, but anyway Leo met the kid after school one day and gave him the song to give to Rosalie.

That's how "I'm Eighteen" got put on rotation at CKLW. Score one for Alice. In my naïveté, though, it had not occurred to me that if a song got radio play, the record had to be in the stores so kids could buy it. The better the sales, the more radio play it would get. No sales, and radio would drop it. So when I called Clyde and told him "I'm Eighteen" was on CKLW, he said, "You can't have it on CKLW. You don't have a record yet. This is a disaster."

Showing a gigantic set of cojones, Clyde got "I'm Eighteen" pressed as a single on Warner Bros. Records, not on Straight, and rushed it out to stations and stores. Warner was Straight's distributor, but Straight was an independent, separate label, so what Clyde did was not exactly legal. We were under contract to Straight. If Straight didn't want to put our record out, technically it shouldn't have been put out. Clyde did it anyway and let the chips fall where they may.

Now that there was an actual record, we got on the phone twenty-four hours a day calling the request lines of every radio station in the country. I had my mother, my uncle, all my relatives calling radio stations. "Please play 'I'm Eighteen' by Alice Cooper." Stations around North America started playing the single. And now Straight sued Warner Bros. over it. As a result, the second pressing of the single went out on the Straight label.

I freaked. I did not want the song on the Straight label. They had treated us so shabbily before, I didn't want them profiting from us now that we had a hit. More than that, our contract with Straight, which we had signed in our inexperience, gave them the song publishing rights to any of our music they put out. Publishing royalties for a hit song could be significant, and I didn't want Zappa and Herb Cohen to get them.

I went right to the top this time: Mo Ostin, president of Warner Bros. Records. Mo was an industry legend. He had started out at Verve, working with all the great names in jazz, then moved on to Reprise and now Warners. He had signed everyone from Frank Sinatra to the Beach Boys to the Kinks and Jimi, whom he signed after seeing his famous Monterey Pop performance in 1967. I had tremendous respect for him, and felt that if anyone at Warner Bros. would do the right thing by us, it was Mo.

He didn't disappoint. When I aired my complaint to him, he said, "Shep, I got you covered. But you got to do me a favor. Don't press the issue. I will get you publishing. You have my word on it, one hundred percent."

So we were back on Warner Bros. And then it went back to Straight. I called Mo, and Mo said, "I got you covered." We were back on Warners. Then we were on Straight again. It was ridiculous. But every time I spoke to Mo, Mo said, "Shep, I got you covered." And I believed him. The more I dealt with him, the more he became, in my head at least, one of those mentor figures I sought out. I trusted that eventually we would see those publishing royalties.

⸻

All this time, "I'm Eighteen" was climbing the charts. Kids loved it. Alice, who wasn't much older than eighteen himself, was speaking directly to the confusion and dissatisfaction a lot of young Americans were feeling in that era of Richard Nixon and the Vietnam War. *Lines form on my face and my hands, / Lines form on the left and right, / I'm in the middle, the middle of life, / I'm a boy and*

I'm a man. It wasn't specifically an antiwar or antidraft song, but a lot of people, adults and kids, heard that in it.

Warner Bros. executives still weren't behind us, though. They seemed to think "I'm Eighteen" was a fluke. I had to fight to get the money to finish the album, with both Richardson and Ezrin producing.

Love It to Death came out in March 1971 and was the band's breakthrough LP, their first gold record. Along with "I'm Eighteen" it included another track destined to be one of Alice's signature songs, "The Ballad of Dwight Fry." Bob Ezrin worked a lot with Alice to develop his character so it wasn't just part of the stage act, but integral to the songs. For instance, this is when Alice started singing "Dwight Fry" in a straitjacket. Bob had him do it in the studio when they recorded the song, so that when he sang "I gotta get out of here," he really sounded like he meant it.

Warner Bros. was finally behind us. They told me they would pay for a big press party for it in L.A. if I organized it. For the first time, after years of scrambling, I had real resources, power, and some semblance of control. I knew it at the time—and it felt good.

"Absolutely I'll organize a party," I said to them. We had been to some record company parties. They were terrible bores. Some executive would give a speech about the record to a roomful of other record execs, publicity people, and press.

I said, "But it's got to be an *Alice Cooper* party." They asked me what that meant. "I don't know," I said, "but I'll figure it out."

Somehow we found out that July, the time for our party, was the point in the year when the debutantes all had their coming-out parties. If Alice Cooper was a good, clean, all-American girl, she'd have her coming out then, too. Where do coming-out parties happen? In hotels.

So that's what we planned, a coming-out party for Alice Cooper. On acid. We took out ads in the society pages of the L.A. papers, announcing the coming out of Alice Cooper along with all the real debutante's announcements. We rented the elegant, mirror-paneled Venetian Room in what we thought was the most appropriate hotel in L.A., the giant old Ambassador on Wilshire Boulevard. It had a lot of history, some of it glittering and some of it grim. In the 1920s and 1930s it was the home of the Cocoanut Grove nightclub, where every movie star and celebrity of the time hung out. In 1968 it was the site of Robert Kennedy's assassination. In the three years since then the hotel had not been able to revive its once-glittering reputation. Still, management did not want to rent rooms for record company parties, so Bob Regehr, a hip publicist at Warners, and I told them we really were booking a coming-out party for a debutante from Pasadena named Alice Cooper. They were delighted. They didn't find out we'd tricked them until guests started arriving on the night of the party and it was clear they weren't there for any debutante. They were really angry but it was too late.

The affair went off on July 14, 1971, Bastille Day, and it was wild. *Rolling Stone* called it "the party of the year." We had mailed out formal invitations, and five hundred guests showed up. Mo was there with his wife, a really nice lady who was celebrating her birthday. Atlantic Records president Ahmet Ertegun was there. Celebrities included Richard Chamberlain, Donovan, Rod McKuen, Randy Newman, some of the Beach Boys, and John Kay of Steppenwolf. Reporters for the society pages came, thinking it was a real debutante affair. At the entrance to the Venetian room, they were greeted by old-fashioned cigarette girls. Only they weren't girls, they were the Cockettes, a San Francisco drag troupe, wearing glitter in their mustaches and beards. They offered cigars, cigarettes, and Vaseline. When you entered the room, the card with your table number was handed to you by a person in a gorilla suit, wearing a bra and panties. The hotel, thinking it was a real society affair, had provided their resident four-piece band, who looked confused as they played standards like "Somewhere My Love."

When everyone settled at their tables the festivities began. "You could tell right off," Mo later said, "even from the preliminary entertainment, that either the world was just about to come to an end, or good taste had simply been thrown to the wind." A six-foot-tall cake with *Happy Bastille Day Alice Cooper* written on it was wheeled out. Miss Mercy of the GTO's burst out of it and threw handfuls of cake and icing at the people at the front tables. We'd hired an enormously fat black stripper named TV Mama and her husband. I asked him if there was any way I could pay her to take her top off and show her gigantic breasts. "She may be TV Mama to you, but to me she's TV dinner," he said. "That'll be five hundred dollars." I paid. She slapped the people up front, including Ahmet Ertegun, with her tits. The band played a short set, including "I'm Eighteen" and "The Ballad of Dwight Fry." Alice wore a silver lamé bodysuit, and put on the straitjacket for "Dwight Fry." As people left, the Cockette cigarette girls offered dildos.

It was a great success. Everybody had fun and it got tons of press. It was the start of a grand tradition. Over the years Alice Cooper became famous for the great parties we threw.

|||||||||||||||||

There's still the question of why Herb Cohen and Frank Zappa were so adamantly against having a hit record in the first place. I don't think it was really to maintain Straight Records' edgy, rebellious integrity. I think it was a strategy right out of *The*

Producers. I'm not one hundred percent certain about some of this, and neither Zappa nor Cohen is around anymore to ask. Not that I'm so sure they'd give a "straight" answer. But this is what I *think* was going on, and it's the only explanation that makes sense to me.

We found out later that Warner Bros. gave Straight a large advance to deliver four artists (four albums). Out of that advance, they had to pay the cost of producing the albums. A typical album in those days cost $150,000 to produce. The artist earned about a dollar in royalties for every record sold, but the record sales had to earn back the initial recording costs before the artist saw any of those royalties.

So Straight got $150,000 from Warner Bros. to make Alice Cooper's album. They spent $10,000 making it, and banked the other $140,000. The only way they'd have to pay Alice Cooper any of that would be if the album really sold. For instance, if Alice Cooper sold 100,000 records, Straight would owe the band $90,000 ($100,000 minus the $10,000 production costs). So, of that $140,000 Straight put in the bank, they would be left with only $40,000.

Obviously, then, the fewer records Alice Cooper sold, the better for Straight. That's why the very last thing Herb Cohen and Frank Zappa wanted was for Alice Cooper or any Straight artists to have a hit record. I think that's why Herb went ballistic and tried to scare me away at our very first meeting, and it's why they wouldn't let us record with Richardson.

6

WITH THE FIRST SIGNIFICANT CHECKS coming from Warner Bros. in 1971, Joe Greenberg and I moved back to New York together, to a really nice rented brownstone on West Thirteenth Street between Sixth and Seventh Avenues in Greenwich Village. Our landlord was a dentist. It was a real New York street, lined with trees, most of the block brownstones, with a couple of night-clubs and a couple of restaurants. We ate almost every day in a classic old-school Italian restaurant across the street, Felix's. Felix and his son were really nice to us and let us build up credit for as much as forty-five days.

Our living room was our first real office. Alice's first fan mail was starting to come in. That was exciting. If I was there I'd get up in the morning and start opening it. One morning I opened an envelope and shook out a little baggy filled with some pale, sticky-looking liquid. *Dear Alice,* the letter read, *You bring out the best in me. I've never been able to tell anyone about my desire for men. I masturbated today thinking of you, and here's the cum.*

I didn't open up a lot of fan mail after that.

The money coming in also let us rent the band a new place where they could all hang together and rehearse, only now they could do it in a style that suited rock stars. It was the Galesi mansion and estate in Greenwich, Connecticut. You entered through a twelve-foot-high iron gate and drove up to the house. It was fifteen thousand square feet, with I think forty rooms, thirteen of them bedrooms, plus a chapel, a beautiful library, frescoes on the ceilings, huge chandeliers, a pipe organ, and a grand ballroom so high and wide that we could set up the entire touring stage and do complete dress rehearsals. We converted the dining room into a recording studio. Alice and his girlfriend Cindy took the vast master bedroom, and the other guys spread out to others.

I knew of the Galesi family from my time in Buffalo, where they were very powerful and prominent. The patriarch, Francesco Galesi, was the son of Italian immigrants. He started out dealing in real estate in and around Buffalo in the 1960s. He was also a pioneer in telecommunications and would later be one of the directors of WorldCom, the second-largest long-distance telephone company in America. He was worth hundreds of millions, married a Russian princess, and had several enormous homes spread around, including a ten-thousand-square-foot Sutton Place apartment in Manhattan.

All the guys started living the way they thought rock stars should. They drove up to the mansion in Rolls-Royces and Jaguars. They bought all the liquor and drugs they wanted. Alice was becoming a drunk. It should have worried us more than it did at the time, but to us the drinking, the drugs, the sex were all perks of the rock star life, and we were only just starting to learn that the lifestyle had consequences. To us, drinking was cool, drugs were cool, sex was cool, and none of them had any serious consequences. You might get hungover, but no one we knew had liver failure. You might get herpes, but there was no AIDS. Jimi and Janis overdosed in 1970, Jim Morrison died in

1971, but we were still pretty slow to realize how dangerous the rock lifestyle could be.

Besides, Alice was a manageable drunk. He had started out drinking whiskey all the time, and that he couldn't manage. So he switched to Budweiser in the daytime. From when he woke up he always had a can of Bud, but he sipped it slowly, not to get falling-down drunk, just to relax and help him through the day. It was his way of coping as life got steadily busier and crazier. At night, when his work was done, he'd switch to V.O. and Coke.

To me, the drunk was Alice, not Vince. They were still definitely two distinct personalities at that point. Vince was a sweet, funny, grown-up kid who was so gentle he wouldn't swat a fly. His favorite activities were watching old movies and corny TV shows, and, after Joe Gannon introduced him to it around 1973, playing golf. His favorite music was Burt Bacharach. Although he drank, he did not, at that point, do any drugs, not even pot. He even forbade anyone from smoking pot around him on tour. On the road, when everybody else was partying, he was in his hotel room, watching the Marx Brothers on TV and practicing putts.

Basically, Vince and Alice were black-and-white opposites. For a while, he only became Alice when he put on the outfits and makeup and hit the stage. But slowly, Alice was taking over off-stage as well. I admit I pushed hard for that to happen, because Vince wasn't really a rock star—Alice was. And we needed the rock star not only onstage, but also offstage, hanging out with other stars, talking to the press, drinking, having a great time.

Of all the band members, rock stardom had the worst impact on Glen. He became such a horrible alcoholic he almost died from it, then switched to drugs. He was the band's Brian Jones, an integral founding member who lost his way and was barely part of the band anymore. He showed up for rehearsals and recording sessions erratically. We had to hire a session guitarist to play his parts for him. It angered some of the other guys in the band, who wanted to fire him, but Alice loved Glen and couldn't do that to him.

|||||||||||||||||||||

Alice took some of his first real money from Warners and bought himself a nice house in Benedict Canyon, north of Beverly Hills. He bought it from H. R. Haldeman, of Nixon White House and Watergate break-in fame. Cary Grant lived next door, and Elton John had a house just up the road. I woke up the day after escrow, turned on the news, and saw on my TV screen the house burning down. Right to the ground. Apparently Elton John saw flames in the windows and called the fire department.

I called Alice and said, "I have some good news and some bad news."

"Give me the good news first," he said.

"You know that skylight you wanted in the bedroom? No problem."

"Great," he said. "What's the bad news?"

"The house burned down."

He thought I was joking at first. He went on to build a completely new house on the site and lived there for most of the 1970s.

Living in Benedict Canyon made Alice a neighbor of one of his biggest heroes—Groucho Marx. Groucho was in his eighties and frail, Alice was a rock star in his early twenties, but they hit it off. Like me, Alice had been a huge Marx Brothers fan ever since childhood. He had watched the movies dozens of times and could practically quote them line for line.

Groucho had insomnia and would call Alice at one in the morning and ask him to come over. Alice would get on the bed with him and they'd watch TV until Groucho fell asleep—both of them wearing Mickey Mouse ears. It was the cutest thing you ever saw. Groucho chewed on a cigar, Alice worked on a six-pack of Bud, and they watched old movies.

Alice respected Groucho as a living legend, a comic genius, and a virtuoso entertainer. Once he got to know Groucho the man, he adored him even more, and felt very protective of him in his old age. Groucho treated Alice like a son. He liked Alice so much, he started calling him "Coop," which had been his affectionate name for his friend Gary Cooper. They went places together all the time. They sang a duet of Groucho's signature song, "Lydia the Tattooed Lady," at a birthday party for Sinatra. Alice took Groucho to the Polo Lounge for his eighty-sixth birthday. I thought their odd-couple friendship was really, really sweet.

I first met Groucho one night when Alice called and said, "Can you come over to Groucho's house?" I was really nervous about meeting him. I was twenty-two, and as I said, like Alice I'd been a Marx Brothers fan all my life. They made me and my dad laugh so many times. I felt I owed Groucho so much. I found them on the bed, watching TV. We made a little small talk until Groucho fell asleep and we left. The next morning Alice called and said, "You notice there wasn't a nurse last night? He requires around-the-clock care, but he can't afford the night shift of nurses anymore. Can you see if you can put his business back together?"

Erin Fleming, a part-time actress, was Groucho's assistant. She had started out as his secretary, mostly to answer fan mail, and at some point moved in. When they appeared together on Dick Cavett's TV talk show, she said, "I'm Groucho's secretary." And he cracked, "This is the euphemism of the year." He was in his eighties, she was maybe thirty, and he wanted the world to think she was assisting him with more than the mail. When he was alone, he'd slump over like a marionette with its strings cut. But when she walked into the room, he'd perk up right away.

Erin hired me. I never really had a conversation with Groucho about being hired. I brought in a guy named Bill Owen, who worked for me in L.A., and positioned him in Groucho's house to be the point man. We looked into Groucho's financial affairs and they were a mess. He had to be wealthy, but nobody seemed to know where the money was. We found a bunch of freeloaders on the books, whom Groucho was paying for doing nothing. We weeded them out.

I concentrated on finding him more income sources. I was really proud of the first deal I did for him. In London, at the end of the block-long Savile Row, was a top-class men's tailor shop called Blades. When you walked or drove down Savile Row you looked right at their big display window. I licensed them Groucho's image for a sweater they displayed in that window for years. I wear one in *Supermensch*. We also helped get the episodes of his old TV show *You Bet Your Life* back on the air, which took some doing. Almost everyone who appeared on that show was an actor who came under Screen Actors Guild rules, which meant you could syndicate it but you'd lose money unless you cut deals with the actors or their estates to reduce their SAG rates. A lawyer had already outlined the strategy and started making the phone calls, and we helped execute.

In 1972 A&M released the album *An Evening with Groucho,* a live recording of a one-man show he did at Carnegie Hall. TV show host Dick Cavett introduced; Groucho told family stories and jokes, and sang a few of the classic old songs from his films, with Erin singing backup and Marvin Hamlisch on piano. Albums actually made money in those days, so I thought we should ask A&M to give Groucho an advance against potential future earnings, which we could use to pay for nurses. *A&M* stood for Herb Alpert and Jerry Moss, the label's founders, both industry legends. Erin knew Moss and got us a meeting. To me, Moss was larger than life, a guy from the Bronx who had made better than good. I was feeling particularly small and insignificant as we arrived at A&M's offices, which were in the beautiful old Charlie Chaplin Studios at La Brea and Sunset.

Erin and I waited a short while, then Jerry Moss rolled into the room in a wheelchair. I didn't know if he had a permanent condition or had just had an accident or something; he is only about ten years older than me. Erin hugged him.

"Listen, guys, I'm on my way to the hospital," he said. "I'm getting back surgery today. But I figured it was important, and I love Groucho. So what are we meeting about?"

Nervously, I said, "Mr. Moss, thank you for taking the time. I really appreciate it. I got involved in Groucho's financial affairs, and we're looking for ways to get him some income to pay for the health care he needs at this stage in his life. We're wondering if—"

Out of nowhere, like a tiger exploding out of the underbrush, Erin started screaming at him. "You motherfucker! You're fuckin' stealing from him, you cocksucker!" And on and on, raging like a madwoman.

I was shocked. I didn't know her well and had no idea where this was coming from. It was one of the most insane things I'd ever seen. He let her scream like that for maybe thirty seconds, then turned to me and said, "Shep, can I see you outside?"

I followed him to the outer office.

"So what's this about?" he said, remarkably calm under the circumstances.

I explained that I'd gotten involved through Alice, that we were looking for ways to pay for night nurses, etc.

"I'm really sorry this happened, Mr. Moss. I had no idea. This is the last thing I wanted."

Now, this is the kind of mensch Jerry Moss is. He pulled out a checkbook and right there and then wrote Groucho a personal check for a significant amount. I was so moved and touched. Then, as he held it out to me, he got a little glint in his eye and said through a crooked smile, "There's only one thing I ask."

"Name it," I said.

"Don't bring her back!"

Jerry has a coupon with me that goes all the way back to that day. I will gladly pay it back for the rest of my life. I will do anything I can do for him at any time. That's what a coupon is. More than that, I had a feeling that day that we'd become good friends, and we did. I found him a house in Maui, so we became neighbors. I helped to organize the wedding of Jerry and his beautiful wife, Ani, in the heart of Maui. A few friends attended, including Herb Alpert and his wife, Lani. Herb blew a conch shell we found on the beach. I arranged for a helicopter from the Kapalua Hotel to bring in champagne, caviar, and a picnic dinner. A few years ago Jerry asked me where I'd like to go for my birthday. He has his own plane. I said Bhutan, and he and Ani flew me there.

The rest of Erin's story, unfortunately, is a sad one. When Groucho died in 1977 she fought a big court battle with his family over the estate, and lost. The mental instability she flashed in Jerry's office grew more pronounced over the years. She would be periodically institutionalized in the 1990s, sometimes living on the street in between, and she killed herself with a gun in 2003. Still, she did a lot of good things for Groucho in his final years, and he was very happy to have her around.

At some point Groucho got curious about Alice's act, which he'd seen something about on TV, so Alice invited him to a concert in L.A. Alice's stage show was as elaborate as we could afford to make it by then. It was theatrical and cinematic as much as musical. I loved it and pushed for it, because I loved theater and still didn't care much for the music. Alice did "Dwight Fry" in the straitjacket. For "Dead Babies" he chopped up baby dolls with a hatchet and lots of fake blood. It was my idea, even though I had to turn my head for that part of the show. As I said, I feel faint at the sight of blood, even if I know it's fake. If I cut a finger I have to get down on the floor and put my feet up above my head for a few minutes. That's why I wanted it in the show. I figured that if it freaked me out it had to have an effect on the audience. Alice says it was his idea to start performing with a huge boa constrictor curling around him. I'm sure I approved even though I'm very frightened of snakes. I have never touched a snake in my life. We also staged a choreographed knife fight inspired by *West Side Story*. It ended with the band dragging Alice to the gallows and hanging him.

Erin brought Groucho. Wearing earplugs, he watched the fake blood, the mock hanging, the snakes, all of it, and loved it. After the show, a reporter asked him what he thought and he said, "Alice is the last chance for vaudeville."

When Alice read that quote in the paper the next day, he said, "Wow, that's exactly what it is." I thought so, too. It had not occurred to us before then, but vaudeville was the perfect frame to put around what we were doing, a big, freewheeling spectacle of nutty, offbeat novelty acts. Groucho had seen it before we did.

Every couple of weeks a bunch of us went to Groucho's house for dinner. After dinner everybody had to give a little performance for him. Apparently it had been a tradition in the Marx household when he was growing up. Groucho insisted it be something you wouldn't usually do. If you were a singer, you had to dance. Alice told a string of one-liners once. If you wanted musical accompaniment, Jeff Bridges might be there to play guitar, or Marvin Hamlisch or Bud Cort at the piano. (Bud was the young actor in *Harold & Maude*. He often came over to watch TV with Groucho, too.) When it got around to me, I always read contracts to musical accompaniment. Groucho would let me go for maybe thirty seconds before calling, "Get out of here!"

Groucho never turned off the shtick. A group of us would be out somewhere, and he'd turn to me and say, "You're Shep?"

"Yes, Groucho."

"You're my manager?"

"Yes, Groucho."

"Funny, you don't look like a crook."

Or we'd be sitting in a restaurant and he'd say, "It's been five minutes and you haven't sued anybody yet."

Sometimes I still can't believe that I got to work with Groucho Marx. I can't say I ever developed a close friendship with him, like Alice and Bud Cort did. I don't think I ever sat down for a one-on-one conversation with him. I was always too much in awe to talk. And I wasn't trying to develop a career for him at that point in his life. My job was to maximize his assets, and I was proud and happy to do it.

7
||||||

ALICE'S FOURTH ALBUM, *Killer,* came out toward the end of 1971. It got to number 21 in *Billboard. Love It to Death* had peaked at 35, so we were climbing, but we still had a way to go. The rock critics were coming around by then to the music, but they still mostly hated the stage show. They were all sixties people, and their favorite bands were still playing on bare stages in jeans and T-shirts. But I didn't care about the rock critics. I wanted to get all the parents in the world hating Alice Cooper, and the parents weren't reading *Rolling Stone* or *Creem. Rolling Stone* meant nothing to us. We had to jump over the rock media and get Alice in *Newsweek* and *Time* and *BusinessWeek* and the newspapers and tabloids and evening news, all the places where the parents would see him and be revolted by him.

That's how I came up with the idea of wrapping panties around the vinyl in the packaging of Alice's next album, *School's Out.* It started because I read a story about a big shipment of paper panties being confiscated by U.S. customs officials at the port of Baltimore, because they violated something called the Flammable Fabrics Act. That you couldn't bring paper underwear into the country struck me as hysterical. Then, when we were designing the jacket for *School's Out*, we decided it should look like an old-fashioned wooden school desk, the kind where the top flipped up and there was space underneath for your pencils and rulers and such. The album would go in there, and we were thinking about what to put in there with it—something a bad kid would have in his desk. Someone suggested a switchblade, but obviously we couldn't do that. Someone else said bubble gum.

I remembered the panties. What was the coolest thing a seventh-grade boy could be hiding in his desk? What if we wrapped paper panties around every copy of the LP that went out? Parents everywhere were sure to hate us.

When I told Warner Bros., they said it would be too expensive and they'd never sell enough records to recoup the cost. I said fine, I'll pay for it. They still said no. In those days I didn't take no for an answer. Once I had set a goal, there was no such thing as no.

There were only two companies making album jackets in those days: Ivy Hill Lithograph, and Album Graphics. In most cases, they had exclusive deals with the record companies. For example, Ivy Hill did all the album jackets for Warner Bros. Records. Album Graphics really wanted to do business with Warners, but they couldn't get in the door. I said to them, "I can get you in the door. Alice is their biggest act. They won't let me do the panties because of the price. Here's what they want to pay. Can you do it for that?" They agreed.

But Warners still turned it down anyway. That really pissed me off. Now, I knew a secret about a Warners exec involved in giving Ivy Hill its deal: he lived in a very nice house that he rented from Ivy Hill Lithograph. I went to him and said, "You're not gonna fuck up my artist just because you have this nice setup with Ivy Hill. I'm going to give you up to your bosses if you don't let me do this deal with Album Graphics." Miraculously, Ivy Hill matched the price, and the world got just what it needed—an album wrapped in panties. Thank you, thank you.

So I bought perfectly legal, flameproof paper panties in Canada, and Ivy Hill made the jacket and slipped the panties onto the albums.

At the same time, I called up a friend of mine, Tom Zito, a big writer at the *Washington Post*. I told him I had a great story for him, if he could get it on page one. I explained that these panties were being shipped to Warner Bros. for Alice's album, and if Customs found out they were going to seize them under the Flammable Fabrics Act. I gave him the shipment number and everything he needed. I bought an additional one hundred thousand *not*-flameproof paper panties made in France and had them shipped to Warner Bros. Records. It wasn't a huge outlay of cash, just a few pennies each. When they came through the port of Baltimore, Customs confiscated them, and Tom was there to write the story.

His article ran on page one of the *Washington Post*, with a headline about the "Largest Panty Raid in History," explaining that the panties were supposed to be wrapped around Alice Cooper's new LP, *School's Out,* which was coming out that week. Other papers picked it up, and that's how parents throughout the land learned not only that this outrageous Alice Cooper had a new album coming out, but that it was supposed to be wrapped in panties. How disgusting. It was one of my greatest PR coups.

Warner Bros. was furious with me. They thought all the panties wrapped around the albums were flammable, and they were going to have to pull the albums from the stores and remove the panties. They'd be out millions. I let everyone know the truth—Warners, the distributor, the stores—and they all calmed down. It was win-win for everybody.

I like telling this story because it's a good example of my modus operandi: *creating history instead of waiting for it to happen.* In this case, I knew my goal was to get parents to read about Alice Cooper's new album over breakfast and hate his guts. Okay, how to get there? Then I saw the article about the confiscated panties. Then—probably twenty-five joints and a lot of time in the Jacuzzi and alone in hotel rooms later—I made the connection. Alice plus panties equals lots and lots of angry parents. Every father in the land with a young daughter would be pissed.

Once I had a path to my goal, I didn't let anything or anyone deter me from following it. So when Warner Bros. didn't want to use Album Graphics or pay for the panties, instead of just giving up I figured out how to make them do it—and I wasn't above using a little nonviolent, gentle extortion on that exec to make it happen.

That brings up another component that was very important to me: *No one got hurt. I drew no blood.* In fact, everyone came out a winner. It could have gone wrong, in a lot of ways. It could have all blown up on Alice or Warners or that exec or Tom Zito, but I put the extra work and time and money into it to make sure it all came out win-win. When you're creating history instead of just reacting to it, you have that control. Visualize what you want the history books to say, then you can make it happen the way you want it to happen.

This is where I feel very blessed, in a way, about my childhood, because it taught me how to be alone. Thank you, Skippy, you miserable mutt, for all that time I spent trapped in my bedroom as a kid, thinking, creating my own worlds in my head. Because it's not like you just snap your fingers and things happen. It's hours of work. It's waking up earlier, maybe getting higher, not allowing distractions to deter you, and then working your ass off to reach the goal you set yourself.

It all starts with the end, the goal. I always tell my clients the real value in me is that I can get a year ahead of you, see where there's a pothole in our road, and figure out how you don't fall into it. That's what I do.

||||||||||||||||||

Both the single and the album *School's Out* shot straight up the U.S. charts. The album peaked at number 2 in *Billboard*, the single at number 7. It was time to break Alice in England. England was still considered the nerve center of rock music. London was rock Mecca. If you made it there the whole rest of the world opened up to you. And we wanted the world. I booked Alice in Wembley Arena, a ten-thousand-seat venue, for Friday, June 30, 1972. But England hadn't really heard of Alice yet, and as the day approached we had only sold five hundred tickets. I knew I needed to get Alice's name out to the British public in a big way, and quick, or we were going to flop.

Some brilliant people in London helped me do that. One was Ian Ralfini, the new head of Warner Bros. Records for England. He was a wonderful man, a true gentleman. He always dressed very nicely and wore a tie. At the time we couldn't get over a guy wearing a tie treating us so well and saying yes to our crazy ideas.

Ian walked me into Derek Taylor's office. Another amazing man, a huge legend in the music business, Derek had been the Beatles' publicist in their early years and was chiefly responsible for whipping up worldwide Beatlemania. Derek was a beautiful character, very cool, always elegantly smoking a cigarette, a man of few words and many great ideas.

Derek's office was circular, furnished more like a living room than an office. When I walked in I was stunned by the assortment of music business legends hanging out there. George Harrison was there, in white robes. He had just come back from India. And a fellow named George Melly, an old-time jazz player who would have been in his early fifties then, a cult hero in England who never made it in the United States. He was a fantastic character, and a total alcoholic. He looked and dressed like a mafioso, with a wonderful face and style. To British musicians he was something like Arthur Lee was to the Landmark crowd, someone they all respected and looked to even though they had larger public profiles. When he played in London clubs the audience was all other musicians.

Roy Silver, yet another legend, was there as well. He managed Bill Cosby, Tiny Tim, and a bunch of others, and he co-owned Tetragrammaton, the record company that had a huge hit with Deep Purple's first LP, and later distributed John and Yoko's *Two Virgins* in the States when Capitol refused to because of the nude cover photo. When you sat in the waiting area at Silver's office in Los Angeles, they didn't ask if you wanted a glass of water—they poured you a glass of delicious first-growth Bordeaux. He later opened a legendary Chinese restaurant, Roy's, where the House of Blues is now. No one went there to eat, but everyone went in the bathroom and got high. At this point Roy was managing an all-girl group called Fanny, who looked like they were going to have a moment, and they were on Warner Bros., so he was meeting with Derek about how to make that work.

At some point Carolyn Pfeiffer came in. Carolyn was an American who had a top-flight public relations firm in London. She was very, *very* good. As a young woman she had started out as an assistant to various luminaries in film, including Omar Sharif, Claudia Cardinale, and Alain Delon. As a publicist her extraordinary client list included Liza Minnelli, Robert Redford, Barbra Streisand, and the Beatles' company, Apple. I think she represented Cannes Film

Festival winners ten or twelve years in a row. She was very powerful and very respected, and couldn't have been nicer, the most refined, perfect lady. And now she was representing us.

I had been hanging out a couple of hours, just soaking it all in, when Derek finally turned to me and asked me what my story was. It turned out he had not heard of Alice. We drank and talked until ten or eleven o'clock. I explained our theory that anything we could do to get parents to hate us was good public relations. We came up with this amazing stunt, guaranteed to piss off and disgust the maximum number of parents.

First we hired one of those trucks that drive around with advertising billboards on them. Then we had to come up with the most shocking image for the billboards. Carolyn and I went through a lot of photos of Alice and hit on it: a Richard Avedon photo of Alice, naked on the floor, with a boa constrictor wrapped around him, just barely hiding his genitals. Richard Avedon was the leading fashion photographer in the world, so, using my guilt-by-association principle, I had arranged for him to shoot Alice. It was his idea to photograph Alice naked with the snake.

We made the billboard—a huge image of Alice, naked, with the snake, under some copy about the Wembley show. Then we put Derek's genius plan in motion. We had the driver of the truck go into Piccadilly Circus, the heart of London, the busiest, most densely trafficked and pedestrian-crowded spot in the city, at rush hour. He drove around the circle a few times—and then faked a breakdown. At rush hour. The traffic jam was a nightmare. For two hours black London cabs and big red double-decker buses were backed up as far as the eye could see in all directions, horns blaring, drivers shouting, a giant crowd of pedestrians just standing there staring. It was pandemonium. Bobbies surrounded the truck, trying to get the driver to move. I had told him, "No matter what they say, do not move the truck."

"But I'll get arrested," he said.

"I know," I said. "Don't worry, I'll take care of you."

He did get arrested, and I paid him very well for it. Not my proudest moment, but it turned out a win-win anyway: the money saved him from losing his house.

Carolyn's job was to get all the press there. There weren't really paparazzi at the time, but there was Fleet Street, where there was a group of photographers who serviced all the magazines and tabloids everywhere. Fleet Street was where you went to find the photographers who could take the shot heard around the world. Unlike American photographers, Fleet Street photographers didn't just go out and try to catch news when it happened. They'd work with you to create the news—and create history. It was good for you and good for them. It was a very different attitude and approach than in America. Carolyn had informed them all that if they were in Piccadilly at such-and-such an hour, they'd get great shots.

It was a big success. We made all the papers, all the evening news shows. Everyone was shocked and outraged. A member of Parliament called for the show to be banned. There were headlines like "Ban Alice the Horror Rocker. He's Absolutely Sick." And the show sold out. The single "School's Out" went to number one in England, and then around the world. That August, a woman named Mary Whitehouse, a famous, self-appointed moral watchdog who was always trying to get what she considered offensive songs, TV shows, and movies banned, wrote to the BBC to complain about their playing "School's Out" on *Top of the Pops.* "Because of this millions of young people are now imbibing a philosophy of violence and anarchy," she wrote. "It is our view that if there is increasing violence in the schools during the coming term, the BBC will not be able to evade their share of the blame." That got us on the front page of the newspapers. Not back in the music section, but page one. There wasn't enough money in the world to pay for press like that. I had a bouquet of flowers delivered to her every couple of hours for days, to thank her for the excellent publicity.

||||||||||||||||||

After Wembley we came back to the States and began a massive tour that started in Pittsburgh's Three Rivers Stadium on July 11 and went all over North America, ending in October. By far the most fun was the extravaganza we threw at the Hollywood Bowl on July 23. The album and the single were getting played everywhere, and we sold the place out. I felt this was our moment. Everything I had done with Alice had already been so overproduced that I had to take this to an even higher level. So I had mariachi bands playing, and more people in gorilla suits wandering around, and bubble machines and balloons and fireworks and all sorts of ridiculous things going on. I was friendly with Wolfman Jack, one of the biggest disc jockeys in the country. He agreed to emcee the show and introduce the bands, and let me come up with spectacular, ridiculous productions just for the introductions. He was a great character and happy to play along. For one band's intro I had him come out on a minibike with a Harley-Davidson crew, another time on horseback; another time he wore a wizard costume. To introduce Alice he would come out riding a camel, dressed like a sheik with an enormous golden turban, surrounded by a dozen harem girls.

This was one of the first really big productions we put on where

I had to use a union crew. Very, very, very difficult. The Hollywood Bowl is probably the toughest union house in the country. I was in way over my head to begin with, even if it wasn't a union house, and I was way overaggressive in what I tried to pull off. It was a really tough day for me, and expensive. The union crew was killing me. By around five o'clock I knew we were losing money on the show. Then Joe Gannon came over to me and said, "We have a problem. We have to hire two more union guys."

I lost it. One of the few times I remember really blowing my stack.

"I ain't hiring any more guys!" I yelled. "I've had enough. I'll cancel the show. I can't take it. Why do I have to hire these guys?"

Joe brought the union steward to me. "If the camel shits," he said, "and the shit steams, it's a moving prop. I need two guys on it. Union rules."

"What if it doesn't steam?" I asked.

"If it doesn't steam you're okay."

So I took Joe over to the corner.

"Here's what you're doing," I instructed him. "You're standing next to that camel the entire time it's onstage, with a towel, and if that camel shits you're throwing that towel on that shit so fast it can't steam."

The show starts, Wolfman rides out on the camel, and of course the camel shits on the stage. And Joe is standing there and throws the towel on it before it can steam. No moving prop, no union house rule violated, no extra two guys.

At the high point of the show we unleashed my pièce de résistance: a helicopter hovered over the Hollywood Bowl and rained panties of different colors onto the crowd. The place went wild. A sea of arms reaching up for those panties, people fighting over them. Elton John was in the crowd that night and fought to get a pair of those panties along with everyone else. He says that night inspired him to make his own shows more spectacular.

Just like the truck driver in London, the helicopter pilot was arrested, and his license was suspended. But he knew that was going to happen. We discussed it all beforehand. And I paid him very well for it. It was his choice. Luckily, he was the last person in Alice's career we had to pay for getting arrested. Thank you, thank you!

||||||||||||||||||

Life on the road was an exciting sensory bombardment, but it was also grueling. For the band it was hours and hours of doing nothing, then two hours of hard work onstage, then more doing nothing until the next night's show. Alice had more work than the other guys, because he was the media point man, and there were always press conferences and interviews for him to do.

For me, though, it was constant, all-consuming work. However hard they worked, I worked ten times harder. In the early days, when we didn't have a lot of money for crews, a lot of times Joey and I drove the truck, loaded and unloaded equipment, then took a shower and were the management collecting the money. Even when we started to have more money, there were never enough hours, and I never got enough sleep. Every day there was another mountain to climb. At one point when we were touring there was a big national gasoline strike. All the gas stations shut down. We had to organize people with ten-gallon drums to meet us along the highway to fill up the tank. Then there was the ASPCA, who had people at every one of our shows after the Canada chicken thing.

Meanwhile there was everything else a manager had to do, including dealing with the record company, coordinating with the producer of the next album, working with the agents and the publicity people, dealing with the press in every city, and, as we managed to make Alice more and more an infamous character, having to meet with and mollify city councils and other committees of concerned adults. This was all before cell phones, emails, and faxes. We fed rivers of coins into pay phones and spent a small fortune on telegrams.

This left me no time at all for relationships. But I did finally become sexually very active. I was in my twenties and finally having sex—a lot of sex—which was really exciting. But how I was getting it soon made me uncomfortable. It was all sex with groupies, which at best meant one-night stands, and often not even that. Groupies were a constant presence on the road. They were in every city you went to, not just where you might expect them, in L.A. and New York, but even in places like Salt Lake City. Girls were always hanging around, wanting to get backstage, wanting to get to the guitar player or the lead singer. I'd give them access to backstage, and when they couldn't get to the singer or guitarist, they'd settle for the manager. I'd tell them I loved them, get them undressed, and tell them I loved them again after sex. Then I either tried to get them out of the room before I went to sleep, or tiptoed out in the morning when the bus was leaving.

It was all a lie on top of a lie. We were lying to each other. They wanted to be with the singer. Nobody wanted the manager. But they'd go with me in hopes of getting through me to the one they really wanted. And I would be saying "I love you," even though I didn't care at all about them. It wasn't even that most of these girls needed to hear it. It was just how the game was played in those days.

All that lying made me really unhappy. I'm not a good seducer. Not my thing. So I came up with the most direct solution I could think of. I got a T-shirt made that said, NO HEAD, NO BACKSTAGE

PASS. If a girl came up to me, I pointed to those words on my chest and said I really meant it. If she wanted a backstage pass, she had to give me some head. Then I'd be fine for the night, and she could go on and try to score the guitar player. It was as honest as I could make it. I didn't want to be lying to some girl, schmoozing her and saying "I love you." I just wanted some head. You see me wearing that T-shirt in *Supermensch* and I probably look like some kind of sexist schmuck, but that was my reasoning behind it: *Let's cut the bullshit*. It worked, and it was great.

I applied the same principle to hiring an assistant to help handle all the paperwork and phones and logistics. I was very honest about it: I'm hiring you to be my assistant, and to give me head. She said okay, and she turned out to be great at both jobs. I know how that sounds, but it worked out perfectly for both of us.

|||||||||||||||||||

By 1973, Alive Enterprises had grown to the point where Joe and I kept two offices, one in New York and one in Los Angeles, and I was renting a place in each city. The one in Manhattan was a two-bedroom apartment near Max's Kansas City.

Socially, I still had no serious attachments, and wasn't looking for any, either. I was dating gorgeous, sexy women, the kind of women I used to only dream about. But I knew something was missing. Then Fat Frankie Scinlaro, Alice's road manager, set me up on a blind date.

He said, "I know this beautiful girl, Winona Williams. You should meet her. You'd really like her." I set the date for the Hippopotamus, a chic disco on the Upper East Side run by a Frenchman, Olivier Coquelin. All the celebrities were going there then, from Jagger to Sinatra. I knew I could get us in.

I went to her place in a cab, and when she got in I saw that Frankie was right. Winona was a stunning African-American girl, a Wilhelmina model from Jersey. Beautiful smile, beautiful face, beautiful figure, beautiful manner. We talked a lot that night at the club and really hit it off. She was my age, twenty-seven, and we had a lot of other things in common. She was sweet, classy, intelligent, and funny.

Around three thirty in the morning we grabbed a cab to head back downtown. The driver fell asleep and smashed into a *Daily News* delivery truck. Winona and I both banged our heads and gashed our eyebrows in the same place, blood flowing. When I told the cabbie to take us to an emergency room, he said, "No! Get out! You are bleeding all over my cab!" That was New York City in the 1970s. We caught another cab and went to the hospital, where each of us got about a dozen stitches.

By now it was five in the morning. We went to my place. We were both exhausted, banged up, stitched up, and on pain-killers. I told her it made no sense for her to leave at that hour. She stayed the night. In fact, she basically moved in. With her stitches over her eye, which I felt sort of responsible for, she wouldn't be modeling for a while, and I was happy to have her hang out with me. I felt there was something special here, some-thing I hadn't felt dating anyone before. Looking back from a great distance now, I'm not sure that it was love, but I think I wanted it to be.

The next day, Winona told me she had an eight-year-old daughter, Mia. Winona's mother, Ruth, was babysitting her in Newark. She asked if Mia could come over and I said of course. Mia was a beautiful little angel, warm, happy, a very calm pres-ence. A week went by, then a month, and it felt very comfortable.

It was the first time I'd been that comfortable with a woman. And I really enjoyed Mia's presence, her innocence, her laughter. I'd buy her a little dress and she would be thrilled. I loved her childish exuberance. Sometimes I'd take her out with me at night, just me and Mia, to music clubs I was checking out. I remember her falling asleep in my lap one night at the Bottom Line. This was all new to me, too. Even when I was a kid myself, I didn't spend a lot of time with other kids.

We moved into a fantastic brownstone on West Ninth Street and Sixth Avenue. I had the whole house. Down a few steps from the sidewalk was a semi-basement level with a pool table and a sauna. There was a private movie theater on the next floor up, then a kitchen and dining area on the next floor, then three bedrooms above that. I didn't cook yet in those days and I don't think I ever turned the oven on, but the great food market Balducci's was right on the corner and I could bring prepared meals home.

It wasn't like we became a traditional family unit. Winona was a model; I was a rock manager. We both lived in the fast lane. In my house on a given night would be Salvador Dali or Alice Cooper or Ronnie Wood. There were always a lot of high-profile people around the pool table and in the sauna. Having a child in the house, I'm sorry to say now, didn't put much of a damper on the drinking, drugs, and sex that went on.

When I got another significant check from Warner Bros., Winona and I took a limo north from Manhattan about a hundred miles to Copake Lake, a wealthy vacation and retirement area not far from the Massachusetts line. Late in the afternoon the limo turned up a long driveway to this unbelievable brick mansion. I had never seen anything like it in my life, except maybe in a movie. Joe Perry of Aerosmith later said it looked like the Addams Family house. It had ten or twelve bedrooms, an amazing dining room with blown-glass chandeliers, a gigantic den with a fireplace you could stand in. From the back of the house you looked down a huge lawn to the lake, with other mansions around it.

I loved the house. I couldn't believe I was standing in it, much less thinking of owning it. We asked if we could stay the night in one of the rooms. The people there were very nice. They told us the story of the house. It was called the Brown Mansion and was built in the early 1900s. Brown's wife smoked cigarettes, which in those days women were not supposed to do. He finished the entire huge attic for her as a smoking room. In his older days Brown became very eccentric. There was a gun tower on the property, and he would stand up there shooting at airplanes that flew over. They also told us that Jay Anson had recently stayed there and written his book *The Amityville Horror* in the house. There was talk of the house being haunted by both Mr. and Mrs. Brown.

I bought the house. We didn't go there for the first few months because I'd spent every dime on it and didn't even have enough money left to buy a car. When I did get a car we drove up every weekend, Winona, Mia, and me. I was so proud of myself. When I drove onto the property I felt like a king. I told my parents that I'd bought a house upstate and they had to come see it.

"Where is it?"

"Copake."

"You're kidding. Is it near the lake?"

"It's on the lake."

"We met on the lake!"

My mother was in a rowboat, my father was on the shore, he saw her and fell in love, and they never separated from that moment. I had never heard that story before. They got to spend a lot of time at the house.

I don't know if the house was haunted, but strange things definitely happened there. My mother, who was the straightest, most nonspiritual person you'd ever meet in your life, had her friends up there one night, and the card table they were playing on started moving. She never went back. Later, when Alice and Joe Perry got out of rehab at the same time and wanted to write some songs together, I let them use the house. They said that doors closed on their own, there were loud rumbling sounds from the basement even though they were alone, and things kept disappearing. They ran out after a night or two and never went back, either.

AFTER THE YEARS OF HARD WORK AND STARVING, the band was seemingly poised to take over the world. Instead, they were slowly falling apart. They scattered themselves around the Galesi mansion and lived separate lives. Alice spent much of his time holed up in the master bedroom drinking Bud and watching TV, while the rest of them complained more and more about falling into his shadow. When we brought in a mobile unit to lay down the basic tracks for *Billion Dollar Babies,* Bob Ezrin also decided to bring in a session guitarist to play Glen's parts.

I understood why it upset the rest of the guys that Alice had become the star. They had all gotten into rock because they wanted to be stars. But they couldn't all be *the* star. We had agreed that had to be Alice. We were on track to our goal of becoming millionaires. I couldn't let their bruised egos derail us.

Alice was now an international celebrity, and the guilt by association was working both ways: other celebrities wanted to be seen with him as much as we wanted him to be seen with them. In the art world of the early 1970s no one was cooler than Andy Warhol, or more interested in the workings of fame and celebrity. When Alice and Andy were photographed together at New York clubs like Studio 54 or Max's Kansas City, it made Alice look more acceptable to the art crowd, and Andy look cool to the rock fans. (For one of Alice's birthdays, Warhol gave him a silk screen of an electric chair—the same electric chair Alice sat in when he was "executed" in his show.)

For the same reason, we really wanted to get Alice seen with Salvador Dali. Dali's work had inspired Alice and Dennis when they were still students. Dali was a god to Alice, and Alice was as close to a Dali as the rock world had. Joe had much more to do with hooking them up than I did. He found out that Dali had a manager in Spain, and set up a meeting at the King Cole bar of the St. Regis hotel on Central Park South, where Dali and his wife, Gala, lived.

Gala swept into the room first. She was everything you'd expect Salvador Dali's wife-manager-muse to be: a gaunt, striking, middle-aged lady in a black tuxedo, black silk scarf wrapped around her head, a black walking cane, trailing in her wake a half-dozen cherubic young boys in black silk outfits. They never spoke, just glided around the room like shadows.

Gala set the ground rules. "He is to be addressed always as The Dali. Money is not to be discussed at any time with him. When I say it is over, you leave."

She took the elevator back up to their suite, and returned ten minutes later with The Dali. As I recall he was wearing an artist's smock; at any rate, it definitely had very large pockets. After polite introductions we all sat at a table. The rest of us ordered drinks while Gala ordered a cup of hot water for The Dali. When the hot water arrived, The Dali very slowly and purposefully drew a small jar of honey out of one of those big pockets, placed it on the table, and very deliberately unscrewed the top. It was brilliant theater—you couldn't not watch. Then he lifted the jar six inches above the cup, tipped it slowly, and a slow-motion stream of honey poured toward the hot water. Meanwhile with his free hand he drew a pair of scissors from his other pocket. He used them to cut the stream of honey. Alice, Joey, and I gaped.

The meeting was very brief. We asked if The Dali was familiar with the new, three-dimensional optical art form, the hologram. A guy named Hart Perry, who'd shot some pictures of Alice for New York's WNEW TV, had shown us some. We wanted to know if The Dali would be willing to make a hologram of Alice.

The Dali went back upstairs. Joe, Gala, and I went for a walk in Central Park, with the cherubs floating behind us, and talked business. Gala informed us that The Dali would retain all rights to any work he produced, and we'd get two copies of it.

It took six months to complete the hologram. We didn't see a lot of The Dali during the process. We had a couple of dinners with him and Gala at Trader Vic's, the restaurant in the Plaza hotel. I loved Trader Vic's, and its over-the-top Polynesian tiki bar decor seemed a perfect setting. (Sadly, when Donald Trump bought the Plaza a few years later he closed the restaurant.) Gala did most of the talking. For some reason The Dali started calling me Mr. Blemly. From then on, through our whole relationship, I was Mr. Blemly. I had no idea why; I still don't know to this day. He'd just say things like, "Mr. Blemly, would you pass the egg rolls." Both times, The Dali paid the bill for us all by signing his napkin. It was how he paid for all their meals. "My friend Picasso, so silly, he had only coffee and biscuits in Paris and he signed the whole tablecloth," he said both times. "I have whole meals and I sign just the napkin."

The most time we spent with The Dali was a very long photo session, probably six hours, shot by our friend Hart Perry. Alice had to be photographed meticulously from every angle for the

3-D hologram to work. The finished piece was a rotating, almost-life-size, three-dimensional image of Alice sitting cross-legged in a white silk outfit, wearing a million-dollar diamond tiara that the jeweler Harry Winston's store loaned us for the shoot—complete with security guards. Alice is holding a small *Venus de Milo* statue, looking like he's either about to sing to her or bite her head off. Behind him, The Dali suspended a plaster sculpture of Alice's brain with a chocolate éclair in the middle, covered in little black ants—a signature Dali image. He called it all *First Cylindric Chromo-Hologram Portrait of Alice Cooper's Brain*.

Alice was overwhelmed by the experience of working with and just being around his idol. Every now and then when we were with The Dali he'd catch my eye and give me a look that said, *Oh. My. God*. Remember, we were just a couple of kids in our twenties, and this was one of the greatest living artists in the world. What was most awe-inspiring for us was that The Dali didn't seem to make art only when he was painting or sculpting; he seemed to make his entire life, every minute of it, every word and gesture, art. That was the point of the scissors and honey. It was a living Dali painting. That was exactly what Alice Cooper had been trying to do onstage. Once I went up to the apartment in the St. Regis, rang the bell, and The Dali answered the door sitting in a wheelchair, even though he could walk perfectly. He was wearing the skin of an entire bear, from head to claws and tail, and holding an open umbrella. Another living Dali painting.

What Alice and I always wondered—and we never really got close enough to The Dali to get the answer—was what happened when the apartment door closed. Was he the same in private as in public, or did he and Gala just become a normal couple behind that door? Were there two Dalis, the way there were two Alices?

I got one chance to find out. When the *Chromo-Hologram* was completed, we arranged a major press conference in New York for Alice and The Dali to unveil it. We got all the print there, but we were really interested in TV for this one. This was 1973, and there weren't a lot of TV news outlets. No cable to speak of, no YouTube, just the three major networks, their local affiliates, and a handful of prestigious TV "newsmagazines" like *60 Minutes*. We were very excited when *60 Minutes* and all three networks said they'd come.

The print reporters and *60 Minutes* crew arrived. Then we were told there'd been a fire or a shooting somewhere in the city. The network and local news crews wanted us to delay the conference forty-five minutes so they could go cover that and then come to us. I had a choice to make. Do I let *60 Minutes* leave, or do I try to stall them until the others arrive? I figured there was only one thing I could do that *60 Minutes* could not walk out on—have The Dali speak.

I said to Alice, "I don't know who lives behind the curtain, but I think we're about to find out."

Joe and I went to The Dali. I said, "The Dali, may Mr. Blemly speak to you?" I always had to ask permission.

"Yes, Mr. Blemly?"

We explained the problem. The Dali, who understood the importance of the media and celebrity as well as Warhol did, calmly replied, "The Dali will take care."

He went out there and spoke for forty-five minutes. It was not possible that the newspeople understood much of what he said. It was kind of a Surrealist poetry.

"The Dali, the greatest artist. The Coo-per, the greatest artist. New York City, the greatest city. The hologram, the greatest art form. The Dali, The Coo-per, the world's two greatest artists meet. . . ."

He rolled on that way until the news crews came in. The second they did, he said, "And thank you." And left the stage. For me, it was a sign that he could in fact turn it on and off as needed, the way Alice did. It was certainly beautiful theater, and it worked. *60 Minutes* stayed through the whole strange thing.

That was the last we saw or heard from The Dali. It was one of the highlights of Alice's career. Today there are two Dali museums, one in St. Petersburg, Florida, and one outside of Barcelona, Spain. The hologram is on display at both. In 2013, when Alice had a concert in Tampa, he went to the Florida museum to help them celebrate the hologram's fortieth anniversary. I was recently in Spain with Jerry Moss. We went to the museum and saw the hologram there. Wow.

ııııııııııııııııı

The money kept pouring in. I did what young men did with money in the 1970s: I bought a lot of drugs. I did acid, cocaine, Quaaludes, pot, you name it. Yet the money kept piling up. We had almost a million dollars in the bank between us. Then Joey started to drift away. He was still my fifty-fifty partner, but things got very strained between us. Finally I said, "Obviously we should not be partners anymore. So why don't we flip a coin. We'll put the money in one pile, and we'll put the business in another. Whoever wins the flip takes his choice."

He won the flip, and he took the money. I kept the business. And that was the end of our partnership. We had been the best of friends, followed the same path together for so long, started the business, and made it work together. I can't give him enough credit for how much of our early success with Alice was Joey's doing. And now we were going our separate ways. It was very tough. From here on out it was just me.

Despite the interpersonal problems they were having, too, Alice and the band wrote and recorded their best album yet while they were at the Galesi estate. *Billion Dollar Babies* was their satirical take on their own fame and fortune. Everyone agreed it was the best collection of songs they'd ever put on an album. The baby on the cover wearing Alice makeup was Carolyn's baby Lola. The album came out in February 1973 and went straight to number one in the United States, the United Kingdom, and other places around the world.

The band left the Galesi estate and went in all directions. Four days after the last of them moved out, leaving only Ron Volz in the apartment over the garage, the mansion burned to the ground. Holy shit. We were still on the lease. I got a call that Francesco Galesi wanted to meet with me at his Manhattan apartment. Alice says he has never seen me more scared. I put on a suit and tie. Galesi sent a car for me—a black Mercedes with darkened windows. The driver looked like Cato from the Inspector Clouseau movies. He did not smile or say one word to me as he drove me to Sutton Place on the East Side. The elevator opened right into Galesi's giant apartment. I waited around for a while, then a beautifully handsome man entered the room. He looked like a mafia don from Central Casting, very smooth, in a suit that had to cost twenty thousand dollars. And he was not happy. He was more or less convinced that we had burned the house down, probably doing drugs. I didn't get the vibe he was going to hurt me. I did get the vibe that he could harass me for the rest of my life if I didn't make him happy in some way.

Then his son Jesse came in the room. Jesse was a musician. I got out of hot water by saying I would help him with his career, which in fact I did for years.

We decided that the *Billion Dollar Babies* tour had to be spectacular, and now we had the funds to do it right. Joe Gannon had produced Neil Diamond's *Hot August Night* concerts the year before, the first pop concerts ever to use a full Broadway-style production, with moving stage parts and theatrical lights and effects. I thought that sort of really grand theatrical approach was perfect for Alice at this point, and I paid Joe $25,000—a ton of money in those days—to make it happen. He constructed it on a soundstage at Warner Bros. in Burbank. It was incredible. Nobody in rock had done anything remotely like it. It had big steel towers and multilevel platforms and a Busby Berkeley–style staircase where each step could light up as Alice went up and down. Every available surface was covered in mirrors and metalflake glitter, so that when the big Super Trouper lights hit the set it was almost blinding.

The only problem was, we had not really thought through what it was going to be like hauling this massive production from city to city for weeks on end. Every night it had to be unpacked from the two semi-trailers we rented for it, loaded into the building, constructed, then torn down after the show and packed back onto the trucks, which had to haul ass to make it to the next city. It was a logistical nightmare and exhausting work. Early on, Joe and I were helping the crew lug the giant steel frames into the trucks after a show one night. I looked at him, both of us huffing and puffing, and said, "What the *fuck* did you get me into?" Alice loved the set, but the band didn't particularly like having to work on and around it. They were constantly bumping into things or ripping their outfits on the metalflake-encrusted edges.

While the semis hauled the set and equipment from city to city, we flew in the Starship, the chartered Boeing 720 that all the big acts toured in at the time. The Starship is the jet in the background of rock photographer Bob Gruen's iconic image of Led Zeppelin from the same year. All the conventional seats had been stripped from inside. When you walked up the ramp, you entered a lounge, with shag carpeting, a piano, and a full bar with a butler/bartender standing behind it. The main body of the plane was all plush couches and easy chairs, equipped with seat belts, and some private hideaway cubicles. There were TV monitors and a library of videocassettes, everything from Alice's old black-and-white movies to *Deep Throat,* which had come out a couple of years earlier and launched the notion of "porn chic." Alice felt uncomfortable watching porn and would usually turn away when the other guys had it on. In the rear were a small library-study and a private bedroom with a king-size bed and full shower. He spent a lot of time back there. I had hired the magician James Randi, aka "the Amazing Randi," to play Alice's executioner in the climactic guillotine scene. He loved touring with the band and kept up a constant burble of jokes and card tricks on the plane.

The tour went throughout Canada and the United States from March to June. Alice Cooper was the top-performing act in the world in 1973. We played to more than eight hundred thousand audience members, who together paid $4.5 million at the box office. When you added record sales, merchandising, and other income, Alice Cooper grossed $17 million that year. Considering how they started out, and what a very long shot their amazing success was, the guys in the band should have been ecstatic, but the bad feelings only grew worse. They were exhausted, they were sick of the stage show, and they resented Alice's star treatment. Even Alice was getting bored with the routine.

In November of that year, Warner Bros. released the next Alice Cooper album, *Muscle of Love.* It was their second album in less than a year. That was how it was done back then: a constant treadmill of touring, writing songs, recording them, and touring some more. Recordings made the big money, not touring. The touring was to promote the records and boost sales. Tickets to rock concerts were priced to pack the hall—five dollars was tops. So depending on the size of the hall, after all the expenses, after everyone else got their cut of the proceeds, the band might make a few thousand dollars. This is a major reason bands started touring to larger and larger venues in the 1970s. It was an economic necessity.

We put together the Alice Cooper Holiday Tour, beginning in Nashville on December 3 and winding up in Buffalo on New Year's Eve. It was all stadiums, coliseums, and arenas now. As we were getting the tour ready, a very good journalist with the *Chicago Sun-Times,* Bob Greene, who'd been writing about the band for a few years, got in touch with me. He was not a music critic but was very interested in the way rock was evolving from the soundtrack of the hippie counterculture in the sixties to the global corporate business of platinum albums and arena tours in the seventies. Since Alice Cooper had so much to do with that, Greene was especially interested in us. He approached me with the idea of going along on the tour—not just to observe but as part of the band in some way, so he could get the full inside experience. I cooked up a role for him: he would come out toward the end of the show as Santa Claus, and Alice and the band would beat him up.

It turned out to be the tour that broke up the band. Bob describes it in detail in the book he ended up writing, *Billion Dollar Baby,* one of the best books written about seventies rock. The band was truly sick of the stage show by this point and close to mutinying. Alice was drinking constantly as a buffer, which was

At age four.

My grandma Fannie Frank—I still make her matzo ball soup—
with my brother, Eddie, Mom, and Dad.

My early years at public school.

Boy Scout camp (loved it) with Mom.

The original Alice Cooper band
on their first European tour.

Signing with Atlantic Records for *Welcome to My Nightmare*,
with Jerry Greenberg, Harry Nilsson, and Alice Cooper.

On the set of a music video
with Alice Cooper.

Debbie Harry on the set of *Roadie*,
a film I did, which starred
many of my clients.

An early Alice Cooper recording session, with Liza Minnelli
and Ronnie Spector on background vocals.

At a great party for client Rick James, a Buffalo boy.

A magic moment—being inducted as a commander of the Honor of Bordeaux by Alexis Lichine, along with Roger Vergé, César, George Greif, and Dennis Marini from Maui.

The Gipsy Kings Arrive in L.A.

Teddy Pendergrass at Live Aid with Ashford & Simpson . . . WOW.

At the Cannes Film
Festival, with Prince
Charles and Lady Diana.

Michael Douglas
and I at a morning
shower in Hana.

A tough day at the office with my assistant.

A birthday party for Sharon Stone in Maui—a wonderful night.

Family trip to Universal Studios Orlando with Ruth Stewart; and Amber, Chase, Keira, Monique, and Winona Williams.

At Universal Studios Orlando with Ella Furnier; Sonora, Sheryl, Alice, and Calico Cooper; and Winona Williams (*back*); Dash Cooper; and Chase, Monique, Amber, and Keira Williams (*front*).

Cooking for friend Robert De Niro and Daniel Secunda at Jean Pigozzi's house in the South of France during the Cannes Film Festival.

With Peter Max, Arnold Schwarzenegger, Roger Vergé, and Sylvester Stallone at the launch of Hawaiian regional cuisine.

Dinner for Roger Vergé at my house in Beverly Hills,
hosted by me, Michael Douglas, and George Greif.

Dinner for Roger Vergé.

I cooked with Roger Vergé for James Coburn's wedding; Rod Stewart serenaded.

Tibet Fund Gala Dinner with Michel Nischan,
Jean-Georges Vongerichten, Emeril Lagasse, Nobu Matsuhisa, His Holiness
the Dalai Lama, Roger Vergé, and Kerry Simon.

A great night at Emeril Lagasse's New Orleans restaurant with
Michael Douglas, Sharon Stone, Emeril, and Sammy Hagar.

With His Holiness the Dalai Lama.

Opening night of
Planet Hollywood Maui—
an imu in my backyard.

In Aspen at a benefit for His Holiness the Dalai Lama
that Willie Nelson performed at . . . a magic moment!

A great night at my house with Don Ho,
Paul Stanley of KISS, and Ratan Tata. Quite a crew!

My wedding in my backyard on a beautiful night.

Solving the world's
problems with
Sammy Hagar and
Mick Fleetwood.

One of my favorite spots on Maui—Willie Nelson's poker room with Maui's finest.

With Johnny Depp and Steven Tyler at the *Dark Shadows* after party.

Supermensch South by Southwest party with Tom Arnold, Mike Myers, Nancy Meola, and Willie Nelson on Willie's bus.

The original team a few years later, backstage after an Alice Cooper show—with Jon Podell and Joe Greenberg.

At my Maui home with Mo'o; Chase, Zada, Amber, Monique, Keira, Karter, and Winona Williams; and Ruth Stewart.

Filming Anthony Bourdain's show for CNN—Kris Kristofferson was a big fan.

I was honored to deliver the commencement speech at the Culinary Institute of America (CIA) in 2015.

Golf trip to St. Andrews with Woody Johnson,
Michael Douglas, and Jack Nicholson.

Another magic moment—Alice Cooper and I bought
an "O" from the original Hollywood sign.

His Holiness the Dalai Lama in Maui before addressing
the largest crowd in Maui history.

The original Alice Cooper band, minus Glen Buxton,
inducted into the Rock and Roll Hall of Fame.

Life at 70. Makena Golf Club with friends Tommy Armour III,
Steven Tyler, Mike Meldman, Dante Jimenez, and Dale Ray Akridge.
I birdied the first hole the day before!

More fun at Makena with Chuck Bergson, Jimmy Story,
Willie Nelson, Ray Benson, and Chris Stutts.

ruining his health. Winter weather made moving the band and the equipment from city to city nerve-racking. Meanwhile, I was busy dealing with threats from parent groups and city councils in various cities to ban us. Again, to me this was gift-from-God publicity, as long as they didn't actually go through with their threats. The most serious came from the city of Binghamton, New York, where the band was scheduled for December 29. The city fathers of Binghamton were especially concerned about our beating up Santa Claus. They sent a four-man commission eighty miles to the War Memorial Arena in Syracuse on December 15 to judge for themselves how evil the show was.

I met with them backstage before the concert and put on a real show myself. Bob Greene describes the hilarious scene in his book. Four middle-aged guys in jackets and ties sat in a row of folding chairs while I addressed them in my most polite and persuasive manner. Bob writes that I reminded him of a minister giving an Easter sermon. I introduced Bob to them as a highly respected gentleman of the press. When one of them asked Bob what he thought of the Santa Claus part of the show, I pounced: "Gentleman, Mr. Greene *is* Santa Claus in the show." Then I introduced them to the Amazing Randi, a middle-aged man like themselves, who told them he found the show entirely respectable and professional. After that I introduced them to Alice himself, who was also at his most polite. He explained to them that part of the purpose of the show was to introduce the young audience to the cultural significance of Busby Berkeley–era spectacle, and that rather than promoting immoral behavior, the show was in fact "a morality play" in which the evil figure of Alice Cooper is punished in the end for his misdoings.

Then I went into my routine. I explained to them that the Alice Cooper group were all serious, hardworking young men who would never jeopardize their careers by promoting violence or immorality. Yes, they depicted it onstage, but only to entertain and educate young people, not to incite them. I told them that I had written the show myself, and as a former probation officer (I didn't say for only about four hours) with a degree in sociology, I cared deeply for America's youth.

"They say that you can't get young people to care anymore," I somberly told them. "But we do it." I told them that when they saw the show, they'd see young people laugh, cringe with fear, and applaud with delight. We were an outlet for them, a release valve. I told them how hurt and indignant we all were about some of the terrible things written about us in the press, and that I completely understood how that press might have given them a false perception of the show.

I went on like that for thirty minutes. Then I escorted them to the stage, where they watched the show from the wings. After that I met with them again for another hour.

In the end, Binghamton canceled the show. I protested to the Binghamton press, but I wasn't surprised. I had already gotten our agent to book a replacement gig in Utica for that night.

‖‖‖‖‖‖‖‖‖‖‖‖‖

That was the last tour of the original band. The bitterness and resentment toward Alice and me had made things too difficult. For a year, a year and a half, on more occasions than I can remember, I had to have very heavy conversations or they would refuse to go on. They hated that Alice was the star and focus of all the attention, on stage and off. They hated all the theatrics of the show. They wanted to go back to T-shirts and dungarees.

I would take the position, "That isn't what we agreed upon. That isn't Alice Cooper."

"Well, people are laughing at us," one of them would say. "They don't think we're good musicians."

"I don't know what to tell you," I'd say. "We're sharing equally. You don't get paid any less than Alice. I can't help it if your ego is suffering. I can only do what I know."

Now, after the holiday tour ended, they called a group meeting. That had never happened before in all our years working together. Group meetings only happened if I called them. I went expecting nothing good, and that's what I got. They wanted no more theatrics. They wanted time off to record solo albums. They wanted the world to know they were great musicians, not just some anonymous flunkies playing for Alice Cooper.

"Listen, we all made a deal," I said. "We agreed to do this until we were all millionaires. We're not millionaires yet. If you guys break this deal, I hope you understand that leaves Alice free to use the name to do what he wants, and it doesn't mean he has to come back. Once you break this deal and let him out of the cage, he's free. And I'm going with him. I can't work with you on solo projects after you've broken your word to me. I have killed myself to make this thing happen. We're right there. We're the biggest group in the world. What do you mean you want a year off? I am not taking a year off. And if you let me out of the cage, I may never come back, either."

A few of them countered by saying that they wanted to make solo albums. That left Alice free to make one of his own.

So that was it, the end of the original Alice Cooper group. I feel bad about the way history subsequently played out, because none of them managed much in the way of commercially successful careers on their own, but it was their decision. We were all on the gravy train together, and it was just about to pull into the station, and they jumped off.

Now Alice and I had to reinvent the wheel. If his next project was his first solo one, it had to be huge, bigger than anything we'd done before. We came up with *Welcome to My Nightmare,* which meant taking every dime he and I had in the world and reinvesting it. Luckily we won. But it's not how we had wanted to do it.

9

EVERYTHING I'D DONE FOR ALICE I HAD INVENTED. Was it just luck that it worked? Or did I really have a knack for this that I could apply to other kinds of artists? I had to know. I had to challenge myself.

I got an opportunity to do that while we were touring Canada in 1973 and I met up with the Canadian record producer Brian Ahearn. We'd met back in 1969 when I helped organize the Toronto festival. He wanted to talk to me about the singer Anne Murray. She'd had a big hit single in 1970 with "Snowbird." She was huge at home in Canada, but that's a limited market. Outside Canada, where a longtime friend named Leonard Rambeau was her manager, she needed the help of somebody who could take her to the next level.

I agreed to meet with her. Partly that was because I liked her music. I thought she had a beautiful, pure voice. Most everyone in the rock world thought her stuff was corny, but the truth is that rock was never my favorite music. I liked music that emphasized good singing—soul, rhythm and blues, and yes, Anne Murray. I encouraged all the theatrics of Alice's show partly because, at least in the early days, I didn't think the music alone was strong or distinctive enough to carry them to where we all wanted to get. Alice knew that and it never bothered him; when he was offstage, he didn't listen to much rock, either.

But I had a bigger reason for seeing Anne Murray. The success I had with Groucho was nice, but it was a limited demonstration of my skills. He was a giant in the industry who only needed some help getting his affairs in order. No one was farther from Alice Cooper than Anne Murray, or would present more of a challenge. She was squeaky-clean, straight as a pin, middle of the middle of the road, and as white as white bread gets. She was the girl next door who happened to have a few hit records. She appealed to a totally different market than Alice did. If I could successfully apply what I'd learned with Alice to an artist like her, then I'd know that it wasn't just luck, but a set of operating principles I could use for any client. If I failed, that would be an important lesson, too. I didn't want to spend my life doing something I wasn't really good at, just lucky at.

So we met. She said she had talked to other managers but liked what I had done with Alice. She'd had those hit singles but almost no name recognition. She wanted to be a star. She wanted to headline in Vegas and be on *Midnight Special,* the new late-night rock concert show. Did I think I could do something like that for her?

I said I'd try. Everybody thought I was crazy. What could the guy who managed Alice Cooper do for an artist like Anne Murray?

Exactly.

As talented as she was, Anne didn't have much of what you could call star quality, and she was pretty much the antithesis of cool. But I'd learned two things with Alice: stars aren't born, they're made; and if you put someone with people who are acknowledged to be cool, they become cool by association. One of the coolest clubs anywhere in 1973 was the Troubadour in Los

Angeles. All the female folksingers who people thought were hip and cool played there—Linda Ronstadt, Judy Collins, Joni Mitchell. I wanted Anne Murray to be seen as one of them.

When Alice moved to L.A., he and some friends had formed a drinking club that met upstairs at the Rainbow Bar & Grill on Sunset. They called themselves the Hollywood Vampires. Alice was the club president; Keith Moon of the Who was vice president; other founding members included Harry Nilsson, Elton John's lyricist, Bernie Taupin, and Alice's neighbor Micky Dolenz of the Monkees. Harry's friend John Lennon frequently joined them. He was going through a dark period when he'd left Yoko back in New York and moved to L.A., and was doing an awful lot of drinking and carousing with Harry, who was one of the biggest drinkers and carousers on the planet. Photographers were dying to get shots of Lennon, but he was doing a good job of evading them. I knew that if I could get a photo of John and the Vampires that just happened to include Anne Murray, heads would spin at every newspaper and magazine in the world. The elusive John Lennon seen out on the town with . . . *Anne Murray?* The what-the-hell factor would get the photo everywhere, and her coolness would increase a thousandfold.

I went to the Rainbow and upstairs to their hangout, called the Lair of the Hollywood Vampires. I actually got down on my knees and said, "Guys, you gotta help me. I need a very big favor. I booked Anne Murray in the Troubadour. If I can get you guys to go and get your picture taken with her, I swear to God I'll come to the Rainbow every time the Vampires meet, and I'll drive you all home at the end of the night for the rest of my life."

They all said yes, and I recruited a group of paparazzi, TV, radio, and press people to ensure maximum coverage.

Anne debuted on Wednesday, November 21. Thanksgiving

was the next day, so we organized it as a Thanksgiving party. Staff dressed as pilgrims and Indians served turkey and all the trimmings to the three hundred handpicked guests. We handed out little old-fashioned snuff boxes and copies of Anne's records. To start her show, Anne stepped out of a big wooden turkey. She did a great set, and the audience, who were already having a good time, applauded enthusiastically. Then I herded the Vampires around her for the all-important photo. Anne Murray smiling, looking pretty, with John Lennon, Harry Nilsson, Alice Cooper, and Micky Dolenz all standing behind her, looking drunk as skunks.

Of course, that picture went everywhere, and had a fantastic impact. *Rolling Stone* called for an interview. So did *People* and *Time*. Several music magazines put her on the cover. Overnight she was the coolest woman in music.

NBC's *Midnight Special* came on Friday nights after Johnny Carson at 1 A.M., and right out of the gate it was a big hit with rock fans. There was no MTV in 1973, no Internet where young fans could easily check out new music and bands. A show like *Midnight Special* was a godsend to fans, and everybody in the business wanted to be on it. As Alice's manager, it wasn't hard for me to swing a deal: I not only got Anne Murray on the sixth week of the show, March 2, 1973, but I got her the host position. We gave her a hipper look—not radically different, still squeaky-clean and innocent, just bell bottoms, a velvet vest, and a softer hairdo instead of the knit sweaters and curly Raggedy Ann hair she'd had. She sat on a stool in a spotlight and sang her cover of Kenny Loggins's "Danny's Song" ("Even though we ain't got money . . ."). It was slated as the title track and first single from her next album. When the single came out the following month, it went straight to the top ten in the United States, and I high-fived myself in the mirror.

The experiment had worked. The same principles of management I had used for Alice worked for Anne Murray. Let the games begin! After this I went on to manage dozens of great artists in a wide array of musical genres—from George Clinton and Parliament-Funkadelic to the Manhattan Transfer, to King Sunny Adé, to Rick James, and on and on. Lucky me!

IIIIIIIIIIIIIIIIII

So many times in my life, I wake up and things happen. The important thing is to be open to whatever comes and remember to say yes. One morning in 1973 I got a call in my L.A. office.

"Shep Gordon?" a woman said.

"Yes."

"Are you the young man who made that freak Alice Cooper famous?"

"Well, I helped."

"This is Raquel Welch," she said. "And you could help me. If you'll take me to the Academy Awards next week, I'd like to talk to you."

Raquel Welch was inviting me to the Academy Awards? Little Shep from Oceanside? How could I say no?

The following week she appeared at my house in a limo. She looked absolutely stunning in a pink chiffon, low-cut, no-bra evening dress. She was maybe thirty-three, and stunningly gorgeous. I was twenty-eight and feeling like the kid back in Oceanside who didn't know how to act around girls. I'm sitting in a limo beside Raquel Welch, heading to the Academy Awards show. I had no idea what to say. But she was very nice, easygoing, and kept the conversation rolling. She told me that she was getting a little old for a "sex star" (her words), and roles for women her age were hard to find in Hollywood. She had recently been divorced for the second time, had two children to support, and was worried about her income. She'd seen other former sex stars like Ann-Margret doing song-and-dance shows in Vegas and thought that was something she could do, too. Then she went to see one of Alice's shows, and that led her to me.

At that point the limo rolled up to the red carpet. In those days, the radio host Johnny Grant, the "honorary mayor of Hollywood," stood there with his microphone to greet the stars. It wasn't like today with hundreds of reporters and television cameras and photographers. He was the only one. He actually got in the car with you. He was saying, "Miss Raquel Welch, ladies and gentlemen!"—forget me, he had no idea who I was—when Raquel turned to me and whispered through her dazzling movie-star smile, "*Could you grab the back of my dress? The clasp just broke. It's going to fall off.*"

Her door swept open, she started to slide out, and I scrambled across the seat right behind her, grabbing the back of her braless pink chiffon dress to keep it from falling off. My knuckles are white. *Wow. I'm holding Raquel Welch's dress together. I'm touching her naked back.* Bill Graham later sent me the photo that ran in *People,* captioned, "Raquel Welch and unnamed escort."

We marched up the red carpet that way, Raquel sweeping along in front like the great star she was, me trying to look natural coming along right up behind her with my hand on her back. I'm sure people were wondering who the hell that guy was Raquel had brought to the ceremony. We made it backstage. I surrendered her to the costume crew, and they sewed her back together. But what a moment. What an introduction.

We started to work together shortly after that, developing her new stage act. Vegas was our goal, but I thought we should try it out before we took it there. I knew the guy who booked the entertainment at the Concord Hotel in New York's Catskill Mountains;

it was the flagship resort of the Borscht Belt. He asked me why he should book Raquel Welch.

"Are you kidding me?" I scoffed. "What would old Jews rather do than slobber over Raquel Welch?"

He laughed and said, "Okay, you got it."

I had forgotten one ridiculous tradition at the Concord: the audience didn't applaud, but banged these big wooden clackers instead. It was loud and obnoxious, and Raquel did not appreciate it.

At John Ascuaga's Nugget Casino in Reno, Nevada, her second gig, a pair of elephants, Bertha and Angel, always opened the show. They did a whole "showgirl" routine and were a famous draw. Just before Raquel was to go on, she watched from the wings as one of them took a big dump onstage. I don't need to tell you she was pretty upset at having to follow that act. I never again made the mistake of not knowing in advance everything there was to know about a venue—especially anything that could upset or distract my artist.

After that I helped negotiate a long-term contract at Caesars Palace in Vegas, and things went smoothly. The audiences loved her show. She rehearsed seriously and was very successful.

I knew TV would be key in breaking this new Raquel. People seeing this beautiful, sexy woman singing and dancing on TV would want to come see her live. So how to get her on TV? HBO had been launched in the early 1970s, and Michael Fuchs, who ran it now, was a good friend. I kept trying to get him to do music specials featuring my artists, and he kept saying that the only programming that seemed to work on pay cable was pornography. HBO was a family channel, so he couldn't do porn, but he didn't think music was the answer.

One night after a number of drinks I said, "What about a sexy

Raquel Welch in concert?" HBO's broadcast of Raquel live in Vegas, the first music special on HBO, was the result. High five!

When I look back at my life, managing Groucho and Raquel were amazing moments in an incredibly lucky journey. Sometimes I think it was all a dream.

Thank you, thank you.

|||||||||||||||||||||

In 1974 I decided to quit smoking. I had a lot of people working for me or with me who smoked. I made them all an offer: whoever wanted to spend a month with me in Hawaii, we'd all go and quit smoking together. I was friends with Tom Moffatt, the DJ and concert promoter in Honolulu who had been behind Elvis's concerts there. He knew all these great houses that Colonel Tom Parker had rented. I thought, Oh my God, I can sleep in the same bed as Colonel Tom Parker.

Carolyn Pfeiffer, Joe Gannon, and seven or eight others came to Honolulu with me. I don't think any one of us actually quit smoking on that trip, but we had a great time. I got in with Steve Rossi, half of the comedy duo Allen & Rossi. He was a great guy but a party animal, and after a few days of hanging with him I realized I needed more seclusion if I was going to seriously try to quit the smokes. Tom Moffatt had a tour going to the outer islands. I asked if I could come along and sell T-shirts for him.

In those days you took a hydrofoil from Honolulu to Maui. It landed at Maalaea Harbor, a beautiful, serene place with yachts and pretty sailboats parked all around and palm trees waving and low green mountains behind it rising to blue skies. Hawaii is the youngest landmass on the planet. It has the innocence of a baby. It even smells like a baby. As I was getting off the hydrofoil, I put one foot on the dock—not even both feet—and turned to

Joe and said, "I'm living here the rest of my life." I had never been there before, and it felt like home. I saw the house I wanted on that trip, on Keawakapu Beach in Kihei, and bought it soon afterward.

The following year I moved out of New York. Winona and Mia came with me to Los Angeles. I got us a great little house at the end of a dead-end street in Bel-Air, with a huge rose garden, and a pool with a postcard view of L.A. But Winona and I broke up and gradually lost our connection. Still, I stayed in touch with Mia for about five more years. I'd get a letter or a call every now and again, and I always sent her money. Finally, I realized that the *only* times I heard from her were when she needed money. I suspected it was going to no good use, so I just stopped. If there are a few things I'd like a redo on, that would be one. I probably should have gone to her, sat down, and had a conversation with her. But I didn't; I just stopped. I don't have a lot of regrets, but that's one.

||||||||||||||||||||

Breaking up with Winona hurt. That was a new feeling. I had never been in that situation before, where I cared enough about a relationship that it could be painful when it ended. It's something everybody goes through, but I think most people probably experience it when they're younger than I was and in far less of a position to self-medicate with drugs and dating more pretty women.

I even bought myself a place where I could do that.

In the mid-1970s the three hottest rock clubs on Sunset Strip were the Roxy Theatre, the Rainbow Bar and Grill, and the Whisky a Go Go. The producer-manager Lou Adler, known for his work with Sam Cooke, the Mamas & the Papas, Carole King, and a long list of others, owned and ran the Roxy. Upstairs was a private club called On the Rocks, which you could only get into if

Lou gave you a membership key. Lou gave keys to Alice, Raquel, Groucho—though I doubt he ever used it—but I never got one for myself. I'd go with Alice or Raquel.

One night I went there alone and they wouldn't let me in. I called Lou and got his secretary instead. She conveyed his reply: "You're not a member." I said, "Tell him to *make* me a member." Lou refused. That stung. Maintaining an inner sense of self-esteem, even now that I was successful, was always hard for me. Inside I was still Shep, the kid from Oceanside. Lou Adler was basically telling me that my clients were cool enough for his exclusive club, but I wasn't.

This was another occasion for me to think, Don't get mad. Accomplish your goal. I could have been really angry at Lou, but that wouldn't have gotten me anywhere. What was my goal? To have a private club I could get into. So I opened one.

I remembered Carlos'n Charlie's in Acapulco, one of the most fun places I'd ever been. Since then they had opened franchises all over Mexico. I got Alice to fly to Acapulco with me and see if it was still as fun as I remembered. We were sitting there having dinner when a guy came to our table, whipped out a red bandanna, and started wiping out our ashtray. Since he clearly recognized Alice, I asked him, "You know who we can talk to about opening one of these clubs in L.A.?"

He sat down. "I'm Carlos Anderson. You talk to me."

In fifteen minutes we had a deal.

Alice and I came back to L.A. and found out that Micky Dolenz's dad had a restaurant on Sunset Boulevard he wanted out of. We rented the building from him and opened our Carlos'n Charlie's. Upstairs I put my own private club, El Privado. In L.A., if it's new and exclusive all the big names flock to it. We had Sugar Ray Leonard, Eddie Murphy, Hugh Hefner, Lakers owner Jerry Buss,

Saudi princes, and assorted other millionaires. And they attracted the hottest, wildest, loosest women in Los Angeles.

I felt like I was the king of L.A. I had the hottest club in town, I had the Rolls and the silk suits, I had all the drugs and sex I could handle. My little house in Bel-Air was the site of some of the hardest partying of my life. I loved it all. But I also knew that it was all superficial. Something was missing.

10

AFTER HIS BAND BROKE UP, Alice and I committed ourselves to making his solo debut the biggest, best, most spectacular thing he'd ever done. And I didn't want Warner Bros. to get it. My relationship with Mo Ostin was the reason.

For a couple of years after all the back-and-forthing over "I'm Eighteen," life rushed by in such a blur that I completely forgot that we had never seen the publishing royalties Mo promised me. When it hit me, I called him and asked him for the money.

"I can't give it to you," he said. "It's in escrow. Herbie says it's his, you say it's yours."

"Yeah, but you said you'd take care of it."

"I am taking care of it, Shep," Mo said. "But I have to do it the right way. It's there, you're covered, don't worry about it."

A while passed, and still no money.

"Mo," I finally said, "you leave me no choice. I have to take it to court."

"Yeah, you probably should," Mo replied. "But don't worry, I got you covered."

All this time, Mo was becoming more than a mentor in my head, more like a father figure. I don't think he saw it that way, but I did. I got to be friends with him and his wife. They had me to dinner. In some ways they became a surrogate family to me, since I was so detached from my own. This was all inside me. But it meant that when Mo said not to worry, he had me covered. It felt good and I believed him.

So now I brought my lawsuit against Straight Records, thinking that I had Mo in my corner. And Mo testified against me. It came down to me or his good friend Herb Cohen, and he backed Herb.

I was extremely hurt. It felt like such a betrayal.

I went to Alice and said, "This is personal. But it's also professional. In the first place, anybody who stabs us in the back like this can't really think we're going to have a long-term career with his company. But also, I have to teach this guy that he can't fuck with us like this."

Once again: Don't get mad. Accomplish your goal. I read our contract and saw that it granted Alice Cooper a one-time exclusion to record a soundtrack album on another label, if Warner Bros. was unable to obtain the rights. I knew that if we put out a soundtrack on a rival label—Columbia, say—Warner Bros. would sue. But at that point Steve Ross and his Kinney National company had bought three record labels—Warner Bros., Atlantic, and Elektra—and packaged them under the umbrella Warner Communications. I figured that if we did the soundtrack for either Atlantic or Elektra, Warner Bros. couldn't sue.

If we had waited around for some movie producers to come ask Alice to do a soundtrack, my idea might not have gone any further. But that's not how I do things. I decided we would create the show *and* the soundtrack. I went to ABC TV and said, "We want to do an Alice Cooper special. Alive Enterprises will produce it. I'll give it to you for costs."

They jumped on it. Alice Cooper was one of the biggest acts in the world, and they were getting him for nearly nothing.

Then we recorded the soundtrack, working with Bob Ezrin again. Dick Wagner, who had filled in for Glen on guitar, really stepped up as a cowriter with Alice, and they loaded the album with great songs, including the title track, "Department of Youth," "The Black Widow," and "Only Women Bleed." I worked up my nerve and got a meeting with Jerry Wexler at Atlantic. Jerry was another giant in the industry. They credit him with inventing the term *rhythm and blues* when he was a young reporter for *Billboard*. He and Ahmet Ertegun had run Atlantic since the 1950s, making careers for an incredible list of stars from Ray Charles, Aretha Franklin, and Wilson Pickett to Led Zeppelin.

"Mr. Wexler," I said, "I want to be honest with you. One way or the other, Warner Brothers is not getting the next Alice Cooper record. You'd provide me with a great insurance policy if you take it, and you'll make a ton of money."

Jerry said, "Play me something from it." I played him "Only Women Bleed," and he loved it.

"I'm in," he said. He went to his bosses at Warner Communications and convinced them it was best to keep Alice Cooper's next record in house. I'm not sure, but I don't believe he and Mo ever spoke again.

So *Welcome to My Nightmare* came out on Atlantic, and went platinum in the United States and double platinum in Canada. Alice was still in a multiyear contract with Warner Bros., and would record five more albums for them before we could finally leave in 1981. But I felt we had made our point. It may have been like a flea biting an elephant, but it must have stung a little because they never messed with us like that again. For his part,

Jerry Wexler went on to be a great friend and advisor to me, another mentor.

||||||||||||||||||

For the TV special Alice wrote a story around the songs, about a boy named Steven who can't wake up from his nightmares. We shot it in Canada, with a Canadian choreographer and a Canadian director, Jørn Winther. That way we came under the Canadian content law and got a bit of a government subsidy for it. We were very excited to get Vincent Price to play the narrator. Price was another god to us, like Dali and Groucho. We knew him a little from when he and Alice were both on Dinah Shore's show. When we did the album he had recorded his part at a different studio, so we didn't spend time with him. Now I called his agent and got him to come to Toronto for a couple of days to be in the special. Alice and I were in awe. We addressed him only as "Mr. Price." Then, on our first day of shooting a scene, over the loudspeakers we heard Winther say, "*Hey, Vinnie, could you move over to the left?*"

Hey, Vinnie? Alice and I practically melted into the floor with mortification. Mr. Price, though, was so cool that he just let it pass. We loved him for that.

I arranged for the *Nightmare* tour to start in Lake Tahoe, at the Sahara Tahoe Hotel, in December 1975. It was a way of announcing that this wasn't just another rock concert; this was the new Alice Cooper, putting on a show. It was the first time a rock band played in a major Vegas-Tahoe casino, and the first time an American rock band performed live with a full orchestra. (The British band Procol Harum had done it a few years earlier.) And when Price agreed to be in that performance, it was the first time that I know of that a major film star performed onstage with a rock star.

We hired a 727 to fly some celebrities up to Tahoe for it. Of course we did that Alice Cooper–style. Our leading celebrity was a dog—the German shepherd from the new movie *Won Ton Ton, the Dog Who Saved Hollywood,* a takeoff on the old Rin Tin Tin movies. The studio paid for the jet because they were having trouble getting press. We loaded everyone else on the dog's flight.

The morning of the show we arrived for a rehearsal with the orchestra. The band had never played with an orchestra before. The conductor came over to me and said, "Can I get the charts from you?"

"What charts?"

"For the orchestra."

As a former trombone player, I should have expected that they'd need charts of the songs.

"We don't have charts."

"Okay," he said. "Just have one of the guys write out the chords. We'll listen to the record and work it out."

These were rock musicians. None of them could read or write music. I asked the conductor to give me a few minutes. In the dressing room I put five hundred-dollar bills in an envelope. I handed the envelope and a copy of the album to him and said, "Just make me look good."

We worked it out that I conducted the orchestra for the rehearsal, while he observed and took notes, and then he did it for the show. Another first—me conducting an orchestra.

Since Won Ton Ton paid for the flight I figured he should have VIP treatment. I reserved him a table in the front row, with a dog bowl. As we were getting everything set up, security called me.

"We have a big problem, Mr. Gordon. It's Won Ton Ton."

I said, "Listen, I worked this all out with hotel management. The dog's allowed in. I need him here."

"No, no," they said. "The dog's fine. But the trainer's drunk and vomiting in the lobby!"

I had to get the hotel to find two dogsitters to be with Won Ton Ton during the show. Add to my manager's resume: *Obtains dogsitters.*

To enhance the sense that this was a big event, I had an assistant start calling the hotel an hour before the show. For an hour you kept hearing over the loudspeakers, "Paging Mick Jagger . . . Paging Frank Sinatra . . ." So everyone in the hotel thought all these celebrities would be at the show. Who's a star? Someone who attracts other stars. Guilt by association. Early on I used to hire people to crowd around the band in public, pretending to be paparazzi. Flashbulbs would be popping off all around them, but there was no film in the cameras. Film and processing were very expensive. This was just for show, to attract actual photographers. Who's a star? Someone who has flashbulbs going off around them all the time.

One of the great Fleet Street figures Carolyn introduced me to, Terry O'Neill, totally understood guilt by association. Terry was the king of Fleet Street. He shot iconic portraits of the Beatles, the Rolling Stones, Elton John, and on and on. When *Welcome to My Nightmare* was coming out, I called Terry and said I wanted to get Alice in *Newsweek*.

He said, "Do you have a pool?" When I said yes, he said, "Buy an inflatable shark. I'll be out there tomorrow."

I didn't ask him why an inflatable shark. It was Terry. I trusted he knew what he was doing. I called Alice and said, "Come up here tomorrow and bring a swimsuit." I sent a kid to the toy store to buy the shark.

The next day Terry had Alice get in the pool with the blowup shark and started shooting.

"Terry," I asked, "why are we doing this?"

"There's a movie coming out this week called *Jaws*," Terry said, "and it's going to be the biggest thing ever. The day after it opens, we're going to send these pictures out."

And it worked. Pictures of Alice and the shark hit every magazine and newspaper in the world. That was Terry's genius. Whenever we needed press, I'd call Terry. We'd fly to London and arrive at the airport with, say, a guy dressed up in the cyclops costume from Alice's show. In those days security at airports was far more lax than it is now. The cyclops from the Nightmare show would go through the passport checkpoint, and Terry would be there to take the shots. We'd turn right around and fly back home. Terry's photos would be in all the papers the next day. Win-win. You couldn't work with American photographers that way. You had to go to Fleet Street.

Alice hit the road for *Nightmare* in March 1975 and toured it all over the United States, Canada, Europe, Australia, and New Zealand for the next two years. Australia originally banned him in 1975 for being a "degenerate," but a new government got elected and let him come in 1977. He did two hundred shows during those two years and they all sold out. The show was even closer to a Broadway musical this time. The set was huge and elaborate again, basically a stage version of the sets used in the TV show. There were dancers, the giant cyclops, a giant spider, and all sorts of props. Alice was entirely the star now—the set hid the band for most of the show.

Nightmare was a triumph, for Alice and for me. We proved that we were right. We never got mad, we just reached our goal of being millionaires.

As for the other guys in the band: Sadly, Glen passed away in 1997, just short of his fiftieth birthday. We all miss him. He was the James Dean of the band, always with a cig and a buzz going. The rest of us remain good friends to this day. Alice and the guys help each other in any way they can. They play and record together occasionally, and it's always special. They were all there to be inducted together into the Rock and Roll Hall of Fame in 2011.

After *Nightmare,* there was no star in the world bigger or brighter than Alice Cooper. All sorts of other acts, like KISS and Elton John, were imitating Alice now, putting on lavish theatrical productions. But there was still one dark cloud. All through this period, Alice's drinking got worse and worse. Periodically I would read him the riot act, and he'd clean up for a while, only to slip back into it. When the *Nightmare* tour ended, his wife and I staged an intervention, though they weren't called that yet. We made him go to the Cornell Medical Center in White Plains, New York, where they locked him in for two months. It wasn't the worst place to be shut in for two months. It even had a golf course. I still owned my house on Lake Copake, maybe an hour's drive from the clinic, and stayed there so I could visit him almost every day.

He came out clean and sober, and stayed that way for a couple of years before falling again as hard and far as before. Eventually he'd have to hit rock bottom, the way they say true addicts do, before he really quit.

IN 1977 I STARTED A WHOLE NEW JOURNEY. I got into producing movies. I did it as a favor to a friend.

It started on a terribly sad note, when Carolyn's baby Lola, our Billion Dollar Baby, died in her crib, which happened more often then than it does now. Carolyn worked out of her apartment in London, and just couldn't bear to be there anymore. She asked if I might have a spot for her at Alive. Of course I said yes. I loved Carolyn and there was no question that I would make a place for her in my company and give her whatever she needed to recover and be happy. She started out helping to manage artists, then said that what she really wanted to do was make movies.

Okay, I said, then we'll make movies. First, though, we had to learn how to do that. Despite her experience in the film world, Carolyn had never made a movie. I had only done some video and TV. When I asked her who might be a good teacher, she thought of David Puttnam, a British producer. He and his partner Sandy Lieberson had made some terrific films, including *Performance*, the Nicolas Roeg movie starring Jagger, and Ken Russell's *Mahler* and *Lisztomania*. Later David would make *Chariots of Fire, The Killing Fields,* and *Local Hero*.

We met up with David in New York and he agreed to go in with us. We formed Alive Films. David was the chairman, and Carolyn worked with him. It was a very small, independent film company, something that didn't really exist in America at the time. The first movie David wanted to make was called *The Duellists,* with a screenplay adapted from the Joseph Conrad novella *The Duel,* about a pair of officers in Napoleon's army. I didn't read the script; I wasn't involved on that level at all. What I did was put up some cash—I think it was a quarter of a million dollars—for overhead.

David set up a meeting at Paramount Pictures to see if they'd give us the money to make the movie. A fellow named David Picker was running Paramount at the time. Wonderful man. His father was one of the founders of United Artists. He said, "I love Carolyn. I'll do anything for Carolyn. I'll give you a million dollars, just don't embarrass me."

As we walked out of the office I asked, "Was that good?"

David said, "Good? Are you kidding me? This is probably the first time in the history of the studios that they didn't even want to see a script. We just got a million dollars for nothing."

He hired a director—some guy named Ridley Scott. This would be his first feature film. And they cast Harvey Keitel and Keith Carradine as the two officers.

One day, a couple of weeks before shooting was to start, Keith called me. We'd known each other peripherally. Apparently we were fronting some money for him to take fencing lessons. But he was getting worried because he hadn't heard from us about his travel arrangements to France, where the movie would be shot. About three days before Keith was supposed to leave, David called me from London.

"We have a problem, Shep. We're two hundred thousand dollars short on the budget. We need that much more to start making the movie."

"Well, where are you going to get it?" I asked. He was the producer, after all.

"Do you have it?" he asked.

"No. What have you been telling Keith? He thinks he's leaving in three days."

"Shep, when you make movies, you never tell anybody the whole truth."

Really? I was a pretty successful businessman by then, and that's not how I ever conducted things. I called up Keith and told him the truth: "We have two more days. I'm going to try and figure this out, but I'm not in a position to put up the money myself. I just didn't want to call you five minutes before you're supposed to leave."

He was in a panic. I didn't blame him. Then I woke up the next day to see in the news that there had been a sterling crisis in England, and the pound had been drastically devalued overnight. The new exchange rate meant we were instantly $200,000 richer. We started shooting the next week.

We finished the film in time to enter it in the 1977 Cannes Film Festival. David and Carolyn went. I didn't. I was still so green at this business that I even forgot to have my name put in the credits as one of the producers. We won the Best First Work award. It was Ridley's first movie, our first movie, total cost $1.2 million, and we won. Man, were we proud. We were convinced we were going to waltz back into Paramount and be handed a ten-picture deal. We called the studio to set up a screening for David Picker and the other bosses, because they'd never seen it. That's when we were told David had just been fired. That's Hollywood. Two new guys were taking over. One was Michael

Eisner. The other was Barry Diller. They set up a screening for two weeks later.

Carolyn, David Putnam, Ridley, and I went into that screening room very excited. We were sure they were going to love us. Ridley was already staking out his position for his next movie. The lights went down. Nobody said a word. We heard the door open behind us. Still nobody said a word. The movie started. When it had been running maybe fifteen minutes, a guy behind us called out, "Lights!" The movie stopped and the lights came on. Two guys were sitting behind us. They were about our age, mid-thirties, but otherwise they couldn't have looked more different from us. They looked like corporate suits, and they had that corporate suit attitude, deadpan and hardass. One of them stood up.

"I'm Barry Diller," he said. "This is Michael Eisner. We just took over the studio. We came from ABC TV, and the one thing Michael and I have in common is, we don't like art house movies. We're not going to release this. But very nice to meet you."

And they left the room. Paramount never did a real release of the picture. After their reign at Paramount, Diller would go on to create the Fox Television Network, and Eisner would run the Walt Disney Company for twenty years.

||||||||||||||||||

Now it's 1979, and my life is like a carnival ride. I'm dividing my time between L.A. and Maui. Carolyn and I are growing our movie company. I'm managing Alice and an expanding roster of performing artists, and have a growing staff to help me do that. I still have Carlos'n Charlie's, and still bring women home from there. I'm drinking, drugging, partying.

One night I let a married friend of mine bring a girl up to

my house in Bel-Air. When I came home they were in the living room. She was a gorgeous blonde, Marcy Hanson, who had been *Playboy*'s Playmate of the Month for October 1978. She invited me to a party at the Playboy Mansion in Beverly Hills a night or two later. I was so excited. Me, Shep Gordon, at the Playboy Mansion!

To start with, Hef's estate was incredible. The house is enormous, sprawling, all Gothic arches and turrets, like a medieval castle. And the grounds were beautiful, with a tennis court and a pool that was fed by a waterfall and a sauna and peacocks wandering the lawn. And then there were the women. It was Pajama Night or Lingerie Night or something, and hundreds of beautiful women were there.

Marcy took me to the famous grotto, a man-made cave of carved rock with steam rising off Jacuzzis and hot tubs, romantically lit, like something out of Disneyland if Disneyland wasn't for families. Marcy and I got undressed and soaked and got to know each other. When we were ready to get out, our clothes were gone.

I said, "Hey, somebody stole my clothes."

Marcy laughed and explained that while you were in the grotto, staff took your clothes and pressed them for you.

We went for a walk on the grounds and came to a big, hollowed-out tree with a mattress in it, and that's where we made love for the first time. Now it was after midnight and I was hungry. Marcy said she could eat, too.

I said, "Great. Where should we go?"

She smiled at me again. "Oh no, Hef keeps kitchen staff twenty-four hours a day."

So we went up to the mansion and a chef came out, took our order, and cooked us some eggs.

The whole experience overwhelmed me and swept me away,

THEY CALL ME SUPERMENSCH

and in no time Marcy and I got married. It wasn't something I thought through. Like a lot of other decisions in my life, it was just what I did at that moment. I was in my early thirties. Maybe after the previous few years of sex with strangers from the club I felt ready to settle down.

I sold the party-hardy house in Bel-Air and bought us a beautiful mansion on a gated property on Oakmont Drive in Brentwood. It was designed by the great African-American architect Paul Revere Williams, who designed homes for a lot of Hollywood celebrities, like Tyrone Power, Frank Sinatra, Lucille Ball, and Bert Lahr. James Garner and Zubin Mehta were our neighbors. Our first week there, around three in the morning, Mrs. Mehta called. I had a dog I'd rescued from the pound. Marcy loved dogs, so I thought I'd try to get over my fear of them. He had dug under the fence, swam through the pond outside the Mehtas' bedroom, come in the bedroom, and jumped into bed with them soaking wet. He did that three more times, until I felt so mortified I gave him up. A few months later I found a note from them in the mailbox. They missed the dog and hoped he was okay!

That house was immense. I don't think I lived there long enough even to walk into half the rooms, because it soon became obvious to Marcy and me that our hasty marriage had been a mistake. We worked at it for eight or nine months, then got it annulled. I never heard from her again until *Supermensch* came out and she wrote me a beautiful letter from Galveston, Texas, where she ran a bed-and-breakfast, and we had a really sweet phone conversation.

After the annulment went through, I sold that house and bought Alice's Benedict Canyon place from him. He and his wife, Sheryl, moved to Phoenix. The house was listed on all the maps to the stars, so people used to ring the bell all the time, hoping that Alice Cooper would answer the door. I put up a sign:

ALICE DOESN'T LIVE HERE ANYMORE.
GO BACK AND GET A REFUND.

I didn't have my dog anymore—sort of a relief—but I had a cat, the Sensitive One. He must have learned something from the dog, though, because he also went next door to get cozy with the neighbors—Mr. and Mrs. Cary Grant. I went over to their place and rang the bell. When his assistant answered the door, I could see through to the backyard, where Cary and the Sensitive One were hanging out together, obviously enjoying each other's company. Cary had retired from pictures a decade or so earlier and was in his late seventies, I think.

I went out there and said, "Mr. Grant, that's my cat."

His wife Barbara—his fifth and last, almost half a century younger than him—was out there, too, and said to me, "You can't take the cat away from him. That cat has brought him back to life."

So Cary Grant and I agreed on joint custody of the cat.

Maybe both my pets knew that in L.A. you don't meet your neighbors, and they were trying to do something about it. The Alice house was almost at the end of a long, windy road. There was only one more house past it, where the road dead-ended. I lived there for five years and never met the neighbors in that house, though once in a while I'd catch a glimpse of this pretty young woman going in or out.

This went on for years. I would keep that house as my L.A. residence until 2000. The day I left, my moving van blocked the road, and those folks couldn't get out. They sat in their car and honked for maybe twenty minutes, and then finally rang the doorbell. It was Ric Ocasek of the Cars. I was really good friends with him and his very pretty wife, Paulina. We had gone to dinner three or four times while I lived in that house, and never knew we were next-door neighbors until this moment—when I was leaving.

When I first got there, Elton John was still on the street as well. He moved out, and the house was bought by a pornography company that shot a lot of videos there. Heidi Fleiss, the Hollywood Madam, also lived on the street.

Only in L.A. Sometimes my life there felt like I was living in the Hollywood Wax Museum.

12

WHEN CAROLYN HAD COME BACK FROM CANNES IN 1977, she'd told me about an incredible dinner party at "this great place in the mountains." It was a Michelin three-star restaurant called Le Moulin de Mougins, up in the hills outside Cannes in a refurbished, sixteenth-century olive mill. "Shep," she said, "you have to go to Cannes and the Moulin. Everyone goes there. It's very cool." She described the spectacular setting, the amazing nouvelle cuisine, and its owner, a famous French chef named Roger Vergé.

I had never heard of him, or his restaurant. Or nouvelle cuisine. Food didn't matter to me much. I was a burger-and-fries, macaroni-and-cheese guy. But I was intrigued for some reason, so I filed it away in my head.

After that we made a couple more films with Hollywood studios. One of them was *Roadie,* a rock-oriented thing starring Meat Loaf, with small parts in it for some of my artists and friends, including Alice, Debbie Harry, Ray Benson, and Roy Orbison. We did that one for Warner Bros. Neither Carolyn nor I liked working with the studios, making movies by committee, dealing with the alpha dogs in Hollywood.

Then we made *Return Engagement.* It was a political documentary directed by Alan Rudolph, who loved eccentric characters. We created and filmed a national debate tour of two infamous guys from the sixties and seventies: Timothy Leary and G. Gordon Liddy. Leary, for those of you too young to remember, was a former Harvard psychologist and hippie guru who became the leading spokesman for LSD and popularized the mantra "Turn on, tune in, drop out." Liddy was his opposite number, a former FBI agent turned prosecutor who busted Leary for marijuana possession, then was arrested himself as Richard Nixon's ringleader on the Watergate break-in. Leary had spent three and a half years in prison, Liddy four and a half. Now they went on this highly successful college speaking tour, two old warhorses arguing about whatever popped into their heads—revolution, evolution, national security, LSD, prison, religion, abortion. They traded radical theories and nutty humor and outrageous insults, and the college kids loved it. They were still as opposed as comic-book rivals, but they began to like each other a little.

We all flew over to Cannes together to have it in the festival in 1984. It was my first trip. I definitely wanted to experience the festival, but I also remembered what Carolyn had told me seven years earlier about that restaurant. I asked her to book us a dinner there, and we took Leary and Liddy along.

Moulin de Mougins was just a ten-minute drive out of Cannes, but it felt like a different world. During the festival, Cannes is one long crazy party scene, crowds circulating everywhere, tourists and locals and celebrities and paparazzi all swirling around. As we drove up the mountain out of town it got rural and dark, really quickly. No crowds, no lights, very serene. We turned at a big sign that said Moulin de Mougins, and went down a very steep, very short gravel driveway that bottomed out in front of the old stone mill (*moulin*). A young valet in a bow tie and white shirt parked our car in the big gravel lot, which was already packed. This place was clearly popular. Carolyn explained to me that it was an inn, with six rooms upstairs and the restaurant on the ground floor.

We walked through a glass door into a little vestibule that could maybe fit ten people standing. Behind the wooden counter was a maître d' in a black tuxedo who was very lofty and formal in that way only a French maître d' can be. He didn't even look at you when he spoke. In fact, the whole staff was very French, straight out of Central Casting.

As the maître d' led us toward the dining room I noticed a little boutique off to the right, displaying small, one-of-a-kind antique objects—a beautiful old vase, a tea set, things like that. There were also products from the Moulin's owner, Monsieur Vergé: cookbooks he'd written, bottles of his olive oil, mustards, Moulin aprons. We also passed the old mill, a large circular stone for mashing the olives.

The decor in the main dining room beautifully balanced the formal and the rustic. It was mostly ancient stone and wood, with glass doors opening onto a garden terrace lush with gorgeous flowers. More flowers stood on the ivory tablecloths. There were maybe a dozen tables, and I noticed they were all were round. Original artwork hung everywhere, and I could see right away that it had been chosen with care. I saw a Picasso—he had lived and painted very nearby from the mid-1950s on. And a sculpture by César Baldaccini, an inventive avant-gardist and probably the best-known sculptor in France at the time. They named the César du Cinéma, France's equivalent of the Oscar, after him, and he designed the trophy. He and I would become good friends. I began to feel there must be something very special about a restaurant where the art and the artists all had relationships to the place.

From the main dining room archways led off to others. There

was seating for eighty and the place was full. I'd learn that it always was. This place was ground zero for nouvelle cuisine. Every time you went in there Japanese tourists were photographing every dish. Everyone was dressed to the nines, seated in soft lighting on chairs with linens draped over the legs. Two or three wineglasses stood at every setting, along with stylish silverware and plates with little painted flowers. There was a wood-glass-brass Lalique cheese cart, thick with fresh cheeses.

We were seated at a corner table and handed beautiful menus bearing a soft, antique portrait of an older woman's face. Carolyn told me she was Célestine, Vergé's aunt. Célestine taught him about cooking when he was growing up in the 1930s. Every week, she took him to the market to show him how to pick the best food. If it was chicken, she'd check that everything looked healthy: comb, feet, gizzard, eyes, examining it like a doctor. She taught him the correct way to buy butter: if it was bright yellow, that meant the cow grazed on buttercups and the butter would be too strong.

I was impressed again. How respectful and completely lacking in ego it was for him to honor his aunt this way.

Now, I was not in any way a foodie. I was less interested in reading the menu than in observing the crowd. On any given night it's the crème de la crème. You might be looking at royalty or aristocrats. This night, some exiled African dictator, a giant man—it might have been Idi Amin, I wasn't sure—held court at one table. Because of the festival, some of the world's biggest stars were there. I remember Kirk Douglas, Luciano Pavarotti, Clint Eastwood, James Coburn, and Anthony Quinn, as well as Jack Valenti, head of the Motion Picture Association of America.

I sat and observed the ballet as four waiters with white linens on their arms carried large, covered platters to a table, then

removed the covers in unison. It was the first time I had seen anything like that in a restaurant. I mean, I'd seen it in movies, and
I'd been to expensive restaurants where they did something similar, but with nowhere near the well-practiced precision and grace.
This Monsieur Vergé was intriguing me more and more. He was
producing the meal the way I produced a show, everything pre-
cisely organized, everything as scripted as one of Alice's concerts.
And he made each and every person in the place feel like a king or
queen. Since the tables were round, everyone was equal. No one
sat at the head, no one was served first. My business and my life
were all about service to others, which often meant making them
feel all right about themselves. It was obvious that Vergé took great
care to do just that for his clientele—all his clientele, no matter
who they were.

Despite the excellent food and elegant presentation, no one
else was paying their food much attention, either. They were too
busy looking around at each other, and admiring the theater of it
all, the presentation. We had Tim Leary and G. Gordon Liddy at
our table, and everyone was checking them out, too.

After we ordered, Liddy got up to find the bathroom. Leary
got a prankish look on his face and said, "Don't say a word." He
opened a salt shaker and poured out six neat lines on the ivory
linen tablecloth. They looked exactly like lines of cocaine. When
Liddy came back, Leary had rolled up a bill and started to lean
over the table like he was going to snort the lines.

"Timothy . . ." Liddy and I both hissed. Leary leaned back and
grinned, and we all relaxed for a second. Then he stood up and
began to bang on his glass with a spoon. Loudly, repeatedly, until
the whole dining room fell silent and every set of eyes was on him.
I wanted to slide under the table.

"Hello, everyone," he said. "Some of you may know me. My

name is Dr. Timothy Leary. I've been arrested many times in America for using drugs. When I cross borders it's very difficult for me to bring drugs with me. But I was able to sneak about a hundred hits of acid into France."

He reached inside his sports jacket and produced a sheet of paper, presumably blotter acid.

"But I need other drugs to maintain my life," he went on. "I'm sure that in this room there are people with sleeping pills and people on diets with speed. So I would love to come around and introduce myself and trade you acid for your pills."

Then he actually began to go around from table to table, while a whole lot of powerful and celebrated people sat there looking outraged, aggravated, squirming, puffing on cigarettes. It was insane.

At that moment, maybe sensing that the tenor of the evening had shifted from serene to surreal, an elegant gentleman glided into the room. His white jacket matched his pure white hair and mustache. He was the calmest, most beautiful, quiet pool of light that I had ever seen in my life. Everyone in the room stared at him.

It was Roger Vergé. I felt the entire balance of power in this room filled with the rich and famous focus on him. Their faces lit up. James Coburn leaped out of his chair and hugged him. Coburn had been Vergé's very first guest at the Moulin when it opened in 1969. Coburn had been filming in Monte Carlo, and on a day off, while driving through the village of Mougins, he saw a very old inn with a restaurant sign and pulled in. They served him lunch, and he decided that the food, the inn, and Vergé and his wife were so charming that he rented one of the six small rooms upstairs. He stayed two months. Vergé always called Coburn his first "guest." He called all his patrons guests, not customers. That's worth repeating: *guests,* not customers.

Just by entering the room, Vergé had calmed everyone down. Everyone was smiling again, relaxed. Watching Vergé, I sensed his inner peace and happiness. It was something I had only read about. Joseph Campbell had said, "Follow your bliss." But where do you find your bliss? I had no clue yet, but I knew by now that money, success, fame, sex, and drugs—all the typical American keys to happiness—weren't doing it for me. This man had clearly found his bliss. What was his secret? I flashed on the seventies TV show *Kung Fu,* in which David Carradine was "Grasshopper," student to Master Po, played by Keye Luke. Po doesn't teach Grasshopper kung fu just as a way to fight, but as a way of life, a spiritual path. It was very clear to me that if I didn't change my life soon, didn't find someone who could lead me down some new path, then I was going to become like everybody else in this room. And I decided right there and then that this man, this serene pool of light, was going to be my new mentor, my Master Po.

So when we were done with dinner and everybody else went off in the car, I stayed and waited while the restaurant cleared out. Vergé came out of the kitchen to have a quiet drink with a stocky little bald man at the bar. I watched for probably fifteen minutes before a waiter came over and asked me in very broken English, "Mr. Vergé he ask you are not waiting to him?"

I said, "Yes, I am. I would like to talk to Mr. Vergé."

The waiter gave a little nod toward Vergé, who waved me over. He stood up politely and introduced the man with him as Pablo, who lived next door to the restaurant. Pablo was stocky and bald, and I was sure he was Pablo Picasso. Someone had told me he lived nearby and that the Moulin was his favorite restaurant. That's the way I told this story for years—until I found out that he'd died a decade earlier.

Drunk, nervous, I asked Vergé, "Sir, can I speak to you privately?"

"Certainly," he said, calmly, politely, in a strong French accent. We went a few steps away from the bar and I launched into it.

"Well, um, I was a guest here tonight and the food was amazing and everything was amazing and I had a movie in the film festival and in America they have this TV show with the Grasshopper and I'm gonna really be in trouble if I don't find someone to be my teacher, so can I be your Grasshopper?"

"I don't know what you are speaking of," he said, because of course he didn't.

I tried again. "I just want to hang out with you. Is there some way I can hang out with you?"

"Are you a chef?" he asked. When I said no, he went on, "Well, I am but a simple cook. If you want to work in my kitchen, I would be happy to let you work in my kitchen, but you must be a cook."

He thought I was a foodie who was hitting him up for a job. I didn't want to work in his kitchen, but he was being so nice I said, "How do you become a chef?"

"You go to school."

He wrote down the names of two schools: Marcella Hazan's School of Classic Italian Cooking in Bologna, and another in the Oriental Hotel in Bangkok.

I folded the slip of paper, thanked him earnestly, and left. I was indescribably happy and excited. A new journey was beginning, a new path opening, just when I needed one. I had no idea where it was leading. Never in my life had it occurred to me to go to cooking school. But I was eager to start.

The next day, I remembered that Joe Gannon and his new wife, Beverly, were planning to honeymoon in Italy that year, and had enrolled in Hazan's school. So many opportunities appear in my life just when I need them. They agreed to let me join them, and we all attended cooking school together in Bologna. Later that year I flew to Bangkok and took the course there.

In May of the following year, 1985, we returned to Cannes with another Alan Rudolph film, *Choose Me,* starring Keith Carradine and Geneviève Bujold. (I will tell the strange tale of how that came about later.) I went back to the Moulin, had another sensational meal, and waited for the place to clear out. When it did, I found Vergé at the bar again, sipping a drink just like a year before. When I said hello, it was clear he didn't remember me. Why would he?

"Last year I asked you if I could hang out with you. You told me to go to these cooking schools, and I went to both of them."

"Oh," he said, obviously caught a little off guard. "That is very nice."

I said, "So now can I work in the kitchen with you? I can stay after the festival."

"I am so sorry," he said. "I am leaving for Bangkok after the festival. I am cooking there."

"Well, then can I come to Bangkok with you?" I asked.

He laughed, and then said graciously, "Certainly, if you wish to."

In the year between my two conversations with Vergé, I had learned that we had a mutual friend, George Greif. George had been managing music acts since the 1950s—Barry White, the Modern Jazz Quartet, Lord Buckley, Stan Kenton, New Christy Minstrels, José Feliciano. He and his partner Sid Garris had started their own record label and opened their own club in L.A., with no liquor license so they could let a younger crowd in for what he called "unsupervised fun." In the 1970s he gave George Harrison a tour of Lord Buckley's former L.A. home, Crackerbox Palace, inspiring Harrison to write his song with that name. He mentions "Mr. Greif" in the lyrics.

Greif was a larger-than-life character. He always wore a big felt fedora on his head and a silk handkerchief in his breast pocket. He was boisterous, witty, irreverent, a bon vivant, and extremely generous with his knowledge, which was extensive. He could also be a bit of a pain in the ass when he got on a roll, but he was so funny I didn't mind. I loved traveling with George and took him with me everywhere I could.

I called George and asked if he wanted to go to Bangkok. When I told him I was going with Vergé, he told me he'd been a fan for a few years and said, "When are you leaving?"

"Tomorrow."

"I'm in." He met us there.

My friend Dennis Marini had traveled from Maui to Cannes with me, and I invited him to come along, too.

Since Vergé was guest-cooking at the Oriental Hotel, we rented the Oriental Suite on the top floor. It overlooked the Chao Phraya River and had enough bedrooms for the three of us. The hotel provided Vergé with a small room of his own.

Our first night there, Vergé asked me, "Shep, you are having a tuxedo, *oui*?"

"No. Nobody else has one either."

"But you will be going to dinner tomorrow with Princess Zarina Zainal of Malaysia. You must have wear the tuxedo, you see."

We hired a seamstress to come to our suite in the morning and fit us for tuxes. In Thailand they can make them in hours. That evening we went out for the dinner. When the princess arrived, the whole dining room rose to their feet. Princess Zarina was very pretty, very elegant. Her security guards led her over to our table and then withdrew. She sat between me and George. She was refined but warm, with a stunning smile. She and I engaged in some small talk.

Then George, who was already pretty lit, intruded. "Princess, excuse me. Have you heard the Schmuck Joke?"

She didn't flinch. "No, I don't believe so."

I squirmed. I had heard George's Schmuck Joke a thousand times and couldn't believe he was about to tell it to the princess of Malaysia.

"A wife tells her husband, 'You are the biggest schmuck I've ever met in my life. You do everything like a schmuck. You walk like a schmuck. You talk like a schmuck. You eat like a schmuck. You dress like a schmuck. You comb your hair like a schmuck. If they had a contest for World's Biggest Schmuck, you'd come in second.' She lets that sink in, then says, 'Ask me why you'd come in second.' Husband rolls his eyes but says, 'Okay, why would I come in second?'"

George jumped to his feet, leaned over the Princess, jabbed a finger in her face, and yelled, " 'BECAUSE YOU'RE A SCHMUCK!' "

The whole room held its collective breath for a few seconds of startled silence. Then the princess's security guards came running at us. They didn't hear the joke, they just saw this loud American looming over the princess, jabbing his finger in her face and shouting. The princess, to her enormous credit, was unfazed. She waved the guards away with a smile. She was one of the guys. Who knew? We have stayed friends all these years. When *Supermensch* came out, she friended me on Facebook!

Over the next four days, Vergé and I spent a lot of time together, hanging out and exploring Bangkok. One morning we went upriver to check out the markets. When I was playing with this little knife I really liked at the fish market, Vergé bought it for me. It cost a quarter. He teased me about that for years. I still have the knife; now that Roger is gone, it has even more meaning for me.

It was good having George there to help us all bond. We enjoyed each other like old friends. Vergé must've felt at ease with me, because one night he told me something personal I never forgot. He said he was the son of a blacksmith, and that when he was a young man in his small French village, cooking was considered menial work. So when he dated a girl, he would never tell her he was a chef. Neither of us liked to talk about our private life, so I think this moment added something important to our camaraderie. It got me thinking about how chefs of Vergé's generation were invisible to their culture. That realization would open another path to me soon enough.

Before I met Roger Vergé, I thought bliss was basically wealth and power. But early in our friendship, I came to feel that true bliss was service to others and perfecting your compassion. Unlike so many people I knew then, Vergé always did everything in a selfless spirit of "How can I make your life better?" He was a genuinely humble gentleman; nothing he did was just about him. As a chef, he liked to say, "I try to give pleasure on everyone." What made him the absolute happiest was cooking to please his customers and friends. Doing a service for others.

What I saw in Vergé was that you could be successful *and* happy. I had only seen success and misery—the success that killed Janis, Jimi, and Morrison, and sent Alice to rehab. Vergé was the first person I ever met who had true success: he had mastered his craft, he had respect from his peers, and he was happy, always happy, because his true joy came from putting the comfort of others before himself.

I responded to this on some deep and instinctual level. I never thought of it then, but I've come to believe that in some ways Vergé reminded me of my father, whom I loved wholeheartedly. I think he and Vergé, as different as they were, also had much in common.

I'd spent my adult life up to then in show business and Hollywood, where kindness was considered a weakness. In Hollywood every dog was an alpha dog. Everything was a competition for who could bark the loudest and take the biggest bite out of some other dog. You were either top dog or you were a loser, and God help you because they'd tear you to shreds and never think twice about it. To this day, when I'm talking to anyone in Hollywood I have to consciously put on an alpha dog act. If you're not saying, "You fucking fuck, I'll fucking murder you," they don't hear you. They *can't* hear you. And of course no one is ever happy. It doesn't matter how much money, fame, and power they have. Because in that environment they're anxious and frightened every minute of their lives. They have to be constantly vigilant and on guard, always protecting their turf, always looking out for some bigger, meaner, louder dog. It's a miserable, stressful way to be, and it was the opposite of the way I wanted to live and act.

Vergé was showing me another path—that seeding a little compassion and kindness every chance you get creates an abundance of happiness for all. It doesn't have to be winner and losers. It can be win-win. You make other people happy, they make you happy. It's very simple, and it's probably the most important lesson of my life. It's what I mean by *compassionate business*.

As a young man I was always searching for happiness, but I didn't have teachers. Joseph Campbell said: "If you do follow your bliss you put yourself on a kind of track that has been there all the while, waiting for you, and the life that you ought to be living is the one you are living." Campbell said you don't have to get to heaven to experience bliss: you can grab it right now. He offered one simple, practical way to do that: go into a quiet room and do whatever makes you happy, for thirty minutes a day. Whatever makes you happy—listening to music, sewing, shouting—take thirty minutes out of your busy, hectic, modern-world day to do it. That's following your bliss. Roger Vergé did what made him happy every day.

Our hotel rooms in Bangkok had little books on Buddhism in them, the way American hotels always had the Gideon bible. I started browsing through. Like many other sixties college kids, I had read Jack Kerouac's *The Dharma Bums* and Hermann Hesse's *Siddhartha,* about seeking the enlightenment that brings inner happiness. My favorite *Siddhartha* lines were something like, "Seeking means having a goal. But finding means being free, being open, having no goal." I also liked, "It is only important to love the world, not despise it. Not to hate each other but to regard the world and ourselves and all beings with love, admiration, and respect." That was how Vergé acted. That was how I wanted to be.

I decided that if Buddhism embraced that idea, I wanted to know more about it. My college friend Marty Kriegel, who's about the smartest person I've ever known, had gotten deeply into Buddhism. When I asked him if he could help me understand it, he wrote me a very long, very detailed, very Marty letter about it, basically a scholarly thesis on it. Marty's an intellectual; I'm not. I would never really study Buddhism the way he did. But he said that was all right. At the end of his letter, he wrote, "But Shep, you don't really need to know any of this. Your walks on the beach are what it's all about."

I'm starting to understand that now.

13

I STARTED GOING TO CANNES EVERY YEAR, for both the festival and the Moulin. I loved it. For me, Cannes was like no other place in the world. Business-wise, everything you did mattered. It even mattered where you stayed. The Hotel du Cap was the epicenter of lodging the way the Moulin was to dining. It was built as the palatial Villa Soleil in 1869 and became a hotel twenty years later. It's one of the most elegant, luxurious hotels in the world, on some of the world's prime real estate, twenty-two acres of lawn and garden just down the coast from the city, at the tip of the Cap d'Antibes, looking out at the ocean. It was a power statement to stay at the du Cap. If you didn't stay there, you were nobody. If you couldn't afford it, or couldn't get a room, you lied and *said* you stayed there. Of all the people in the film industry, there are only twenty or thirty who have the power to green-light a feature. At Cannes, they all stay at the du Cap.

Carolyn got me my first reservation. During the festival they won't reserve you a room for under two weeks. Most people are at the festival for only four or five nights. It doesn't matter. You must book for two weeks. And they are *very* expensive rooms. When I went to pay the bill with my credit card, they informed me that they only took cash. They also charged me for three hotel dinners I didn't eat. I ate all my dinners out. And three dinners at the hotel added up to something outrageous like $2,500.

I spoke to the guy at the front desk, who went and fetched the general manager, a Monsieur Arondel. He started out very polite.

"Mr. Gordon. I understand you are questioning the bill for these dinners?"

"Yes. I didn't eat any dinner here."

At that he turned frosty and, well, French.

"Mr. Gordon, we do not appreciate guests who challenge our bills. That is not what our guests do here. We do not prefer such guests. I understand you do not have cash. So I will allow you to pay by check. But you will no longer be welcome at this hotel."

It seemed like an old-time shakedown to me. I had to stay at the du Cap when I was at Cannes. He knew that. He knew the hotel could get away with charging me anything the hotel wanted to, and threatening me with banishment when I dared to speak up. Because if you wanted to do major business at the festival, you did have to stay there. And it *is* a beautiful hotel. When you're in the movie business, you get used to being squeezed by people in power positions. So you paid what the hotel said you had to pay. In cash.

The following year, I was worried that I really wouldn't be allowed to book a room. I asked my friend Tom Pollock, chairman of Universal Pictures, if he could make a reservation for me.

"I can do better than that," he said. "I got a room for De Niro, but he's only going to be there for three days. I had to reserve it for two weeks. Fly on the Universal plane, the office will bring you the key at the airport, and just go use the room."

I flew over, got the key, and went to the hotel. I hid my face as I passed through the lobby, so no staff would recognize me as that troublemaker from the previous year who had the balls to question his bill. When I walked into the room, my friend Michael Fuchs, the head of HBO, was there.

"Michael, what are you doing here?"

"Hey, Shep. I rented the room for the festival. Just got here this morning."

"They charge you for two weeks?"

"Yeah."

I cracked up. They double-booked the room. What a racket.

For years I financed all our pictures, five or six pictures a year, sitting in the lobby of the Hotel du Cap, scribbling deals on hotel napkins. After my very first trip to Cannes I had flown back with Jim Fifield. He was the head of 20th Century Fox Video. Later he'd be chairman of EMI and Capitol Records. We are good friends; I'm his daughter's godfather. Jim explained that where movies had traditionally made virtually all their money in movie theaters, now in-store videocassette sales (DVDs were still a decade off) and TV pay-per-view rentals were very important secondary markets. Theatrical distribution was still critical, because if your picture got into X number of theaters, the people who bought those secondary market rights automatically calculated X number of sales and rentals, for which they paid you X dollars.

But theatrical distribution was in the hands of a few big guns, and a small independent company like Alive had no leverage with them. So it seemed to me that for us, controlling both the production of a picture *and* its distribution was the key. For example, if I could raise a million dollars to make a picture, and then guarantee that it would be in X number of theaters—which we could do if we distributed it ourselves—it would trigger strong secondary rights. We could then put that into making and distributing the next film.

Those are the deals I cut at the du Cap. For instance, I would meet up with Andre Blay, who ran Embassy Home Entertainment in America, and sell him what was called an output deal. This meant I would guarantee him that I would put, say, five movies a year in X number of theaters. He would block-buy the video rights to that entire output for X dollars. That frontloaded us a lump of money for the films.

We became a model for this whole subculture of younger people who wanted to do what we did. One of them was Harvey Weinstein. I'd known him since he and his brother started out producing rock concerts in Buffalo. They formed Miramax in 1979 and started out distributing concert films. He would come to Cannes and try to get into the game, but it was a tough game to get into. I don't know if I can say I mentored him, but I did try to help him out and give him tips, and when Miramax got to be really successful in the 1990s, it was to a significant degree because they followed in our path.

I only actually stayed at the du Cap a couple of years. Then Vergé said, "Shep, you must stay at the Moulin with me." After that I would book a room at the Moulin, and one for George Greif. We slept until late morning, then went down in our bathrobes. One of Vergé's sous chefs made us breakfast. That sous chef was Daniel Boulud, long before he became a world-renowned chef himself. He made incredible breakfasts and we became good friends.

|||||||||||||||||||||

One day I said to Vergé, "You work hard during the festival. I work hard. When it's over, why don't we get a bunch of our friends together and take a bus trip somewhere beautiful? Go drink wine and eat food and have fun."

He agreed. He lived for food, wine, making people happy, and service. I just presented him with another avenue to do what he loved and share it with our friends.

We both invited people. I found us a great touring bus that belonged to Team Porsche and came from Germany with a driver named Adolph. It was big, black, shiny, and new, ominous-looking with its opaque black windows. Inside it was all high-tech and luxurious from its leather couches and seats to its dining area to the private compartment in the back. It was like a rock-and-roll touring bus, but without the beds.

On the last day of the festival for the next five years we loaded up that beautiful bus and took off on an excursion. We went to Burgundy, Champagne, Italy's wine country, Cognac, and once to Hungary, to visit these amazing caves that hadn't been opened in years, where they stored a great Hungarian after-dinner wine. The trip was usually six or seven days. It was a different mix of people each trip, but the core group was Vergé and me; George Greif; César the sculptor; and François Mazet, the famous, flamboyant race car driver, one of the group's heroes.

On these trips I first observed how in Europe a great chef like Vergé was revered the same way a great rock star or great sculptor was. People in Europe understood that they were all artists, just working in different media. Gradually, I learned the history behind the rise of Vergé and other chefs to this status of recognition.

The French had always appreciated the culinary arts. But it was only with the creation of nouvelle cuisine in the late 1960s and early 1970s that the chef rather than the institution became important. Before then, great dining was always identified with a place, usually a hotel restaurant: the Savoy, the Ritz, the Plaza. Pretty much the only chef whose name was well known was Georges Auguste Escoffier, back around the turn of the twentieth century.

In the late 1880s, Richard D'Oyly Carte, famous for producing Gilbert & Sullivan, opened his new Savoy Hotel in London, and brought Escoffier and a Swiss hotelier named César Ritz to run it for him. When they left a decade later, Ritz opened the Hotel Ritz in Paris and the Carlton in London. They were the most elegant and opulent hotels in the world—the adjective *ritzy* comes from this time—and Escoffier had what were considered the world's best restaurants. Escoffier was the first to get the British to eat frog legs; he called them "Cuisses de Nymphe a l'Aurore," Thighs of the Nymph of Dawn. He was so important to Ritz's business that Ritz named the restaurant the Escoffier Room, the first time anyone invested in making a chef a known entity in his own right.

Escoffier retired, and died in 1935. After that, there were no really well-known chefs until Vergé, Paul Bocuse, and the Troisgros brothers, Pierre and Jean, completely renovated French haute cuisine as "nouvelle cuisine," a lighter, fresher, less sauce-dependent style. They organized themselves as the Association de la Grand Cuisine Française, identifying nouvelle cuisine not with a place, but with themselves. A really smart Belgian promoter and marketer living in Paris at the time, Yanou Collart, had a lot to do with spreading nouvelle cuisine around the world, and making Vergé and the others celebrities throughout Europe. She urged food critics to go taste their food for themselves and, if they liked it, to tell their readers about it. She'd arrange for movie stars or other celebrities to come to the chefs' restaurants, where she'd make sure there was a photographer or gossip columnist on hand to capture the moment. (So she was practicing my trick of "guilt by association" before I was.) She was also the first to arrange for them to go on tour, introducing their cuisine and wines.

So, by the time I met Vergé, he was as famous and loved in Europe as César Baldaccini or Mazet. Vergé and Mazet had a long friendship going back to when Vergé cooked for Team Ferrari, which bought a big double-decker bus and put a kitchen in the bottom so Vergé could make meals for the drivers at all the Formula One races. I loved Mazet. When he got married, George Greif and I flew to Paris to be surprise waiters and serve champagne at his wedding.

After we decided each year's destination, Vergé would plot out the details of the journey. As we left the Moulin, Vergé would serve us cheese and crackers and a bottle of wine. As the French countryside slid by he'd say things like, "Oh, Shep, look out the window."

"Yes, Mr. Vergé. Very pretty."

"You see this little farmhouse?"

"Yes, Mr. Vergé, very nice."

"You know this cheese, it was make by this farmhouse. Mr. Gateau. He is third generation of making cheese. He send over this cheese in morning for us."

That was the nature of the entire trip. Vergé had friends all along the route. We ate at their restaurants, drank at their vineyards. They were always very excited to have a Vergé, César, and a Mazet walk into their spaces all at the same time. Vergé had César do a sketch in pencil for each place we visited. Vergé himself brought aprons and signed books. For a week we rolled from one beautiful space and excellent meal to another. One restaurant had an entire truffle menu. And every piece of foie gras and every truffle they had in the place came to our table, because Roger Vergé was in their restaurant. Out came the oldest bottles of wine from their cellars, and they wouldn't let us leave until we drank twenty, thirty bottles.

I can remember only one night that went a bit off the rails. In Umbria, Giorgio Lungarotti invited us to his winery. Since the 1950s, the Lungarotti name was famous for raising Umbrian wines to the level of art. When we got into the little medieval town of Torgiano, where the Lungarotti winery was, it was late at night. We took a very narrow street to a beautiful fifteenth-century hotel where we were all staying for the night, then headed to a late dinner with Lungarotti. Vergé always organized everything on these trips. For example, we always, always ate at one table. Always. Our group was pretty large this time. In addition to our core group we had picked up a couple of César's sculptor friends, the restaurateur Paolo della Pupa—maybe fourteen of us in all. It was late, around eleven o'clock. We were the only people in the restaurant.

As we entered, I saw they'd set two tables for us.

I asked the maître d', "Could you please reset those two tables to one table? We always eat at one table."

"Mr. Lungarotti said it is two tables," he replied.

"Well, could you tell Mr. Lungarotti we always eat at one table?"

He went off, came back, and said, "Mr. Lungarotti says it must be two tables."

"Really?" Now I saw there were name cards. Vergé's table had what Lungarotti must have thought were all the heavyweights at it. My table was George, me, Paolo della Puppa, and a couple of others.

To miss a night eating together, which was what the entire journey was about, was a big deal to me. Lungarotti walked in, wearing a suit and tie. He walked right past our table without saying a word, then greeted Vergé and everyone at his table and sat with them. The waiter brought them olive oil and bread. I saw that it was a different olive oil from the one they brought us. Theirs was in a beautiful square bottle; our bottle was round.

I asked the waiter, very politely, "Could we get a bottle of that olive oil?"

He went over, whispered to Lungarotti, came back, and said, "I'm sorry. It's only for that table. It's a special bottle just for them."

"We can't have the olive oil from that table?"

"No, I'm sorry. Just for them."

That was it. I got up, walked over, and said, "Mr. Vergé, we are leaving. Not just the restaurant, but the hotel."

"Oh, but Shep. There is not a hotel in two hundred miles."

"Mr. Vergé, we are leaving right now. It's different olive oil!"

He had no idea what I meant. I pointed out the different bottles. Vergé spoke a little French to Lungarotti.

"Oh, you cannot go," Lungarotti said. But no apology, no one moving to set things right. So I led our entire group out of the restaurant and back onto the bus. After a moment Lungarotti sent a guy out to say okay, you can have the olive oil. We marched back into the restaurant. They made one long table out of the two, with two square bottles of the special olive oil.

My goal was to have us all sitting at one table, all with the same olive oil. I hadn't really gotten angry, but I knew that storming out and leaving Lungarotti alone at his table would accomplish my goal: a beautiful evening, a great meal, and lots of laughs.

And it was the best olive oil I ever tasted in my life. No wonder Lungarotti was hoarding it. Before we left, we arranged for Paolo della Puppa to get the U.S. distribution rights. He built a career on exporting that oil. I still have probably twenty cases of those beautiful square bottles at my home.

One year we learned that César was scheduled for cancer surgery at the end of the trip. We were going to Italy and then back to Paris, where the bus would drop César at the hospital. I thought we'd need something to lighten the mood, so I walked into a porno shop in Cannes and bought blowup dolls for everyone. A black one, a Swedish blonde, an Indian one. When we got to the French-Italian border, an immigration official came onto the bus and saw all these blowup dolls lying around. He was concerned. But then he recognized César. Everybody in France recognized César.

Another Formula One racer, Clay Regazzoni, came on that trip. He'd been paralyzed from the waist down in a crash at the Long Beach Grand Prix in 1980, then came back and raced in the Paris-Dakar Rally using a special hand-controlled car. Paris-Dakar is the most demanding automobile race in the world, and here he was, a paraplegic, competing in it with all the other drivers. The French called him "the Animal" after that. Whenever people saw him, they'd scream, "*L'Animal! L'Animal!*" He was the biggest pop star of our bunch. He brought no attendant with him. Yet he was the first up and dressed every morning, with the biggest smile you ever saw. We carried him into and out of his wheelchair and it never added one second to our journey.

When we dropped off César in Paris at the end of that trip, Mazet picked up a car there. Mercedes made custom vehicles for race-car drivers to use on the streets. They had eight wheels, a double set at each of the four points, in case a tire blew—because they all drove so fast on the streets. George, L'Animal, and I got into Mazet's eight-wheeled Mercedes, and he proceeded to scare the daylights out of us with his driving. (Well, maybe not L'Animal, but George and me for sure.) He's speeding around Paris like a madman. He has the car phone in one hand, speaking to Vergé, and a cognac in the other, steering with his knees, blasting a hundred miles an hour through city traffic, down one-way streets the wrong way, stopping for green lights, going through red lights. He drives that way any time, but now he's also drunk. He's laughing on the phone. "Hey, Chef, we are having a great time! I am driving the wrong way and people are going crazy! Why are you not with us, Chef?"

I was terrified. How could I get this crazy man to stop? Then I remembered that Jeff Kramer, Bob Dylan's manager, had told me that Dylan was playing a concert in a Paris cinema that day.

"Hey, François, let's go see Bob Dylan."

"Perfect! We go see Bob Dylan!"

At the speed he was driving we got there in no time. I clearly remember seeing the exterior of the movie house rushing toward us. It looked just like one of the old, giant RKO theaters, with maybe a dozen glass doors flanking the ticket booth. Then Mazet driving up onto the sidewalk, scattering pedestrians. Then Mazet driving *through* the doors. Then us sitting in Mazet's eight-wheeled Mercedes in the middle of the lobby, Mazet on the phone yelling, "Chef, we are in the lobby to see Bob Dylan! You should be here!"

The theater manager was running toward us, with a policeman, who was reaching for his pistol. The policeman yanked open Mazet's door and looked inside the car. His jaw dropped.

"Mazet! L'Animal!"

He holstered his gun. And pulled out a pen and a notepad. And asked them for their autographs. I am not making this up.

Mazet handed him the keys, like he was a valet, and the theater manager ushered us into the concert. While we enjoyed the show, the cop backed the Mercedes out of the lobby and parked it out front for us.

⠀⠀⠀⠀⠀⠀ⁱⁱⁱⁱⁱⁱⁱⁱⁱⁱⁱⁱⁱⁱⁱⁱⁱⁱ

In the mid-1980s Alive Films evolved into Island Alive Pictures. That's a complicated story I'll explain later. Island Alive was producing some great films. In 1985 two of our movies earned Oscars: a Best Actor for William Hurt in *Kiss of the Spider Woman* (the third movie we screened at Cannes) and a Best Actress for Geraldine Page in *The Trip to Bountiful*. So we were pretty hot at Cannes. If you were a player there, it was a tradition to throw a big party. I decided to throw my first big party at the Moulin.

I spoke to Vergé. I knew it would be a lot of work for him. I always had to be careful what I asked him for, because very rarely would he give me a no.

"I want to throw a private party for fifty or sixty people in the Moulin during the film festival. Would you do that for me?"

"It will be difficult," he said. "But for you, I would of course do anything."

I had the best possible venue. Now I needed a celebrity cohost to draw the other celebrities—guilt by association again. I thought of Michael Douglas. We had met in a funny way. Phyllis Somer, a former model I was dating, invited me to go to Santa Barbara with her for a party at Michael and Diandra Douglas's house. The Oceanside kid in me thought, Michael Douglas, wow. Then Phyllis called and said, "There're no rooms in Santa Barbara."

I decided that wasn't going to deter us. I went out and rented a big black rock-and-roll tour bus, just for the two of us. We drove up to Santa Barbara and pulled into Michael's driveway.

When Phyllis introduced us, Michael asked, "Where are you staying?"

"In your driveway," I said.

"What?"

I walked him outside and showed him the bus.

"Jesus!" He laughed. We went into the bus, and in a little while half the party was in there.

Michael and I drank some cognac. He has so much life in him; he's so available and easygoing and funny. We clicked right away.

Michael Douglas had just come through a frustrating period in his career and was on an upswing.

"You know, Mikey," I said, "these chefs are all great artists. But nobody gives a shit about them. They're treated like garbage. Look at Vergé. He's the best chef on the planet, even his peers say so, but he can barely earn a living. We need to help our fellow artists make more money. They should all be stars like you guys are. I'm going to throw him a dinner party at his place. All the biggest stars in Cannes are ready to kill to get into these parties. It'll be fantastic. Why don't you cohost with me?"

It was a gigantic success. Everyone came. I mean *everyone*—the world's greatest stars all had their assistants call to get invitations. Everybody at the festival buzzed about it the next day.

That's how we started hosting special annual dinners at the Moulin for fifty, sixty invited guests. It was the most sought-after invitation at the festival. Every producer, director, and movie star in Cannes wanted an invitation. Only the top players got one. Every table was a power table. The next morning at breakfast, every conversation was about who was at the Moulin last night, who sat with whom. Lots of movies got funded at those dinners. It was great for Island Alive's prestige, good for Michael's profile, and fabulous for Vergé. If he'd spent a million dollars he couldn't have bought that kind of publicity. Once they'd eaten at the Moulin, every big name in Hollywood was a Vergé fan. To them, *he* was the superstar, and the Moulin was hallowed ground. A true win-win.

My company always paid the bill. And it was always a big one, fifty, sixty thousand dollars, depending on the wines. After a few years, Michael said to me, "This year I'm paying."

"Mikey, believe me, you don't want to do that."

"No, man, I've had a great year," he said. "I'm back in action.

You've done it every year, Shep. I'm taking care of the bill this year."

"Absolutely not. You're not paying this bill."

"If I'm not paying the bill, I'm never coming again."

When the bill came at the end of the dinner I grabbed it. It was, I think, $56,000. He tried to snatch it from me.

"Mikey, you can't do this."

"Shep," he insisted, "I'm paying the bill!"

So I let him take it from me. And watched a slight look of shock cross his face when he read it.

But then there was this beautiful moment when he looked up at me with a huge grin and said, "You will never know how happy I am that I can pay this."

You get to see somebody's true character through their choices. And Michael's choices are always to do the right thing, every second of every minute of every day. Just a remarkable man. I've never had a better friend, or known a human I respect more.

||||||||||||||||||||

After we had hosted a few of these dinners at the Moulin, I said to Michael, "Why don't we bring Vergé to L.A. and throw a dinner there? We'll invite a Hollywood A-list, and really try to get across the idea that great chefs like Vergé are great artists who aren't getting the respect or the money they deserve." I thought we should do it in Los Angeles, rather than in, say, New York, because for everyone in Hollywood the high point of Cannes was already dinner at the Moulin. I knew if we put out an invitation in L.A., we would get a turnout that would blow everybody's mind. Everyone would want to know who this Vergé was and why all these amazing people gathered in one room for him. Then I took the idea one step further. Why not put all these celebrity guests in white cooks' jackets, so that they're tacitly showing their respect to the culinary arts? Which led me to think, And why don't we do for Vergé what he does for us? Why don't we serve and be the staff for the party?

We threw the first one at my house. Vergé cooked, Michael was the head waiter, and I was the head sommelier. We served sixty guests—a Hollywood who's who, people like Jack Nicholson, Sylvester Stallone, James Coburn, Anthony Quinn, Danny DeVito, Rhea Perlman, Wes Craven, the heads of all the studios. Michael and I and other staff bringing plates around to all the tables, pouring their wine. Being of service.

I paid for it all. I was making rock-and-roll money, movie money—money was of no importance. I felt that Vergé had saved my life without saving my life. He probably wasn't conscious of it, but meeting him and being in his presence had been the turning point of my life. So I felt a great debt to him and was honored to help him get the respect that he deserved. I always paid for everything around Vergé anyway. In all the years I was with him I never let him put his hand in his pocket, ever. He never paid for a hotel room, a meal, anything. He shared with me what he had, and I shared with him what I had. It was a great exchange.

My favorite moment of the evening came after dinner broke up at around eleven. Most of the guests went home, but Michael, Jack Nicholson, Danny, and a few others hung around. I went to sleep. Around one thirty I woke up and went into the living room, and the only person left was Jack. He was leaning up against the wall by the door, obviously with a good buzz on.

I said, "Hey, Jack, how you doing?"

He said, "Oh man, come here."

I went over to him.

"Shep, tell me something," he said. "Which one of us has to go home?"

||||||||||||||||||||

We did a few of these dinners, and they were all great events. Vergé was very pleased. He was a proud man, he always enjoyed having all of Hollywood come to him at Cannes, and to have them all gather to honor him in Hollywood itself brought him great joy and satisfaction.

I still love to throw dinner parties at my house in Maui. It's one of my favorite things to do. I apply everything Vergé taught me about the art of doing it correctly. The goal is to make every single guest feel as good as you can. You focus completely on them. It's never about what *you* want. It's all for them. For example, if your guests are young people, give them bright lighting, because they want to see and be seen. For older people, use soft lighting. The round table is very important. It creates a sense of equality. Nobody is at the head of the table; nobody is more important than anyone else at the table. If you have enough servers, serve everyone at the same time, the way I first saw Vergé's staff do at the Moulin.

At my parties, there are often celebrities. If you're a celebrity trying to relax and enjoy your meal, you don't want other people gawking at you and bugging you for an autograph. At my house, you will never be asked for your autograph. I try to invite people who maybe have never met each other but would like to. Vergé taught me that if you have a guest whom everyone else at the affair wants to meet, leave an empty chair at each table. Then that someone can go around from table to table. And there's no doing business at my house. If I hear somebody starting to talk shop or hustle another guest, I get right over there and end it. It's not about business. Business is what you do elsewhere at other times. This is all about living the moment, enjoying the moment, being thankful for the miracles of good food and good friends.

14

AS INVOLVED AS I WAS IN THE MOVIE BUSINESS AND CANNES, I continued to be as busy as ever managing musical artists. In fact, our roster just kept growing. Blondie, the Pointer Sisters, Kenny Loggins, Stephanie Mills. My relationship with one singer in particular gave me some of my highest highs and lowest lows as a manager. My work with him also had a big, weird impact on the movie side of our company. It's a complicated tale with some fantastic twists and turns.

It starts back in 1975, when the soul group Harold Melvin & the Blue Notes put out what became my all-time favorite song, "Wake Up Everybody." It's such a beautiful, hopeful song. I still listen to it all the time and it always lifts me up.

The Blue Notes were on Philadelphia International Records (PIR), the soul machine founded and run by the producers and songwriters Kenneth Gamble and Leon Huff, who were also responsible for the success of the O'Jays and other big R&B, soul, and disco artists. Although Harold Melvin was the group's founder, the star was the drummer and singer, Teddy Pendergrass. Although I liked the song a lot, I wasn't aware at the time that it was Teddy singing it. I think I just assumed it was Melvin.

Teddy left the group for a solo career that year. His manager, Taaz Lang, also became his lover. One night in 1977, as she was getting out of her car, she was gunned down execution-style. Her murder has never been solved.

I got a call from Goddard Lieberson, the head of Columbia Records, as well as the executor of Groucho's estate. Columbia distributed PIR. He asked me if I'd be interested in managing Teddy. You did not say no to Goddard Lieberson. I agreed to go see Teddy perform in Philadelphia and meet him afterward. It was in a small theater, maybe fifteen hundred seats. A lot of them seemed to be filled by women, who seemed to love the show. I did not. I thought it was really hokey. Teddy had an album that was climbing the charts, and he seemed really cocky to me, really not authentic. He was wearing these long white capes, surrounded by dancers and backup singers, a really corny production. But when he sang "Wake Up Everybody" I realized for the first time that it was his voice on the record I loved so much.

I went backstage afterward, and there was a traffic jam outside his dressing room of Jewish managers, most of whom I knew, lined up to get an audience with him. It was like a cattle call for guys auditioning to handle him. I didn't want any part of it and went home. About a week later I got a call from somebody at Columbia asking what I thought. I said I hated the show, loved the artist, didn't meet him. They asked me to please try again. He was talking to some managers they didn't think were right for him.

So I went down from New York. Outside Teddy's building was a white Rolls with TEDDY license plates. I took the elevator up to the penthouse, and a gorgeous girl wearing what was almost lingerie answered his door. Then I met Teddy, who was the most beautiful thing in the world. A dazzlingly handsome, very virile, very macho man. It was obvious why his audience was predominantly women. Still, all I wanted to do was get this meeting over with, go home, and get back to my life. So I said the most outrageous thing I could think of to say to a guy like Teddy, figuring that would be the end of it.

"Listen," I said. "There are not a lot of things I'm sure of in this life. One thing I know for sure is that you are not qualified to judge which one of us Jewish managers is the better bullshitter. That's what we do for a living. We talk, you sing. I was backstage a few weeks ago and saw that you had the best of the best lined up to pitch you. There's no way for you to know who's better for you and who's worse, who's going to deliver and who's not. But another thing I know for sure: I can get higher than you, I got better women than yours, I can get drunker than you, and when you fall down I can take the cash out of your pocket and make sure it's safe."

I figured Teddy was going to throw me out of the building. Instead, he said okay, let's make a date and find out. Now I had to make good. But I had that high tolerance for drink and drugs, so I knew I had a fighting chance. One thing I've always done is to try to make every moment special for whomever I'm with, so I had a beautiful wooden briefcase made and filled it with every drug known to man. A record company, maybe Warner Bros., gave us a two-bedroom suite in the Regency Hotel on Park Avenue. Teddy and I went head-to-head there, drinking and drugging and fooling around. When he collapsed after two days, I was still standing. I called a friend at Columbia, who came over and took a picture of me standing over Teddy with my foot on his chest. We sent it to Goddard Lieberson. In his memoir, *Truly Blessed,* Teddy wrote: "Who'd imagine I'd be out-partied by a white boy from Oceanside, Long Island? But I was. And it was one of the best things that ever happened to me. We shook hands and that's been our contract ever since. No paper. His word was enough."

It was one of the luckiest days of my life, the start of a new and incredible journey. Teddy had some dates booked, so I went on the road with him to get a feel for it. The first one was in Hampton Roads, Virginia. I knew the building because Alice had played there. It was a big barn of a space, like a hockey rink, that seated six thousand. You had to put up your own stage and bring in lights and sound. When we got there Teddy's equipment was set up on-stage, but there were no lights, no PA, and no promoter. Around five in the afternoon a van rolled up and the guys unloaded a Shure PA, really small, like you'd use for a shopping mall event or a Holiday Inn lounge, and a few small lights on poles. Really bush league. But I was new so I didn't say anything. A decent-size audience showed up, maybe three thousand people, and they seemed to have a good time anyway.

At the end of the show I found the promoter and said we'd like to get paid.

"Oh, we're not paying," he said, nonchalantly.

"What do you mean?"

"We didn't do as much business as we hoped so we're not paying."

I said, "You've got to pay him. If you don't, I can't stop these guys from coming in here and killing you. They've got guns. If a stray bullet hits me I don't mind. I don't have any family. But you're out of your mind. You're going to lose your life for two thousand dollars or whatever it is?"

He had a ring on one finger. He took it off and gave it to me as payment.

I took it to Teddy and asked, "Is this how you normally get

paid? I've got to change this. I can't take twenty percent of a ring, and I'm not doing this for fun."

That's when I started to hear how things worked on the Chitlin' Circuit, not just from Teddy but from Earth, Wind & Fire and other black entertainers. The Chitlin' Circuit was the traditional name for the black touring circuit. It had been around since vaudeville, and it had always exploited and ripped off acts. What I saw that night was just the way business was done. The entertainers put up with it to promote their records, and because things could turn ugly if they didn't. There was more than a little reason to believe that Taaz had been murdered because she crossed somebody on the Chitlin' Circuit.

I sat Teddy down and said, "I can't do it this way. I can either resign or I can break these motherfuckers, but I can't do that without you."

Teddy said, "Let's go after them. I want to change it, too."

I booked a small tour. The first date was the Roxy in L.A., for a number of reasons. One, I wanted to do a press launch. Two, I wanted Teddy to play in a white-owned building. I wanted to see what reaction we'd get in a venue where I had some control; L.A. was my town. Teddy worked meanwhile on changing his show from the cheesy affair I'd seen. He didn't tell me how he was changing it, and our relationship was still too new for me to meddle.

As the date approached, Teddy and I both started getting death threats. Some came by telephone, and one or two on paper. Those were classics, like something from a movie, with the letters cut out of magazines and glued to sheets of paper. We contacted the police and the FBI. They never found out who sent them, but they took it seriously enough that Teddy and I had to decide if we were going to go through with this. We decided yes.

So he played the Roxy. The audience was almost all white. And the show was awful. He had gone completely in the opposite direction from his former show. This one had no razzle or dazzle at all. He just sat on a stool through the whole thing and sang. It was like he went from James Brown to Vic Damone. I thought it was horrible. When it was over I headed backstage with a full head of steam. I discovered that the women in the audience must have liked the show even with no show business in it, because a constant stream of them were going in and out of his dressing room. It went on for hours. I was still the new guy, and his bodyguards would not let me in. The parade of women went on until 2 A.M. When I could finally get into the dressing room I charged in there with smoke trailing from my ears.

"You motherfucker. Who the fuck do you think you are? I ain't getting paid. I'm getting death threats. I risk my life to watch you sit on a fucking stool the whole show. Then I stand outside your dressing room until two in the fucking morning? Are you out of your mind?"

Teddy said, "Well, what kind of show do you want me to do?"

I said, "I want you to do a show that gets every woman in the house so horny that they all jump on me, because I'm the only guy out there. You're a sex magnet, but you're singing *at* them. You need to sing *to* them."

And as I said it, in the heat of that moment, I heard a concept. It was right there, fully formed. Teddy was very macho and manly, and women found him extremely sexy. Women made up a large part of his audience, and he got them really worked up. Any husbands or dates who happened to come along with them were pretty sure to be rewarded for it later that night. My idea played off that. Teddy Pendergrass was going to perform "for women only."

Once again, everybody thought I was crazy. How could you

keep men out? It had to violate some sort of civil rights laws. And once again, I just put my head down and steamed forward. I knew instinctively that it would work, and it would get Teddy a ton of press. I hedged the legal issue by deciding that though the ad would say that tickets were only available for women, we wouldn't actually refuse to sell a ticket to any man who wanted to buy one. So we weren't barring men, we were just discouraging them. I also didn't want Teddy to appear to be too arrogant about it. He would not say in public, "I'm only letting women into my show." It took a while, but we came up with a beautiful ad that struck just the right tone. It featured a stuffed teddy bear with a note attached: *Come spend the night with me. Love, Teddy.* We were consciously evoking Elvis: "Baby, let me be your loving teddy bear." Sexy, but also romantic. And just to drive it home, we would hand out chocolate teddy bear lollipops to the ladies to lick during the show.

Teddy's For Women Only tour hit five cities, from New York to L.A., and was massively successful. The press stepped right up and started calling him the Black Elvis. When he bought a big house outside Philadelphia they even compared it to Graceland. (He bought it from the Philadelphia-based TV host Mike Douglas, who would later show up unannounced and drive friends around the property, showing them where he used to live.) Over the next few years Teddy was the top-selling male vocalist in R&B. We had the greatest time. I loved being around him, loved going on the road with him. We went to boxing matches together, Ali fights, Sugar Ray fights. I got to know all the NBA greats through him—his best friend was Dr. J, Julius Erving.

Working with Teddy gave me some of my deepest satisfactions as a manager. There was Alice, but Alice goes way beyond being an artist I manage. Alice is like a body part to me. Strictly as an artist's manager, my relationship with Teddy was the most rewarding and involving. Partly that was because I could really get in his face and tell him exactly what I thought. That's very hard to do without upsetting your relationship in some way. And with celebrities, who get used to being pampered, stroked, and lied to on a daily basis, it can be really damaging. Especially when what you say to them goes to the core of what they do. Teddy was not a prima donna that way. He and I had what we called "don't be a schmuck" conversations. He'd see me coming after a show and groan, "Oh shit. Is it 'don't be a schmuck' time?" I would proceed to tell him exactly what I thought, and why. Not attacking, but also not having to package it the way I had to do with other artists. He didn't listen to me every time, but there is no other artist I could be that open and honest with.

One of the wildest times with Teddy came when he was booked to play two shows one night at the Apollo Theater in Harlem. The shows sold out well in advance. The audience for the first show was predominantly women, and with them came every pimp in Harlem, taking their ladies out for a good time.

When Teddy left the stage at the end of the first show, he refused to go on for the second one. He absolutely would not go on, and he wouldn't tell me why. We went back and forth about it for a while, and then he simply walked out. Black Elvis had left the building. Which was packed with a sold-out crowd for the second show. Whom I was supposed to tell that the show was canceled. And that there was no money on hand to pay them refunds, because we had sold out both shows days in advance, so the money was already in the bank. They'd have to come back tomorrow after the bank opened.

That was not a conversation I wanted to have with an auditorium filled with sexed-up women and pimps. I called Bert Padell, my business manager, at home. It was about nine thirty.

"I need $87,500 in cash delivered to the Apollo in the next fifteen minutes," I said.

You can imagine what he said back. When I insisted, he told me to get myself down to the Lower East Side, to a certain restaurant that I won't name, which featured cuisine of a certain nationality I won't identify, and ask for a certain guy. He'd give me the money. I had my driver rush me down to this restaurant, I met the guy, and he handed me a brown paper bag stuffed with cash. We head back uptown, I'm starting to relax a little, thinking a real crisis has been averted—and the car breaks down ten blocks from the Apollo. So at 10:15 P.M., this white boy from Oceanside is running through the streets of Harlem, clutching a brown paper bag stuffed with $87,500. *Holy shit holy shit holy shit.* But I got there, put the money in the box office, and we were able to pay back all the ticket holders. The night ended peacefully. Just another night in the life of an artist's manager.

The next day Teddy told me why he wouldn't go back on. While doing the first show, he'd seen a gun in the audience. That was not too surprising, considering the number of pimps in the crowd. But Teddy was scared it was the same person who had killed Taaz Lang, coming to wipe him out, too. I couldn't really blame him for not going back out there.

One other time, in 1982, Teddy canceled a sold-out show in England. Again he wouldn't give me the reason, he just refused to go on. I pleaded with him: "Teddy, you sold out in a day. These are working people. They all have jobs. They all had to get babysitters. They're sitting there waiting for you. Just get out and do the show." He wouldn't do it.

The next month, Teddy was in a horrendous car accident in

Philadelphia. He lost control of his Rolls and crashed it into a tree. His passenger, Tenika Watson, walked away with some bruises and a chipped tooth, but Teddy was trapped in the wreckage while it took rescue workers forty-five minutes to cut him out. It was not at all certain that he was going to live.

When I found out about the crash, I flew to Philadelphia overnight and met up at the airport with Danny Markus, my partner and good friend, and we drove straight to the hospital. Teddy's mother, Ida, his girlfriend, Karen, and his assistant, Sedonia, were there. The doctors informed us that Teddy might survive, but he had severed his spinal cord, and if he did live he would remain paralyzed below the chest for the rest of his life. He would never walk again, never have the use of his arms and hands. They also said that from their years of dealing with quadriplegic cases, they were convinced that the patient had to be told immediately.

They led us into the room, which I remember as a sort of white void with Teddy in the middle of it, on his back on a kind of table-bed, with ugly clamps to keep his head still. His eyes were open.

A doctor said, "Teddy, do you recognize these people? Blink once for yes, twice for no."

Teddy blinked once. We proceeded to tell him he wasn't going to walk again. We told him that he was in the right place for rehabilitation, to try to stay strong, that we loved him and were with him one hundred percent—all the things you say in a situation like that. In the middle of it some nurses came and flipped him over, which they had to do every ten minutes, so for the last part of it he wasn't facing us anymore. I couldn't even imagine what was going through his mind. Teddy was the top R&B singer in the world, and might never be able even to speak again—if he were lucky enough to live. The day before he'd been the king of the world, the sexiest man alive, strong, virile, macho. Now he would never walk, would never feed himself again, would be lifted in and out of a wheelchair forever. I can't believe how many times my journey keeps bringing me back to friends in wheelchairs.

It was horrifying. I loved that man, still do, and I can't describe how sad it was to see him like that. I think in some ways it was the beginning of my not enjoying what I did for a living anymore.

Still, it was time for a reality check. Teddy had no financial resources. He'd spent every dime he made. He had kids with different women. It was really not clear that he was going to live. I doubted it. And even if he did, he would certainly not be able to provide for his family. My job at that moment was not to feel sorry for him, but to get to work making this terrible situation as bearable as I could for him and them.

Every type of media wanted to photograph him, video him, do an interview with him. I decided he absolutely should not be seen—and absolutely would not want to be seen—in that condition. We had to save every bullet we had in the gun for one big shot at resurrecting his career, if and when the time was right.

Meanwhile, I thought about who I could get to jump in quick, set up a trust fund, and earn a lot of goodwill from it. We had a very good sponsor relationship with a beer company. They more or less agreed to set up some sort of a charitable foundation for quadriplegics, which would include some financial help for Teddy and his family financially. I went to sleep thinking that maybe I had it solved.

When I woke up the next morning, all the newspapers had the story that Tenika Watson, the woman in the car with Teddy, was really a man.

We never heard one word from the beer company ever again. I never really got the story on Tenika until very recently. Teddy and I never spoke a word about it. There was nothing to be gained from it. A lawsuit was filed for Teddy against Rolls-Royce, charging that the engine and hydraulics had failed, so the steering went out. It was settled out of court. The story *I* heard was that Teddy had met Tenika in a bar after a 76ers game. He had gotten Dr. J to take his date home, while he went off with Tenika. It was a very rainy night, and he was driving on a very curvy road. At some point while he was driving he put his hand between her legs, felt a penis, freaked out, and crashed the car.

I believed that for two decades. In 2014, I told it to Oprah Winfrey. We're friendly acquaintances. She has a beautiful up-country farm on Maui. We see each other at social functions and once were in a group on a trip to Africa. Oprah had her staff find Tenika and did an interview with her. It was the first time Tenika had ever spoken publicly about that night. It turns out that she had the full sex-change operation five years before meeting Teddy, so the penis story was false. According to Tenika, Teddy simply lost control of the Rolls on the slick road.

After the beer company vanished I had nothing. No sponsor, and not much hope of finding one. The prospects of Teddy's ever being able to perform again and earn new money seemed very dim, if he lived at all. I wondered if he might have any previously unreleased tapes lying around. His mother let Danny and me into the house. In a couple of days of rooting around with the family we did in fact find enough tapes for a new album.

So far, so good. But this is where the story turns really dark and twisted. I'm sure other players who were involved in this stage would tell different versions. I can only tell it as I experienced it.

Kenneth Gamble was a member of the Nation of Islam, and in my dealings with him and Huff I became convinced that they really didn't like white people, and *particularly* despised me. They paid Teddy very little for recording his albums. Apparently the Chitlin' Circuit mentality applied as much to record labels as performance venues. They were old friends of Teddy, so he never let me go after them to get him better pay. Yet he paid my fee as though they were paying him well, so I don't know if he ever made any money on his albums.

All my dealings with Philadelphia International Records were very, very tough. Anytime I wanted to do anything for Teddy, it felt like they did everything in their power to obstruct me, to undermine my relationship with him, to go behind my back and turn him against me. One of several shots across my bow came at a point where Teddy's material was getting really weak. His last couple of albums hadn't sold as well as the previous couple. I was representing James Mtume, known simply as Mtume, the hottest songwriter in R&B. He had written a great many top-selling and Grammy-winning songs for artists like Roberta Flack, Donny Hathaway, Stephanie Mills, and others. Mtume loved Teddy and was excited by the idea of working with him. But Gamble and Huff did not publish Mtume's music, and the majority of the tracks on Teddy's albums were songs they'd written and published.

I got them to agree to a meeting in Philadelphia to discuss it. I got Mtume to agree to drive down from New Jersey. I called Teddy and said, "I need your support if I'm going to pull this off. I don't need you there for the whole meeting, but I need you to show up when I call you, and to back me up when you get there. I don't care that Kenny and Leon are your great friends. You need a hit. I need you to have a hit. I'm not in this to lose. I'm in this to win."

He agreed. Danny and I took a train down from New York and got to the meeting site, the office of their lawyer Phil Asbury, at noon. We sat there until one, and then two, then three. It was not like Mtume not to show up, but there were no cell phones in those days so we couldn't check up on him. At 5 P.M. a guy stuck his head in the door and shook it.

Asbury put his hands flat on his desk and said, "Well, I guess that takes care of that. He's not coming."

Danny and I went home. I called Teddy and said, "I don't know what happened. I guess he wasn't interested."

Later Mtume told us he had gone to the meeting. They had put Danny and me in one office, Mtume in another, let us all sit there all afternoon, then told each side that the other hadn't shown up. And to top it off, they told Teddy that *none* of us showed up.

That's the kind of relationship I had with Gamble and Huff.

Given our history, I did not want to take these tapes we had found to PIR. I wanted to get Teddy as much money as possible. Walter Yetnikoff had succeeded Clive Davis (who had succeeded Goddard Lieberson) as the head of Columbia. I knew him; he was an old Jew from Brooklyn. Columbia was doing fantastically well as the label of Michael Jackson, Paul McCartney, Bruce Springsteen, the Rolling Stones. I figured he'd be sympathetic.

"I'd give you a million dollars for this, Shepseleh," Walter said. He always called me Shepseleh, a friendly Yiddish version of my name. "But I can't. Legally I can only pay PIR for Teddy's music. You've got to get them to agree that I'll pay them and they'll pass the money to you."

I knew that if I was going to get Gamble and Huff to agree to let a million bucks flow through them, I had to put on a hell of a show. I got Teddy's mother, his girlfriend, and his kids to go with me to the meeting. I explained to Gamble and Huff that this money was solely for a trust fund for Teddy and his family. I wouldn't touch a penny of it. Teddy and his family really, really needed this.

Gamble and Huff agreed. I handed over the tapes. Yetnikoff

said he sent them a check for a million dollars. I don't know if it was in line with Teddy's deal, but the family did not get the full amount.

So now I was really freaking and really pissed off. But here it comes again: *Never get mad.* I had to dissociate myself from my emotions, keep a clear head, and accomplish my goal. I went back to Columbia. I was told privately by one executive that if Teddy filed a lawsuit against PIR, it would stop payments to all of their other PIR artists until it was resolved—because their deal was built around Teddy. If I could get Teddy to serve notice, it would free them up to pay Teddy a million dollars, because they would save six or seven million in the interim by not having to distribute other acts (that they were losing money on). But no one could know that we were told to do it.

So I went to see their outside lawyer, Paul Marshall. I had never met him, but he was a legend in the music industry. His firm represented several of the giant labels, as well as some giant acts like the Beatles. I went to his office on Fifty-Seventh Street. The whole time we spoke he sat on a couch smoking cigarettes and tipping the ashes behind it. He explained that there could not be any written record whatsoever about my deal with Walter; I would just have to operate on trust.

Fine. Now I had to go to Philadelphia and get Teddy to agree to initiate a lawsuit against his good friends. I explained that if he would sue PIR, I could get him a million dollars. I asked him if he was willing to go through with this. He still couldn't speak at this point. It was still one blink for yes, two for no. He blinked once. I brought in a court recorder, we read him the paperwork, he blinked once again, and we filed notice of a lawsuit in his name.

A week went by.

Two weeks went by.

Three weeks went by.

No check for a million dollars appeared. I couldn't get anyone on the phone. I felt the planet dropping out from under me. I shot straight over to Paul Marshall's office. As I started to tell him what his client was doing to Teddy Pendergrass, he actually said to me, "Teddy Pendergrass . . . Teddy Pendergrass . . . I know that name from somewhere. . . ."

Game, set, match. They had me. I had nothing on paper, no recourse whatsoever.

I left Marshall's office in a state of shock, and went straight to the office of Bob Krasnow. Bob had just been named chairman of Elektra a couple of weeks earlier. Bob was a really good friend. Not a business friend, a friend friend. When I got there I broke down and cried.

"Bob, if I had a million dollars I'd put it up myself," I said. "If I had a property I could mortgage for a million bucks I'd do that. I cannot walk back into Teddy's room and tell him I got him nothing, after he put so much faith in me that he sued his good friends. I'll rob a bank first."

Bob heard me out, then said, "Listen, Shep. I'm going to help you out here, but you've got to help me. Is he going to live?"

"I don't think so," I said.

"Okay, then you have to cover my ass. I'm new here. If the guy dies after I've written a million-dollar check to him, I have to have something in my files that shows we expected him to live."

"Got it."

"Now, is there any legal way to get out of this album deal?"

"Yes," I said. "I have a soundtrack clause." (I always included one after Alice's ordeal. Thank you, thank you.) "We can do one soundtrack album that's not on PIR."

"But if he's not going to live, I'll never get a soundtrack," Bob said.

"I'd say that's probably true," I replied.

"Okay. Then what I need is a script for a movie, and I need a tape of a song. If you can get somebody who sounds like Teddy to sing it, that's even better. Then I've got those things in my files to justify giving you the money if the guy dies."

Okay. One song, one script. I can do this.

||||||||||||||||||||||

I had recently started managing another great R&B singer, Luther Vandross. Luther had started out on *Sesame Street,* and had sung backup for stars from Barbra Streisand and Bette Midler to Carly Simon, Quincy Jones, Roberta Flack, and Chaka Khan. He was one of the vocalists on David Bowie's *Young Americans,* and arranged the famous backing vocals on the title song. His first solo album, *Never Too Much,* went double platinum in 1981 and earned him two Grammy nominations, and that was just the start of an amazing solo career. We worked together for almost fourteen years, piling success on top of success.

Our relationship was very different from the one I had with Teddy, or Alice. I never got to know Luther as well as them. We didn't like or dislike each other. Our relationship was almost entirely on a professional level. People in my office did the hands-on work with him. We lived fifteen minutes from each other in L.A. yet in the whole time I managed him he never once came over to my house. I always thought that one of my best services to my clients was in helping them shape their stage acts, but Luther preferred to do it himself. He never let me see a show until he was satisfied it was working.

I did get to know him well enough, however, to know that he could be a real diva, difficult to handle and easy to offend. I got my first lesson in this early on. He was scheduled to perform at a big music awards show. Three hours before the show, I got a call from the guy who handled him for me that he was refusing to go because his pants didn't fit right. I called Luther and tried to talk him into it, but he was adamant. I knew one of Luther's dreams was to have Bob Mackie design clothes for him. Mackie did all the other divas—Diana Ross, Liza Minnelli, Tina Turner, Ann-Margret—and Raquel, which was how I knew him.

I said, "What if I could get Bob Mackie to drive with us in our car and fix your pants on the way to the show?"

"You can't do that," Luther said.

"But if I can, will you go?"

Luther agreed. I hung up and called Bob. Unfortunately, he was out of town. But he put me in touch with his partner, Ray Aghayan, who was famous himself, and Ray agreed. We picked him up, he fixed Luther's pants in the limo, Luther did the show, and Ray designed most of his clothes from then on.

After my meeting with Bob Krasnow, I asked Luther if he could quickly record a song sounding like Teddy. He came back with a tape, of terrible audio quality, of a song called "Choose Me."

I took the song to Alan Rudolph; by then we'd worked together on the Leary-Liddy movie, *Roadie*, and Alice's music videos. I told him the story. "I need a script, quick. I'm never making the movie. I'll get you a few dollars for it if I actually get the million bucks. But I gotta have it and I gotta have it fast." He wrote the movie *Choose Me*.

I took the script and the tape to Bob Krasnow, and he gave me a million dollars.

As it turned out, Teddy lived, so Bob never needed the insurance of the script and the tape. But he earned an enormous coupon with me by taking that risk.

Teddy started to get better. His voice came back. I can't even imagine how hard that was for him, the courage and strength he showed. We decided to record a new album, *Love Language,* which he was now free to do with Elektra. We proceeded very carefully and took our time on it. Now it was 1985, and I had put a lot of thought in how best to bring Teddy back to his public. I had seen that Teddy's target audience—and I don't mean this in any demeaning way—was a middle-aged, probably overweight, black woman who worked as a clerk or a secretary in an office. She came from a gospel background. And her favorite fantasy was a romance with Teddy Pendergrass. She felt that Teddy was part of her life. Then he'd had this tragic accident, and she had not seen or heard one thing from him, not one word or photograph, in nearly three years. It seemed to me that my job was to make sure that the first image she saw of him now, the first song she heard him sing, brought her back into that love relationship with him for the rest of her life. She'd love him more than she ever had, would want to hug him and help him and do for him.

I got HBO to agree to shoot a special, based on the album's release. We decided to do it at his high school gymnasium. I decided we didn't want to hide the wheelchair or do anything gimmicky. We would deal with what we had. We left the gym stark. It was just Teddy and his wheelchair. The camera would start with a long shot, then slowly zoom in until all you could see was Teddy's mouth, so that he was speaking directly to that secretary who had been waiting three years to hear from her Teddy. He'd sing the song I chose for the single, "In My Time," a beautiful ballad in which he'd tell her, "I've lived and loved so much / Through each high and low . . . / After all that I've been through / I'm in love with you."

I had it all set. The single, the album, the HBO special. Every bullet in my gun loaded for this one big shot.

And then I got a call, three days before the special and the single release, that Elektra was changing the single. They had decided to go instead with a duet Teddy sang with Whitney Houston. She was brand-new. Nobody knew who Whitney Houston was at the time. It wasn't like she was a big deal who would add anything to Teddy's comeback. The song was "Hold Me," and Teddy's first line was "I'll hold you and touch you and make you my woman."

Teddy couldn't hold or touch anybody or anything. He was quadriplegic. I could not get through to anyone what a disaster this was going to be. Teddy's first words to the fan who'd been waiting all that time were going to be a lie?

They had switched it at the last minute because they had another single coming out by a different artist that supposedly sounded too much like "In My Time." It put me in a terrible position with Bob Krasnow, to whom I owed so much. Bob had just hired Bruce Lundvall away from Columbia Records to run Elektra. It was a very high-profile, prestigious hire. Teddy's single and this other one were the first ones Elektra was putting out under Lundvall, and it was Lundvall's decision to change Teddy's. It would be very, very difficult for Bob to countermand Bruce at this early stage in their relationship. He would have been cutting him off at the knees on his first project.

Understanding that, I said to Bob, "Let me just buy Teddy's record back from you."

"I can't do that to Bruce," Bob said.

What could I do? It was one of the toughest bridges I ever had to cross, and I didn't feel like I managed to create the right history this time. "Hold Me" went out as Teddy's first post-accident single, and flopped. It was the lowest moment in my managing career. All that work, from both me and Teddy—all that careful planning to get to that moment—scuttled by someone else's decision.

Then, as these things happen, another chance came for Teddy to make his triumphant return to the stage. Bob Geldof, Midge Ure, Dick Clark, and Bill Graham announced that they were staging the Live Aid concerts, to raise funds for famine relief, in two simultaneous locations, Wembley Stadium in London and JFK Stadium in Philadelphia, on July 13, 1985. They would be the largest outdoor concerts ever, with the largest television audience in history. I called Teddy's friends Ashford & Simpson and asked if they'd sing one song with him. They agreed.

Teddy was very scared to get out onstage in front of so many people and sing live for the first time since the accident. We got to the stadium and wheeled him to the ramp up to the stage, and he said, "I can't do it, Shep. I'm just too scared."

"Listen, man," I said, "I love you, but I'm wheeling you up there. There's nothing you can do about it. You don't have to sing, but you're going up there."

I pushed him up to the edge of the stage. When Ashford announced Teddy's name, the one hundred thousand people in the stadium roared. Teddy wheeled out there with a big, relieved smile on his lips, and tears in his eyes. He sang "Reach Out and Touch Somebody's Hand"—admittedly, a song I might not have chosen, with those lyrics—and nailed it. There wasn't a dry eye in the stadium by the end of it.

Teddy continued to record and perform. I stayed very close with him for maybe five or six years, then Danny Markus and Allen Strahl took over as his managers and remained so right until the end. Teddy's strength and dedication were awe-inspiring. He struggled with his health for the next twenty years. He had cancer a few times. He had bedsores every day. Yet he never complained. He carried on with such elegance and dignity. Ida, who is a deep, deep churchgoer, was a pillar of strength for him. He continued to perform almost right up until he died, in 2010.

15

THE STRANGE TWISTS AND TURNS DON'T END THERE. About eighteen months after Alan Rudolph dashed out that script for me, he called me and said, "Shep, I need a favor."

I couldn't say no. He had a coupon. "What's the favor?"

"I want to make the movie."

"Alan, please don't do this to me. You know I can't say no."

"I want to make the movie, Shep."

So I had to make the movie, which meant I had to find a million dollars. Carolyn had a good friend, the godfather of her daughter, who had told her he'd like to come into the movie business with us. He was Chris Blackwell, the founder of Island Records. Chris introduced the world to Bob Marley's music. Steve Winwood, U2, and Roxy Music were also on Island. But Chris had a horrible reputation in the music business. Ahmet Ertegun called him the Baby-Faced Killer. Everybody, including Bob Krasnow, told me, "Do not go into business with him. You'll love him. You'll be best friends. If you fail, he'll stay your best friend. But if you succeed, he'll fuck you over even if he has to fuck himself to do it."

But we had to make Alan's movie. I had Carolyn set up the

meeting. I told Chris, "I'm ready to make a deal with the devil, and everybody tells me you're the devil. I need a million dollars to make this movie. You can't have the soundtrack for Island; it's going to Elektra. But I will build a movie company that you will be proud of and will make money. You will never have to put another penny in." (Pretty cocky, Little Shep.)

That's how Alive Films became Island Alive Pictures. Alan got to make *Choose Me,* starring Keith Carradine and Geneviève Bujold, with Luther's fake-Teddy "Choose Me" as the theme song. Island Alive took off like a rocket ship. Carolyn and I put together a great team, with her as chairman. She was the only woman in the world at the time who could green-light a picture.

I was very grateful to Chris Blackwell. He never put in another penny, never took a meeting, never involved himself in any way after his initial investment. I felt I owed him and asked, "What can I do for you? You got any dreams, anything you need?"

"You know," he said, "I have this one artist that I just can't break. I know you're really good at this. If you could help me that would be great. His name is Robert Palmer."

Robert was an English singer who had been on Chris's label since the mid-1970s, when his albums *Sneakin' Sally Through the Alley* and *Pressure Drop* came out. Over the years he'd moved around from one genre to another, from reggae to Boz Scaggs–style R&B to a New Orleans sound, but he had never been as successful as Chris thought he should. Now in 1985 he had another new sound, more pop and commercial.

I was flirting at the time with managing an all-female swing band in New York City, the Kit McClure Band. They had been getting great buzz in the city for a few years, had sold out clubs like the Ritz, then Cab Calloway heard them and toured with them. Being me, I thought I saw a win-win here. Why not pair

Robert Palmer and this all-girl big band? One plus one might equal twenty. I took Chris to hear Kit, and he liked her and signed her to Island. We booked Robert and Kit at Radio City Music Hall and sold it out.

MTV was four or five years old at that point, and nobody put out records without videos anymore. It seemed a natural to shoot a video of Robert fronting an all-female band, but Chris and his director, the English fashion photographer Terence Donovan, didn't think Kit and her band were pretty enough for MTV. They hired five models, put them in short, tight dresses and high heels, gave them instruments to "play" and taught them a few dance moves, and shot the video for "Addicted to Love." If you remember the 1980s, you probably remember a long period when MTV seemed to run that video at least once an hour, every hour, 'round the clock. The truth is that Robert hated the idea, tried to talk Chris and Terence out of it, and if you look closely at the video, you can see he's really not comfortable doing it. It didn't matter. That video helped make him a big star for a couple of years. And it all started because I wanted to return a favor to Chris Blackwell.

So I thought Chris and I were really good friends. I always had great times visiting with him at his house in Jamaica. He's always had great cooks, which makes sense, given that his family made their fortune in the spice trade. He'd stay with me when he came to L.A.

Then Carolyn and I heard from a fellow independent film-maker we knew. He'd taken a job at one of the big financial houses, and his mission was to make investments in the film business. He wanted to buy into Island Alive. As I recall, he offered to buy 50 percent of the company for twenty-five or thirty million dollars, plus put up another twenty-five or thirty for productions. I thought this was fantastic. Running a movie company had never been my dream; it was Carolyn's. This deal would mean I could step back and go out on a high note. She could keep making movies, which was her passion. And Chris Blackwell would make a ton of money on his original million-dollar investment. Life is beautiful.

I had him, Carolyn, and our prospective investor out to my place in L.A. The investor laid it all out for Chris, after which Chris said to me, "Can I get a minute?" We stepped away from the others.

"Shep, you're going to hate me for this," he continued. "But I'm a businessman. I take advantage of situations. I know Carolyn has a mortgage payment coming up and needs about $400,000. I also know that my vote plus her vote outvote you. So you have two choices. You can take $250,000 and give me all your stock. Or Carolyn and I will vote you out and you get nothing."

I said, "Are you *serious*?"

"I wish I wasn't," he said, "but I absolutely am. I can't help it. This is just who I am."

I can't say it was a total surprise. *If you fail, he'll stay your best friend. But if you succeed, he'll fuck you over even if he has to fuck himself to do it.* But I was still really hurt and pissed. I asked him to give me a few minutes alone with Carolyn. He went outside for some air.

"What do you want to do?" I asked her.

"You know what?" she said. "I'd rather lose the house."

"Okay." I called Chris back inside.

"Two things," I said. "Number one, get packed. Number two, go fuck yourself. Be outta here in five minutes. You can wait for the cab out front."

And that was the death of Island Alive. We went to court, had an arbitrator, split up the company, and disbanded it.

One more twist. In the midst of all this, I was in L.A., driving my white Rolls-Royce one day. A beautiful girl I knew had left me a CD of a group she had heard and loved in St.-Tropez. I was sitting at the red light right in front of the Whisky a Go Go and put the CD in. A gorgeous girl, like a 10.5, pulled up next to me. She started waving at me and called over, "The Gipsy Kings! How'd you get that? I heard them in St.-Tropez. Can I give you my address and get a copy?" Two weeks later another beautiful girl in another car did the same thing.

I knew nothing about these Gipsy Kings, but if all their fans were as pretty as these two girls I was definitely interested. I did a little research and found that they were a group of French gypsies—they sang in Spanish, but spoke French—who busked on the streets and on the beach at St.-Tropez and drew gigantic crowds. They had a French label but nothing in the States.

I was always looking for a way to honor Bob Krasnow's coupon, to pay him back for what he'd done for Teddy. I called him and said, "Listen, I've got a tingle in my gut about this group. I owe you one. Let's go check this out." By this point my reputation was such that when I said I had an intuition, guys like Bob listened. We flew to St.-Tropez, liked what we heard and saw, and Bob signed them to Elektra, while I signed on as their manager.

Now I had to figure out how to put a gypsy flamenco group over in America. I'd seen the effect they had on pretty women, so that was the angle I pursued. I knew Paul Mitchell and John Paul Dejoria, whose hair care products were in every salon in America. I came up with a promotion where we'd bring the Gipsy Kings over for a six- or eight-city tour to promote their first Elektra album. In every city we'd offer all the hair salons with Paul Mitchell products in them free CDs, coffee mugs, and T-shirts—and we'd give them 50 percent of the tickets to the concert in their city, for them to give away to their most beautiful clients. My thinking was if half the house was beautiful women we'd have no trouble selling out the other half to guys.

It worked. Elektra released *Gipsy Kings*, their first LP in the United States—the one with "Bamboleo" on it—and it was a huge hit, eventually going platinum. Women loved them. Every guy in the country thought that if he played the Gipsy Kings for his girl he was going to get laid, and he was probably right. Paul Mitchell was cool and sexy by association with them. And their concerts were full of beautiful women, so I was having a good time. Everybody wins.

Managing them was interesting. They really were gypsies. My defining moment with them came when I read in the paper that the new sneaker company LA Gear, which had just done a huge endorsement deal with Michael Jackson, was now looking for ways to attack the Latin market. The Gipsy Kings didn't speak Spanish but they sang it, so I went to LA Gear's ad agency. They got the idea immediately and made us a *very* big offer to participate in a multimillion-dollar campaign. The Gipsy Kings flew in and did a shoot at Venice Beach with the LA Gear Girls, who were all in T-shirts and white short shorts and LA Gear sneakers.

The Gipsy Kings returned to France. I sent them the poster and asked for them to approve it. A week went by. Two weeks. Then they called me and said, "You better come over here." So I flew over and drove a long way from the airport to this tiny village in the south of France, then followed their directions a little farther to where the Gipsy Kings lived. They had a huge-selling record and were selling out concerts everywhere. But they were still gypsies, and they lived in the modern equivalent of a gypsy caravan, three Airstream trailers under a bridge. The trailers were attached to Mercedes-Benzes, but still. I met the wives, classic gypsy women. It was all very polite and formal.

Then the guys walked me into town to a pub, where they told me they couldn't do the endorsement.

I said, "What do you mean? You don't think the poster is beautiful?"

"Yes," they said, "but if our wives see us with these women, they'll kill us."

"But it's just an advertisement," I protested.

"Yes, but all our wives will see is us surrounded by these pretty girls, and they'll make our lives miserable."

So it never happened and we had to give back the advance we'd been paid. I thought that was a shame, but I respected their decision. We went on working together for years and did very well. To this day, guys looking for a little loving put their music on.

||||||||||||||||||

I also continued to work with Luther, and he continued to be a diva. In October 1988, we were set to open a national tour called "The Heat," with Anita Baker opening for Luther. We were kicking it off with five nights at Madison Square Garden. Anita's agent was a fabulous guy named Oscar Cohen, a throwback to the old days. The agency he ran was supposedly owned in the 1920s either by Capone or a Chicago mob group. Oscar was a great guy, one of my favorites. On paper Anita and Luther were a powerhouse, dream-team duo. Anita was a great singer-songwriter who had just won a couple of Grammys and was very hot right then. So it was a very highly anticipated tour. But Anita could also be a hell of a diva.

We sold out all five nights at the Garden. Oscar and I were walking down a corridor in the dressing room area on opening night. Anita came into the corridor holding a tray of cold cuts and cheeses, which I had sent her. I had thought it was a nice little gesture, but she wasn't looking too happy about it.

Without even looking at me, she said, "Oscar, do you know who this Shep Gordon guy is?"

"This is Shep. I wanted to introduce you to him."

She glared at me and hissed, "I don't accept anything wrapped in plastic." Then she threw the entire platter of meats and cheeses on me, hitting me from head to toe.

Luther just happened to be coming down the hall when she did this. And Luther and Anita already had history. The way I heard it, on a Budweiser show together the year before, she sang his song "Stop to Love." She'd sung it on her solo shows, and left it in for this show with Luther. He got pissed that she did that—he was going to sing it, it was his song, and he felt she should have asked first. They still hadn't resolved it.

Now, Luther loved a good fight. When he saw Anita dump the platter on me, he pulled me aside and said, "I don't want this bitch on the show."

Before I could respond, he continued. "I am going home right now. We're not doing this show tonight. You tell her if I see her again, she's off the show. It's done."

Holy shit. We actually had to cancel the show. A sold-out Madison Square Garden show.

I knew I had to keep these two apart if there were going to be any shows at all. The next day I had the Garden build a plywood wall in that corridor, separating their dressing rooms, so when Anita came out of her dressing room Luther wouldn't have to see her. That night, she left her dressing room, went around another way, stood at Luther's dressing room door, and started taunting him like a little kid. "Hey, Luther, I'm out here!"

Luther went ballistic and threatened to kill the tour if he ever saw *or heard* her again. In the end, the only solution I could come up with, I'm not kidding, was to pay for every building we played to erect a *brick* wall separating the two of them. They went onstage separately, did their shows, and never saw or heard each other. It makes for a funny story now, but it was a nightmare then. It cost us twenty thousand dollars a night to keep those two dueling divas apart.

Yes, Luther was a handful. But we did extraordinarily successful work together. It was deeply sad when he had a stroke in 2003, right after finishing the vocals on yet another great album. He struggled and died of a heart attack in 2005. He had just turned fifty-four. I'm very grateful I had the opportunity to work with such a great artist.

16

IN 1990, I GOT A CALL FROM CAROLCO PICTURES, another independent American production company. I had a lot of business with them. They were taking a new movie to Cannes that year, a sci-fi picture called *Total Recall,* starring Arnold Schwarzenegger and a pretty actress, Sharon Stone.

"We have a jet going. Would you like to come with us?"

"You bet."

I took a limo to the airport. It was the first time I'd ever been driven onto the tarmac, right up to a private plane. When I boarded Schwarzenegger was already there, along with other celebrities I knew. The plane itself was not impressive. The cabin was small and narrow, with crappy seats three across that barely leaned back a couple of inches. It wasn't nearly as nice as my rock-and-roll bus. I asked a stewardess if it was a nonstop flight.

"Oh no. We have to stop twice for fuel."

Oh man. This was suddenly sounding like a long and uncomfortable trip. Then, about halfway down the aisle, I saw there were two cushioned benches, on one each side, dividing all those horrible, narrow seats. I decided one of them was for me. I spread blankets and sweaters and stretched out like I was asleep. Other people were boarding. I opened one eye and saw Michael Douglas. He looked around and got the same oh-shit look I must have had when I got on board. He took one of those awful seats up near the front.

I went up and greeted him. I asked him, "Mikey, do you have a manager?"

"No," he said. "I just have an agent."

I said, "Well, I'm going to show you right now what managers do. Grab your stuff and come with me."

We walked back to the benches and I told him to stretch out on the one across from mine. He grinned. "Very nice managing, Shep." We both slept the whole way over and arrived very well rested, while Arnold and the others twisted and turned all night.

I ended up hanging out a lot with Michael at the festival. One night Carolco threw a party for *Total Recall* at the Eden-Roc, one of the Hotel du Cap's restaurants, and one of the most romantic places I've ever eaten. It's in its own shimmering white building hanging out over the blue sea, with panoramic views of the Bay of Cannes. From the hotel you stroll down the grounds on a long cobblestone path that's lined the entire way with fragrant rosemary bushes. It was the perfect setting for Carolco's party, a formal affair for three hundred, everyone looking very elegant in their tuxes and gowns. The Gipsy Kings, whom I'd been managing for several years by then, provided the entertainment. I would have wanted to be there anyway, but that made it extra special.

I found myself sitting and schmoozing with Michael, his friend Roman Polanski, and Mick Jagger. Over to one side, in a swirl of flashbulbs and jostling, Arnold and Sharon swept into the room. She was the most gorgeous thing I'd ever seen, and right up my alley, a trim, blonde shiksa. I elbowed Michael and whoever was on my other side, Roman or Mick, and said, "You guys are going to have to keep up the conversation without me. I'm leaving with her."

They laughed at me. I myself didn't know what had gotten into me. It was kind of a locker room brag, which was not my style. But I was having such a good time, probably a little high, sitting with the kings of the world, and I got cocky.

I spent the rest of the night failing to make good on my brag. Big shot as I was by then, I was still kind of shy around beautiful women, not a pushy guy, and she of course had a crowd milling around her the whole night. So I never saw my opening, and took a ton of shit from the other guys. "Still here, Shep? Didn't work out?" Oh it was rough.

The next morning I went to have breakfast with Michael. He was staying next door to the hotel at Jean "Johnny" Pigozzi's house. Now, to say "Johnny Pigozzi's house" does not begin to capture what a phenomenal place it is. The Cap d'Antibes coastline below Cannes is just about the most exclusive and expensive real estate on the planet. It's seven or eight huge estates with fairy-tale mansions on them, owned by families like the Heinekens and the Pigozzis, who founded the giant automobile company Simca. Johnny is a photographer, a philanthropist, an art collector, a playboy—a very interesting and fun guy. His estate is just down the coast from the hotel, and I think larger than the hotel, too. He always has celebrities staying there. This time it was Michael and Mick, who is good friends with Johnny. The estate is like a dream, with wide lawns leading to cliffs overlooking the sea. The house, the Villa Dorane, was built in the early 1950s; later Johnny had the great Italian architect and designer Ettore Sottsass give it a lot of playful Modern accents. Inside Johnny displays the largest private collection of African art in the world.

I met Michael down by the pool, which is near the ocean. Staff glided around, bringing us breakfast. Beautiful blue sky above, cicadas ringing in the trees around the pool, the ocean glittering out past them . . . Like a dream.

And then Sharon walked up. Michael introduced us.

"What a beautiful place," Sharon said.

"Would you like me to show you around?" I replied.

Michael's eyebrows shot up and he grinned at me, as though to say, *Where do you get the balls?* I didn't know myself. I mean, I knew the estate about ten minutes longer than Sharon did. I just really, really wanted to be with her.

We left Michael sitting there grinning and walked around the grounds. I pretended to know what I was talking about, and assumed that Sharon thought I was the owner. Later in our relationship I found out that she'd known I was bullshitting. One day she would say to me, "Are you just a schmuck, or do you really not remember that we met before that morning at Johnny Pigozzi's?" The truth is I *had* forgotten—don't ask me how—that I used to date her friend and L.A. roommate, the actress Angela Robinson, a very beautiful girl herself.

Sharon, gracious lady that she is, did not bust me that morning at Johnny's. It was the start of our ballet. We spent the next week or ten days together. She came with me to Dallas, where Luther had a show, and from there to L.A.

We dated for the next few years. Sharon had a remarkable impact on my life, in many ways. She was funny, smart, beautiful— every box gets a check. For her, I think I was easy to be around. I don't ask a lot of questions, and I'm not territorial in the least. She could relax around me. She was so smart and beautiful that a lot of men found her intimidating. By this point in my life I'd been around a lot of smart, beautiful women. I can't say I had entirely gotten over my shyness around women. If she had not walked up to me and Michael that day, I would never have had the courage to call her. But that's been true of all my relationships. I bumped into all of them. I'm very comfortable in the moment once it happens, but I'm not good at the pursuit beforehand.

One of the things I loved most about Sharon was that she was always searching for how to make sense of the planet. One day she asked me if I wanted to go hear His Holiness the Dalai Lama speak. Through my friend Marty and my time in Thailand I had learned a little about Buddhism. Now I did a bit of homework on the Dalai Lama, asking friends, doing some reading—this was in the days before Wikipedia. I learned that Tenzin Gyatso was four years old when he was recognized as the fourteenth incarnation of the Tibetan Dalai Lama. China took control of Tibet the year after he was officially installed. He fled Tibet in 1959 and had been living in exile ever since, traveling the world. He was the spiritual and political representative of the Tibetan people, spoke out for compassion and human rights, and supported the Tibet Fund, a New York–based nonprofit that primarily aids the tens of thousands of Tibetans in exile. China repressed the people of Tibet and refused all overtures for their autonomy, while harassing the Dalai Lama and pressuring other countries not to let him come speak. He won the Nobel Peace Prize in 1989.

Sharon and I went to hear him speak at the Century Plaza Hotel in Los Angeles. It wasn't a big gathering, but I was really interested in who was there: a lot of celebrities who didn't seem to be there to be seen as celebrities, as I was used to. Still, I didn't understand a lot of what he said, partly because of his strong accent, but also because of the content. My mind drifted and I was more interested in studying that crowd. Then we went backstage afterward, and when he walked into the room where we were I felt . . . different. I felt *clean*. It was overwhelming, this sense that just by being in his presence I was somehow cleansed. We joined the receiving line, and when I got to him he had this twinkle in his eye and giggled like a kid. He seemed so innocent. I am powerfully moved by innocence, maybe because in my work I have had to spend so much time dealing with the opposite of innocence. It's why I love kids. It's why I immediately fell in love with Maui. And now I was feeling it in him.

Still, it's not like I became a Buddhist that day. It was more like going to a nice concert, then you move on with your life.

Sharon and I eventually went our separate ways, the way people do. We never had a bad word between us, no ugly scenes. We just went off on our different journeys. She's still a good friend to me. She and her kids stay in my guest house sometimes. For years, I was always introduced as, "This is Shep. He used to date Sharon Stone." It gave me this recurring nightmare. In the Jewish religion, when you've been buried one year they uncover your gravestone. It's called an unveiling. In my nightmare, they unveiled my tombstone and it read:

SHEP GORDON
HE LIVED WITH HER

||||||||||||||||||||

One day in Maui I walked into a Borders, got a cup of coffee, flipped through some books, and checked out their bulletin board to get a sense of what was going on in the community. There was a patchouli-scented flier tacked up there about a three-day retreat the Dalai Lama would be doing at Wood Valley, the Dharma Center on Hawaii's Big Island.

It was 1994, and I had absorbed a lot of Vergé. I thought, I'll feed the Dalai Lama. Then, as I always do, I started figuring out how to make that happen. From the Dharma Center in Maui I learned that if you wanted to do something for His Holiness it was called "an offering." Sharon's secretary gave me the contact info for Rinchen Dharlo, the Dalai Lama's emissary in America. I called and said I wanted to make an offering of cooking for His Holiness, and Rinchen graciously accepted. Then, as I'd learned from Vergé, I started thinking about how to make this special for His Holiness. Somehow I got hold of his travel schedule and saw that it was a lot like a rock tour schedule. I thought it a pity that he was moving around so fast that he never got to really touch where he was. So if I was going to feed him, I would make it more than just a meal, and instead an experience created uniquely for him in that place and moment.

First I asked my friend Piero Resta, the painter and sculptor, to paint a series of plates with images that would reveal themselves to His Holiness as he ate his food, and might make him smile. Piero painted one plate with an image of the Potala Palace, where His Holiness was raised, another with an image of Buddha, and so on. I was friendly with several Hawaiian chefs by then, and they agreed to help out. I asked them to connect me with the people who grew the food we'd be serving, so that, when we served His Holiness eggs, he could look out the window and see the face of the farmer who'd raised the chickens. Every napkin was wrapped around 108 gardenia petals—108 is a special number in Buddhism—so that when he opened it the petals fell all over him. Cindy Dietrich, my go-to girl on culinary stuff, and her mom, Linda (who had been Miss Venice Beach), made white doves out of gardenias to hang everywhere. Every detail I could think up to make the meal unique.

Meanwhile, Rinchen and the Tibetans were being so gentle and undemanding that I couldn't get them to tell me what His

Holiness liked to eat. Other people told me he was a vegetarian, so that's what I was planning. Maybe two days beforehand, I found out that he had stayed in L.A. at the home of Fred Segal, the clothier. I called Fred's chef and he told me, "Oh no, he doesn't like vegetables. He eats meat. He likes beef stew at five in the morning, spaghetti and meatballs."

On my own, meanwhile, I had learned that all Tibetans grow up on yak butter. I have a friend, Ken Ballard, who has lived since the 1970s in Thailand and Bali and leads people on spiritual journeys throughout Asia. He sent me some yak butter. That jar sat in my kitchen smelling up the whole house for three weeks. It's an extremely disgusting, rancid smell and gave me the dry heaves. It was like the house was filled up with thousands of dirty socks. I practiced making yak butter tea, a Tibetan staple.

Because Wood Valley is very remote, out in the middle of nothing on the Big Island, staying at a hotel in Hilo or Kona wouldn't have worked. His Holiness gets up at five in the morning, which meant that we'd have to be up at three or three thirty to get his breakfast ready. So I found a house to rent not far away, pretty primitive but nice, and with five or six bedrooms.

Just before it started, Rinchen said to me, "There's only one rule. You cannot have any expectations that you or anybody with you will meet or interface with His Holiness in any way. If you have that expectation, please don't do this."

Now the first morning arrives. I have one of my elaborate productions planned for His Holiness's first breakfast. As usual, I'm being a neurotic producer, obsessing over every detail. I'm up at two thirty and start getting everyone else up. It's pitch black out. We pile everything and everyone into our vehicles and start driving through the dark toward Wood Valley, when I look down and see I'm wearing no pants. I was obsessing so hard I'd forgotten to get dressed. I threw the car in reverse—and backed it right into the light pole outside the house, knocking it down. That killed all the lights in the house, and the electric-flush toilet. Not how I'd visualized the start of the day.

Finally we get to Wood Valley and set up two trays with His Holiness's breakfast, with the gardenia petals in the napkin and the special plates and everything. Even the trays were special. I'd had a local artist make me them out of koa wood. Then Rinchen said to me, "Shep, would you bring His Holiness's breakfast up to him?"

I was stunned. Cindy and I, wearing our kitchen whites, with white hospital masks covering our mouths, as chefs and food handlers do in many Asian cultures, carried the trays up. She stood outside his room while I took the first tray in, nervous as I've ever been. His Holiness was brushing his teeth in the mirror, with a big smile on his face. He called out, "Hello!"

"Your Holiness," I muttered humbly, "I have your breakfast for you."

"Oh good good good," he said, brushing away. Then he paused and sniffed the air, looking at me in the mirror.

"Yak tea?"

"Yes, Your Holiness."

I was so proud. All that work, months of research and preparation, attention to every detail, culminating in this first moment.

And then he said, "Oh, that's why I leave Tibet!"

He laughed his infectious, childlike laugh. I had to laugh, too. It was an excellent example of the way he can cut through all pretense, all preciousness, and reduce things to their simplest. I think he sensed how nervous I was and pulled me through it with that one line. That's why he is who he is.

The whole rest of the weekend was magical. I have a photo of me bringing his food up the steps of the center that first day, and another of me after I served him the food, sitting on a couch with him. What a moment that was. He said, "Come, come. We take a picture." And then, as we both smiled at the camera, he reached out his hand and took mine. I look at this picture and think, Oh my God, Little Shep from Oceanside sitting with the Dalai Lama—holding his hand. Can anything top that?

That weekend was a huge amount of work. We had planned to feed about twenty people. It turned out that we were supposed to feed more like two hundred—everyone in his retinue, everyone who'd come to the Dharma Center to hear him, the cops on hand, everyone. That was fine with us, but we didn't have enough dishwashers, kitchen help, people to clean up. Feeding two hundred people requires a whole different scale of organization than feeding twenty. We asked for volunteers from the stage after His Holiness spoke. One really small Hawaiian woman and her equally petite teenage daughter volunteered right away. The two of them washed dishes almost nonstop for three days. Joyously, never a word of complaint, washing dish after pot after plate.

At the end of the weekend, Rinchen said to me, "His Holiness was so happy with everything that he wants to thank all your staff personally. He wants to do that the last thing before he leaves. Can you line them up so you'll be the last people he sees on his way to the car? That's what he'd like."

The little woman cried, "Oh, I can't be here! I so wanted to meet him, but I have to go." When I asked her why, she said, "Oh, there's a firemen's strike on Kauai."

I said, "So?"

"I'm the mayor," she said.

She was Maryanne Kusaka, who was in office in Kauai County from 1994 to 2002. That's the sort of thing I love about Hawaii.

Where else in the country would you see a mayor wash a dish, let alone three days' worth of them, smiling and happy the whole time?

Maybe there's something about His Holiness that inspires that sort of dedication to serve. But for myself, in all my dealings with him since that first weekend, I've never been able to tell if it emanates from him, or if it's me, bringing my expectations to it. It's not like we've had much personal interaction. We've actually spoken very little. I know that when I sit in an audience hearing him speak it's beautiful what comes over the crowd. But it's not the same as being in a small room with him. To me, that always feels like it did that very first time I met him backstage with Sharon— that feeling that I've been cleansed, like I just took a shower. It's not as if he dispenses words of wisdom. It's just being in his presence, looking at his face, looking at the way he looks at people. This is not something he's ever said, but I believe that when he looks at anything or anyone, he sees a miracle first, then sees the person or object. And it's impossible not to be compassionate toward everything and everyone if you see that miracle in them.

Maybe that's just me projecting something onto him, but I know it works, and it works for millions of people. I think all of us, even the toughest, look for some light out there that answers some question we have. He seems to hold that light. He seems so happy, even with the unbelievable weight on his shoulders. Meeting Vergé, sensing the peace and satisfaction he derived from learning the path to a life that was so beautiful and fulfilling, the way he cut through life so elegantly, maybe prepared me for this somewhat. But with His Holiness there's that other dimension, that feeling when I leave his presence like I've just stepped out from the most amazing waterfall. Perhaps it's something like going to church and being forgiven your sins.

I continued to cook for him. After the Big Island I got to go to Trinidad with him. We flew on the same plane. I don't think His Holiness quite knew who I was yet. I got up at one point and walked down the aisle past him, and he did give me a big hello. When I went by him again, I could tell that Rinchen had sort of told him who I was, because he said, "The flowers dropping out of the napkins! So beautiful!"

Our first stop after landing in Trinidad was a reception for him at a theater, attended by a small group of the top government and embassy people on the island. Backstage before he was to give them a speech he looked at me and said, "Oh, you cook for me on Big Island."

"Yes, Your Holiness. Thank you. It was such an honor."

"And now you cook for me in Trinidad?"

"Yes."

"So," he said, his eyes twinkling, "you only cook on islands?"

Another zinger.

He went out then to speak to the assembled. Interestingly, they were all dressed in the traditional garb of their homes, some in African robes, some in Native American clothes, and so on. I later learned that in Trinidad all the different ethnicities get along, but they have never blended. Now His Holiness looked around at all these different types of dress and said, "Oh, sorry. Must be wrong room. This is costume party?"

The assembled dignitaries looked kind of startled. Then His Holiness looked down at his own Tibetan robes and said, "Oh perfect. I'm good for costume party."

Nobody outside that very small segment of Trinidadian society seemed to care that he was there. There was no Dharma Center, no Buddhist community on the island. His public speech was at a football stadium that was almost empty. The producer in me was upset, so after he went to sleep the first night I asked his people, "What are we doing here? There are no people, no donations. Why did His Holiness come?"

"Remember the lady you sat next to in the stadium?" they said to me. "She sat next to him at a wedding in India. She asked if he would visit her country and he said yes, so we're here."

That filled me with such admiration. He did what he said he was going to do *because* he said he was going to do it. After my years dealing with Hollywood, where basically nobody's word is as good as his bond and everyone will say or do anything out of self-interest, this had a powerful impact on me. Maybe it reminded me of my father, an honorable man who kept his word. It's how I've always tried to live and conduct business, and why I never wanted written contracts. Once an artist and I gave each other our word, I felt that was all I needed.

At the same time, I never allowed my artists to provide any services for anyone else *without* contracts. It was my fiduciary responsibility to them. So if any of my artists chose to screw me, that was my problem, and if anyone else chose to screw my artists, that was also my problem!

In retrospect, I probably should have signed contracts with my artists. I was always looking ahead to their future, but never to my own. Because I made sure that my artists had strong contracts with their record companies, they've received royalties through their lifetimes. But when my handshake relationships with my artists ended, so did my income, whereas most managers continue to earn a percentage of their artists' royalties in perpetuity. It was in a way very naïve of me to arrange things that way, even though it gave me a sense of inner strength. There's integrity, and then there's stupidity.

After Trinidad I followed His Holiness to New York City. I

had a very good friend, Raymond Bickson, who was the general manager of the Mark Hotel on the Upper East Side. He graciously allowed His Holiness to stay there without charge. In New York the Secret Service detachment assigned to guard His Holiness came more to the forefront of the retinue than they had been before. They were not happy with his going to private homes or eating from private kitchens. They wanted tighter control of his every move. So I was phased out as someone who cooked for him. But I transitioned to sitting on the board of the Tibet Fund.

I also got the bed the Dalai Lama slept on at the Mark and shipped it to Maui. I still sleep in that bed every night I'm home. Thank you, thank you.

One of the amazing things about His Holiness is that somehow he's always aware of everything going on around him—*everything*. He just comprehends it all. It can make things unpredictable for his Secret Service team.

One day, when His Holiness was going to appear at a benefit in Century City in L.A., George Clinton of Parliament-Funkadelic called me and asked if I could get him in.

"Sure, George, but you're in Detroit."

"I'll get there, if you can get me a seat."

At the event, His Holiness sat on a high dais receiving one California dignitary at a time—the mayor, the governor. The Secret Service stood all around. An hour into it, a door in the back flew open and George swept in in full P-Funk regalia, including rainbow dreadlocks down to his ankles. He looked as bizarre as it's possible for a human being to look.

"Can I meet His Holiness?"

"We'll try, George."

As I led George toward the dais, the Secret Service men went into war mode. They grabbed us both roughly. There was no way they were going to let this crazy-looking man near the Dalai Lama.

But then His Holiness stood. He walked over to us, smiling, and gave George a big hug. Then he took him by the hand and had him sit next to him for a while on the dais. He had instantly comprehended everything, and knew that George was no threat.

Another time, I arranged to bring His Holiness to Maui. I was very excited. This time it was all on me. We didn't have the infrastructure, so I had to invent everything, down to the backstage passes. Two weeks before the event, I brought in ten of my best people from the mainland. We got maybe two or three hours of sleep a night, on my office floor.

In the midst of this I got a letter from a man in Honolulu whose nine-year-old granddaughter was dying. They'd been to every doctor and there was no hope for a cure; they didn't have the resources anyway. He believed that if His Holiness would just touch his granddaughter, she would be saved. I got so excited. Now I know why I'm doing this. Thank you.

I shared the letter with everybody and we all cried. I called Rinchen in New York and told him the story. Rinchen was no longer His Holiness's emissary; he passed my request to the man who had replaced him, and he said no, His Holiness could not meet her. He was too busy, he already had a lot of audiences, etc.

I knew they had to be very, very cautious about personal requests like this. What if it was a scam? But I believed in the grandfather's letter. It was so compelling and so heartwarming and pure. And I knew he was a man of very few resources, a local farmer desperate for a miracle. So once again, I didn't get mad, I accomplished my goal. I had the man and his granddaughter flown in, gave them backstage passes, and got them to the stage steps.

The event worked out beautifully, the largest gathering in the history of Maui, twelve thousand people. As we were escorting His Holiness up to the stage, without anyone saying a word to him about the girl, he went right to her, out of thirty people waiting at the foot of the steps, and lifted her up in his arms. He kissed and hugged her, then gently placed her in her grandfather's arms. It gave me goose bumps. I was convinced he'd known—he'd seen it or felt it in her. That's what he does.

Four years later I got a letter from the grandfather that a miracle had happened and his granddaughter lived. Now, it could have been that she wasn't that sick in the first place. But I choose to believe it *was* a miracle, and the fact that the little girl lived was all part of His Holiness's true karma on earth.

17

IN 1991, I GOT A PHONE CALL FROM FAT FRANKIE SCINLARO that Mia's car had been hit by a bus as she was pulling into her own driveway. She had finally been doing well, and now she was dead.

It stopped me in my tracks. It seemed so wrong that someone so beautiful and sweet would have her life ended so early like that. I thought about not having gone to see her, and maybe for the first time in my life, I felt I had really fucked up, that I didn't do the right thing. That life was getting too fast and I was losing sight of what was really important. *That* had been important, but I didn't take the time then to stop my life and try to help her. It weighed very heavily on me; it wasn't the way I liked to think about myself. It wasn't who I thought I was.

I asked Frankie to go to the funeral with me. We drove up to the cemetery in a black limousine, which I shouldn't have done. Worse, I was wearing my current "Hollywood Manager" outfit: silk suit, dark glasses, long ponytail. It only hit me how inappropriate I looked when I got there. Winona waved to me. We hadn't seen each other in years. I knew she was living with her mom and grandmother and working in their basement hair salon. She was cradling a little baby girl.

"This is Keira," she said.

"Who's Keira?"

"Mia's child."

"You're kidding me. Mia had a baby?"

"No," she said. "She had *four*." She pointed out the other three: Monique, nine; Chase, six; and three-year-old Amber holding her grandmother's hand.

"Where's the father?"

"We don't know where they are."

"Well, who's going to take care of them?"

"We've given Keira to a foster home. I'm not sure what we'll do about the others."

I nodded and let that sink in. Afterward, while we were driving from the funeral home to Winona's mother's house, I smoked a joint and tried to think about all this. As gratifying as my career and my success were, I still felt there was something missing. I was surrounded by stars and celebrities, by rich and beautiful and powerful people, but at the end of the day I usually went home or to my hotel room alone. I had always loved kids. I had thought about having a family of my own, but had never met the right person to do that with, and frankly wasn't sure that I was the right person for that, either. Maybe the universe was presenting an opportunity here.

I looked out at Newark as we drove to the family home. It looked poor, beat, and dangerous, like one big ghetto. When we arrived at the house, crack dealers were hanging around out front. I was actually scared to get out of the car. Nobody *wanted* to be in Newark. They were stuck there. By the time we reached the front door I was thinking, I can't leave these kids here. They can't grow up in this. I have to do something.

Without thinking about it any deeper than that, I took Winona aside and said, "Listen, I don't know if I have emotional strength, but I have plenty of resources. I can support all of you. If you're prepared to give up your life for the next eighteen years and raise all these kids, I'll pay for everything you need. Just don't count on me emotionally."

That caught her off guard, to put it mildly. She said, "Well, let me talk to my mother about it."

She did, and came back and said yes.

I said, "Can you get Keira back from the foster family?"

"I think so. They already pierced her ears and put in diamond studs. But I think they'll give her back."

"Okay. I'll go find a house."

That was all it took. We didn't have endless discussions about the particulars of what I was proposing. I didn't do a lot of soul-searching. I just did what I always do: I got to work making things happen. The next day, I got a real estate agent who found a house in rural Monroe, New York, maybe sixty miles north of Newark. Winona and I drove up a few days later. It was a beautiful Tudor house, with a big backyard rolling up into a mountain, and five nice bedrooms—one for Winona, one for grandmother Teri, three for the kids. A good school was practically next door.

I bought it and they all moved in. They lived there about a year. I was really busy then, working in L.A. and traveling back and forth from Maui. And I was a little scared, emotionally, to open up. I hadn't really been emotionally engaged my whole life, since I was a kid hiding out in my bedroom. What kind of relationship were Winona and I supposed to have now? And what about the kids? I didn't know anything about them. How would they feel about this awkward stranger hanging around? For the first year or so I kept my distance and just sent money.

Then I had a thought. Vergé ran the French Pavilion restaurant at Disney World in Florida, and I had never visited him there. I asked Winona if the kids would want to go to Disney World.

"Are you kidding? They'd love it. And *I* would love it!"

Flying to New York to pick them all up, I was nervous about meeting the kids for the first time and started thinking of a way to break the ice with them. I figured I'd do something radical and funny with my appearance. I landed, drove out to the house, and rang the doorbell. Winona opened the door, with all four kids standing there. Their eyes went wide and round as saucers as they gazed up at this big Jewish guy . . . in a Rasta wig. It worked. They started giggling and laughing.

"It's Grandpa Shep!"

I liked the sound of that.

What I had feared would feel awkward and strange felt familiar and comfortable right away. Not that we were a conventional family in any way. I still spent most of my time in L.A. and Hawaii. But we carved out a lot of time together as a unit. Summers, vacations, holidays, weekends. My good friends in L.A. and Hawaii adopted the kids whenever they visited. Alice and Sheryl's three kids loved playing with them. On Maui, Tom Arnold would come over to the house to play pool and other games. They took to calling Don Nelson—the former Boston Celtics star and coach—"Uncle Donny" because of how much time he spent with them at his house just down the beach. My celebrity friends who were constantly at my home spoiled them with attention. A few times the kids and Winona spent a whole summer with me. I took them to Disney World, to Europe, even on tour with some of my artists. They had their own bus, "The Kids' Bus." We had lots of fun and did a lot of bonding, even if it was unconventional and intermittent.

In Hawaiian culture there's a concept called the *hanai* family. Everybody raises everybody's children. It's like one big kibbutz. It only recently occurred to me that what I did with Mia's kids was kind of a *hanai* family. I never thought about "adopting" them in any formal, legal way. I just *hanai*'d them. They needed somebody, and there I was, and it just felt natural. I never questioned it.

One day when she was around twelve, Amber called. She was going to start eighth grade in a few weeks.

"Grandpa Shep, I decided it's time for me to leave here."

I said, "You're not happy?"

She said, "No, I'm very happy. It's just time for me to leave."

"What does that mean, Amber?"

"I looked up a school in Hawaii where I could board and be near you. You don't have to say yes. There's a school in California. If you don't want me to come there, I'll go there."

This from a seventh grader. I said, "Amber, I don't think there's any school here that has boarding."

She said, "No, I looked it up. It's on the Big Island, in Waimea. It's called Hawaii Preparatory Academy."

I googled it and said, "You're right. Okay, I'll call you back."

I hesitated. I knew if she came she'd be my responsibility full-time. I still didn't feel ready. But another part of me was really excited. I flew to the Big Island. Driving to the academy, which is roughly forty-five minutes from the airport, you go up the Waimea mountain canyon, into mist, and there are rainbows everywhere. Beyond gorgeous. The school is at the foot of the Kohala Mountains. I drove through white picket gates, *Bonanza*-style, then up a very long driveway through an amazing postcard campus of horses in rolling green pastures and kids running and playing. Idyllic.

When I met the admissions lady she instantly told me it was way too late to enroll Amber for the coming semester.

"Oh, that's really too bad," I said. "I'd love her to be here. She's African-American, without parents . . ."

Her antennae shot up. "Could she be here in time?"

I didn't know it then, but that decision was one of the greatest breaks in my life. Amber got to come stay with me every weekend. Suddenly I was going to PTA meetings and getting acquainted with her friends and their parents and her coaches and teachers. Amber was a wrestler, the first female wrestler at HPA. At first she wrestled guys—probably not my greatest parenting. I went to many of her matches. At the time, I became friendly with Kris Kristofferson. His son wrestled, so we started going to Kauai together to watch our kids' matches. It gave me this great new rush of pride to watch Amber wrestle, feelings I had never experienced before. I felt like a real dad. For the first time, I got to really feel like a full-time participant, not an occasional visitor. I loved it and I loved her. I loved the problems, too, and the ordinary parent-daughter moments that would arise. Like when Amber wouldn't let me come with her into the drugstore, because she was buying tampons for the first time. Those kinds of moments were so great, so intimate and sweet. And she was my *buddy*. I'd been living alone all this time. Now I had someone to go have dinner with, go see a movie with. Someone I loved.

After Amber went off to Arizona State University, Keira came to the academy and spent four years there and with me. Then she went to the University of Hawaii.

Having Winona visit in the summers was interesting, too. Sometimes it felt like we'd been married for thirty years. We always had a great time together. I had three bedrooms, so she stayed in a separate bedroom, and all four kids would stay in another bedroom, and I was in mine. When we traveled, we would take a room with an adjoining room for the kids. But we didn't have a sexual relationship.

Being in a parenting role with Amber and Keira made me very

happy. I loved putting them first, ahead of my own wants. It felt like the purest way to *be of service* to other human beings, that instinct I must have inherited from my father and honed in my relationships with Vergé and His Holiness. That they weren't my own kids made it feel even more pure. At some point, I realized that parenting these kids was what I really enjoyed doing the most. And I had somebody to cook for, even if all they wanted was mac and cheese. It had real meaning, life-altering consequences. It wasn't like what I did with the rest of my life. It was *bigger.*

Sometimes one of my friends would say, "You saved those kids' lives." I always answered, "No, they saved *mine.*"

18

A PHONE CALL FROM VERGÉ IN THE EARLY 1990S set me off on yet another new journey. He was coming to America to cook dinner at a series of one-night events. A big hotel chain was throwing a dinner party in Palm Springs, California, at their newest location. They were billing Vergé's work as a million-dollar dinner for their best corporate clients, to introduce them to this new product. Then he was going to Santa Barbara to cook at Michel Richard's restaurant there, then Citrus in L.A., then to San Francisco, and from there to the Highlands Inn in Carmel, for a series called "The Master Chefs."

This was not his first time doing one of these trips. As far back as 1972, Yanou Collart had brought Vergé, Paul Bocuse, and Pierre Troisgros to L.A. for the first time. They were supposed to cook a special dinner at a restaurant called Ma Maison. Yanou got Danny Kaye, one of her large coterie of Hollywood friends, to present the chefs. He was not only a fantastic entertainer but also a gourmand and a pretty good chef himself. The chefs discovered they couldn't cook their planned meal in Ma Maison's kitchen, so they ended up preparing it in the home of none other than George Greif. That was how George knew Vergé before I did. Yanou got the chefs written about in magazines like *Food & Wine, Gourmet,* and *Bon Appétit,* which until then had been all about how to stuff a picnic basket or roast a turkey, not about individual chefs.

Almost no one was paying them for these appearances. Not Yanou or anyone else. They did it for food and lodging. The idea was they were getting exposure for their restaurants and any product lines they might have. Just as African-American artists put up with the Chitlin' Circuit because it was a way to promote their albums.

America didn't have enough interest in fine food in the early 1970s for Vergé and the others to get much recognition outside a small and elite circle. But they did start to influence a generation of young American chefs—Wolfgang Puck, Jean-Georges Vongerichten, Larry Forgione. As Chuck Berry is to Mick Jagger, Roger Vergé is to them. In the 1980s they helped America develop its own food culture. All across America young chefs began opening their own places and getting some notoriety. In L.A., Wolfgang opened his first restaurant, Spago, in 1982. In New York, Larry Forgione started An American Place in 1983 and Alfred Portale opened Gotham Bar and Grill in 1984. In 1987, Charlie Trotter's opened in Chicago.

So you'd think that by the 1990s Vergé would be treated like visiting royalty when he came. I was about to find out different. When he told me he was coming, I said, "Let me be the road manager. Let me do what I do for my acts. I'll check you into the hotel, come prep with you, work the gig with you, and collect the money." It would be the first time I ever experienced how these places treated him when he came there to work.

We went first to Palm Springs. Vergé was the absolute focal point of the million-dollar weekend. When I checked us in, the receptionist asked for his credit card.

I said, "No, this is Mr. Vergé. He is doing the event."

"We need his credit card for incidentals," the receptionist said. Incidentals?

After that I went to his room. They had given him this tiny, piece-of-shit room. I went back to the front desk and said, "There's something wrong here. I can't put him in this room."

"That's the room," the receptionist said, deadpan.

I upgraded him. I figured I would take care of it later.

The event went beautifully. When it was over I said to Vergé, "We have to check out tomorrow, so who should I see to pick up your check?"

"Oh no," Vergé said. "I do not get paid for this."

I said, "*What?*"

He said, "Shep, they are very nice people. And they will send business to my restaurant."

I had assumed that since they were basing a whole millionaire weekend on his appearance, *of course* they were paying him.

I checked out, brought the car around, and found that Vergé was not there. He was always on time. I went in to the desk and asked.

"Oh, they brought him down to the pool for a photo session."

I found him at the pool, holding up two bottles of wine for the photographer. Renaissance owned a wine company, and that's what he was holding. Vergé had his own Vergé Wines. Why wasn't he holding, say, one of each? I took the publicity person aside and asked her.

"We're doing a piece for *Bon Appétit*, and we want Mr. Vergé to have our wines in his hands in the shot."

"Are you paying him for this?" I asked.

"Oh no."

I called Vergé over. "What are you doing? You have your own

wines. If you're going to take a picture it should be with your own wines."

He said, "But, Shep, they are very nice. . . ."

I was starting to get a little bit crazed. If someone had tried that with Alice I would have stopped the shoot and destroyed the film.

Next we did two engagements at Michel Richard's. He had actually offered to pay Vergé $2,500. Then he decided that was too much and he was going to give Mr. Vergé only $500.

"I thought you had agreed to $2,500," I said.

He said, "Well, I thought he was going to do a different thing. . . ."

After that we went to Puck's restaurant, and Wolfgang's manager stiffed him completely. On top of that, we had brought a box of Vergé's books and they had all sold, but the staff wouldn't give him the money. It took a year, but Wolf finally had them pay Vergé for both.

When we got to the Highland Inn, I took Vergé's luggage to his room and found that it was next to a garbage dump. I told them we needed another room; they told me they don't have one, because they were booked solid. I could not put him next to the garbage dump, and *I* was not going to sleep next to the garbage dump, either, because this was not a room *anybody* could sleep in. I found a hotel down the road and booked two rooms. What I told Vergé was that the Highland wanted him to be in a nice spot but had run out of rooms so they were paying for him to stay at this other hotel.

The Highland was in fact sold out, generating maybe a quarter of a million dollars, all because Roger Vergé was there. At the end of the event I asked him whom to see for his check.

"Oh, Shep," he said, "I wouldn't accept money. They are nice people."

Roy Yamaguchi was cooking the next night at the Highlands. I knew Roy from Hawaii. I got Vergé to spend one more night so we could try Roy's food. I made a reservation at the Highlands' restaurant in my name. We got dressed up and went back to the restaurant where Vergé had just been the star chef, and as we approached the maître d', he turned white. He asked us to go to the bar. We went and sat in the bar.

About ten minutes later, the maître d' called me outside.

"Mr. Gordon, I have a very serious problem."

"What's that?"

"I just spoke to the owner. I tried to get the rule changed, but he won't change it."

"What rule?"

"Employees of the hotel cannot eat in the dining room. I can serve Mr. Vergé in the bar. I cannot serve him in the dining room."

I was ready to explode. "How is he an employee when you didn't pay him? We even paid for our own rooms."

"Well, technically he is an employee for us. I'll comp the meal, I'll do anything you want, but I cannot let him in the dining room."

I went into the bar and said to Vergé, "I love you so much that if you ever make a deal for yourself again, with anybody, for anything, I am going to choke you to death! I can't take the embarrassment of these deals you make. I love you too much to see you treated this way."

I got on an airplane. I was managing Kenny Loggins then, and he was playing on the Big Island of Hawaii for a corporate event. Wolfgang was there to cook for it.

When I met up with him, I told him how Vergé had been treated by his staff. How could he let his staff give such shabby treatment to the man who had inspired him? And so on.

After a while he put up his hands and said, "But Shep, this is the only way we know. This is our lives."

I said, "What do you mean?"

He said, "No chef expects anything different. We know how we get treated. Nobody expects anything. I go somewhere, they tell me they are going to pay me, but I don't expect to get paid. Let me tell you the story of my weekend here. They promised me two first-class tickets to come over and cook, plus a suite for five days. Three days before I came over, they called me up and said, 'We can't get some of your food, so could you bring it over with you? We'll reimburse you.' So I brought a hundred and fifty pounds of food with me for this big banquet. On arrival, I get off the airplane, and there's no car. I call up the hotel and they say, 'Oh, the cars are all busy. Jump in a cab.' So I jump in a cab, with the hundred and fifty pounds of food. I get to the hotel and ask them to get the food to the refrigerator. They say, 'We don't have any refrigerator space for you. But we can arrange for you to store your food at the hotel next door. We'll give you racks and you can walk it over there.' So I put the food on the racks and walked who knows how far, maybe a half mile, to the next hotel. Then I had to get up early in the morning to walk the food back to the hotel. Oh, and by the way, the tickets were not first class. They were coach. But what was I going to do? I had a hundred and fifty pounds of food with me already at the airport and I can't disappoint all those people who are coming."

I watched Kenny do his show. Kenny Loggins, by the way, got $150,000, and twenty-three airplane tickets, ten of them first class, and two weeks at the hotel.

A week later I was back in L.A. and Wolf called me.

"Can you come over for lunch? I really want to talk with you."

I walked into Spago, the old Spago, and there were maybe

thirty-five of the greatest chefs in the world gathered there. Alice Waters, Dean Fearing, Paul Prudhomme, everybody. I was stunned.

They all wanted to talk to me. Boiled down to its essence, what they said was, "Help us, Shep. Now you see how poorly we're treated. There isn't one of us who can afford a private school for our kids. Please do for us what you do for Alice Cooper and these other people."

That was the day I started my agency, ACR, Alive Culinary Resources. I said to them, "Let's think of ourselves as a union, rather than this as an agency. All I want you guys to do is say, 'No.' Just direct the calls to me."

So now I was managing chefs. I did it all pro bono, because they weren't making anything. It was really an investment of time and money for me rather than something that generated income. I did it because I had come to love these chefs and what they created and I could not stand to see them continue to get shafted.

I framed it as a company designed to bridge the gap between the public and the world's most sought-after chefs by booking them for events. For starters, our who's-who roster of master chefs included:

Wolfgang Puck, Spago, Los Angeles
Alice Waters, Chez Panisse, Berkeley
Daniel Boulud, Daniel's, New York
Dean Fearing, Mansion on Turtle Creek, Dallas
Michel Richard, Citrus, Los Angeles
Lydia Shire, Biba, Boston
Stephan Pyles, Baby Routh, Houston
Mark Miller, Coyote Café, Santa Fe

Larry Forgione, An American Place, New York
Jean-Louis Palladin, Jean-Louis, Washington, D.C.
Robert Del Grande, Rio Express, Houston
Joachim Splichal, Patina Restaurant, Los Angeles
Nobu Matsuhisa, Matsuhisa, Beverly Hills
Pino Luongo, Coco Pazzo, New York
Paul Prudhomme, K-Paul's, New Orleans
Jimmy Schmidt, Rattlesnake Club, Detroit
Celestino Drago, Drago Centro, Los Angeles
Alfred Portale, Gotham Bar and Grill, New York
Jonathan Waxman, Michael's, Los Angeles
Jeremiah Tower, Stars, San Francisco
Norm Van Aken, Norman's, Orlando
Michel Nischan, Heartbeat, New York
Mark Tarbell, Tarbell's, Phoenix
Roger Vergé, Moulin de Mougins, Cannes

To me, one name was missing. There's a story behind that.

‖‖‖‖‖‖‖‖‖‖‖‖‖

Sometime earlier, Jim Fifield had taken over as head of EMI Records. He loved New Orleans, and Jazzfest was the same weekend as his birthday, so he invited George Greif and me to come celebrate with him and his wife, Betsy. My job was to pick our restaurants. I asked Bob Krasnow for suggestions.

"You have to go to K-Paul's, right in the French Quarter," he said. "Excellent Cajun food. Paul Prudhomme is the executive chef."

I didn't know Paul yet, but Bob did. He got him on the phone, told him we were coming, and made reservations for both our nights in New Orleans.

We flew down in EMI's jet. The first night we walked to K-Paul's. When we got there the line was very long. I left the others at the end of it and walked up to tell the girl at the door who we were. She looked at me like I was speaking Martian and informed me that no one jumped the line at K-Paul's.

Things were not off to a good start. We waited a good thirty minutes, shuffling forward one step at a time, getting sweaty and cranky in the humid heat of a New Orleans evening. When we finally got in, the place was mobbed and loud. They put us at a long family-style table with a bunch of tourists. This didn't improve our mood. We were big shots, or so we thought.

We ordered appetizers and drinks. I downed my Cajun Bloody Mary in a few gulps and managed to get the waitress's attention.

"Can I get another one of these?"

"You can only get that with an appetizer."

"Excuse me?"

"If you want another Bloody Mary you have to get back on line, be reseated, and order another appetizer."

I kept my cool. Don't get mad, I told myself.

"Is Chef Paul here tonight?"

"Yes, he is."

I told her to go tell him that Bob Krasnow's friends were in the house and could he please make an exception. Prudhomme himself came out of the kitchen—and told me that if I wanted another Cajun Bloody Mary I had to go back on line, etc. Don't ask me why.

George exploded.

"That's it. Get me out of here before I throw everything on the floor."

We left.

The next day was Jim's birthday. When I asked where he

wanted to go for dinner, he said Commander's Palace, the famous, historic place outside of the French Quarter in the residential Garden District.

George blew up again.

"It's a tourist trap. They drop them off by the busload. I will not eat where they unload them from buses."

On top of that, we found out that we had to wear sport jackets. I'd have to go buy one. George always wore a sport jacket, but he threw a fit about that, too, and said now he *definitely* wasn't going.

I said, "Well then, you're eating alone. Jim wants to go, and it's his birthday, and I'm going with him."

So we got a car and drove out to the Garden District. Commander's Palace is a big, old, wood-framed place, facing a small cemetery. There were in fact tourist buses outside. George grumbled and fumed. We walked up to the maître d'—another maître d' straight out of Central Casting. He was in a tux, standing at a little lectern, looking down at his reservations list through half glasses. He never made eye contact with us as he informed us our table wouldn't be ready for forty-five minutes, but we could wait at the bar. By this point George was punching me in the back.

Another guy in formal attire collected us. At Commander's Palace you walked through the kitchen to get to the bar. As we did, a cook on the line caught my eye. He was a guy with a wide, friendly mug, flipping something in a pan over a hot stove. He grinned at me. I smiled back. He dropped the pan, wiped his face, hustled over to me, and gave me a hug.

"Hey, man," he said, like we were old pals. "They got you hooked up?"

"Well, no," I said. "They told us it's going to be a forty-five-minute wait."

"Okay," he said. "You like champagne? Come with me."

He led us to the bar, ordered a bottle of a nice champagne, and then vanished back into the kitchen.

"You know him?" George asked me.

"Never saw him before."

"So who does he think you are?"

"I have no idea, George."

"Well don't say a word. Whoever he thinks you are, you are."

A few minutes later, our friendly cook came back to the bar. He picked up our bottle and said, "C'mon, bring your glasses." We followed him upstairs to a table overlooking a terrace, obviously one of the "A" tables in the restaurant.

"You want to order?" he asked. "Or do you want me to give you a ride?"

"Give us a ride."

After he went off, George said, "We better order some expensive wine. Because sooner or later this crackpot's gonna find out you ain't who he thinks you are, and then we're outta here."

That didn't make a lot of sense, but okay, we ordered a very expensive wine.

The cook reappeared with some waitstaff and served us our first course. He kept doing that throughout our meal, accompanying each course. We were getting hysterical wondering who he thought we were to deserve such personal service. By the time he brought up dessert George couldn't contain himself any longer.

"Sit down for a minute," he told the cook. The cook sat. "Okay," George said, "who do you think this guy is?"

"I don't know," the cook said. "Who is he?"

"Then why are you doing this?" George cried.

The cook looked around at us and said, "You know, I've been cooking here a long time. I cook the same dishes every night. It gets a little boring. They're not even my recipes. So once a month,

I pick some people coming through the kitchen and take them on a ride. I really enjoy it. When you guys came through, he had a good smile." Meaning me. "So I picked you."

How cool was that? We high-fived him.

Then he said, "What are you doing now?"

"I'd like to try to get into Tipitina's tonight," Jim said. "The Neville Brothers are playing."

I had tried all afternoon to get us in, but it was Jazzfest and booked solid. In New York or Los Angeles I could have gotten us in no problem, but I didn't have any New Orleans connections.

"I got you covered," the cook said. "I'll write you a note that'll get you in."

We thanked him. Jim paid the bill with his EMI credit card. As we were getting into our car, the cook knocked on a window and said, "You guys like cognac?" He showed us an old and obviously expensive bottle of cognac, filled four paper cups, handed them to us, and wished us a great rest of the night.

His name was Emeril Lagasse.

By the time of the chefs' meeting at Spago, Emeril had his own restaurant in the French Quarter, Emeril's. I found him there and he joined ACR.

After Emeril the number kept rising, until at one point we were representing something like one hundred chefs—everybody, basically. Once the word got around, my office received hundreds of letters and calls from people seeking representation. I got dozens of recipes a week from cooks all over the country.

19

TRAVELING WITH VERGÉ AS HIS GRASSHOPPER had opened my eyes to this world of the culinary arts and its artists. I saw that for world-class chefs cooking wasn't labor, it was a labor of love. The more I observed how they worked, the more obvious it was to me that they had not monetized their value. They were mostly one-restaurant guys working six hours a night, and barely breaking even. No one opened a second restaurant. It wasn't even a consideration. If they made guest appearances at other venues they still did it for free, thinking they had to do that because that's why their restaurants were getting so hot.

In my parallel life, my artists were getting more famous and rich every day. I had Luther Vandross making a quarter of a million dollars a night. There wasn't a chef in America making over $100,000 *a year*. One essential difference was that my entertainment clients all had additional revenue streams from selling replicas of themselves and their work—albums, posters, T-shirts. With rare exceptions, a chef made all his revenue from his one restaurant.

I didn't see why selling an artist like Vergé should be different from selling an Alice. I pictured a world where chefs were

celebrities, just like movie stars or rock stars. They would get paid fairly for their work. They would develop products and multiple streams of income. In a way, I thought, it should be even easier to mass-market food than music. There was a very big market for music, as we had shown with Alice and others. Still, not *everybody* loves music. But, as I said to a *New York Times* reporter once we had gotten the ball rolling, "Everybody eats. Not everyone listens to music, but they all consume food. Food is like software for the body. And these days, all software, like CDs, athletic equipment, and cosmetics, is celebrity-driven. Why not food?"

Nobody else, with the possible exception of Yanou Collart, was thinking about chefs this way. And even she doubted I could make chefs long-term celebrities like movie stars or rock stars. My peers in the entertainment industry thought I was nuts, too. I turned down representing Van Halen to manage Emeril Lagasse? Had Shep finally lost his mind? But now that I had the end of the road in my mind, I wasn't going to let anyone else's doubts stop me. I had always grown by setting myself new challenges. They thought I was crazy when I took on Anne Murray. They thought it was a stretch when I decided to work with Groucho and Raquel Welch. But stretching is how you grow. I knew I had to build the highway to get there, just like I had for Alice and my other artists. That's always been my method. If you can see the goal, no matter how distant it might seem at the start, it makes it easier to start creating the path to it.

Not that getting there is easy. I had worked myself nearly to death getting Alice there, and getting chefs there wasn't going to be any less demanding. But having the goal in sight makes each step on the path easier to figure out, and every bump and pothole in the road more manageable. Instead of being defeated by challenges, you think, Okay, how do we get around this so we can

continue the journey? One day and one step at a time, but always knowing where you ultimately want to be.

ıııııııııııııııı

I decided the first step was to raise public awareness—to give the public all the hints and all the pictures they needed to experience chefs as great artists and celebrities, just like other celebrities they knew. Everybody wants to be around a celebrity. From my experience early on with Alice and then with Anne Murray, I knew that one easy way to make somebody look like a celebrity is to get them seen with already established celebrities. Putting Alice next to Warhol, putting Anne next to Alice. Guilt by association. By this point I knew a galaxy of movie stars and music stars I could put my chefs next to. All I had to do was find the picture frame and put them all in it.

A good opportunity came along in January 1993, at the Rock and Roll Hall of Fame induction ceremony, held that year at the Century Plaza Hotel in Los Angeles. L.A. was my turf, and rock and roll was my game, so I thought it shouldn't be very hard to get one of my chefs hired to do the big ceremony dinner. I decided that Dean Fearing was the guy. Dean was a humble, funny, down-to-earth gentleman. And he was a huge music guy. When he wasn't cooking he was playing his guitar. He loved the idea of cooking for everybody in the music business.

I made a reasonable deal. I simply asked what they could afford to pay him. They said $2,500, and that's what we took. The key was that they *were* paying him. A first step.

Dean was ecstatic. But it wasn't going to be easy. He'd be cooking for more than 1,400. And he'd have to work with the hotel's kitchen staff. Kitchen crews always hate when a chef comes in from outside. The Century Plaza was a union hotel, and the union

wasn't happy about an outsider coming onto their turf for this big event. Normally the hotel's banquet chef would cook for an event like this.

When we walked into the kitchen the day of the event, not a smiling face greeted us. The banquet chef took us into his office and started out with, "First of all, *we* should be doing this dinner. But you're here, so I will give you a couple of people to help you. We've ordered all your food, but you'll have to put it together."

"A couple of people" turned out to be one guy—a dishwasher—to help Dean prep all those meals. Dean didn't seem fazed. As a chef he'd seen this before. He got to work prepping. In the middle of prepping, he heard some familiar music and couldn't resist wandering out to the ballroom. Cream and Bruce Springsteen's band were doing their sound checks, and Dean got to be the only one in the hall listening. Later that afternoon I pulled him out of the kitchen again to meet Joe Perry, Eric Clapton, Jackson Browne, and Bonnie Raitt.

As Dean labored away all afternoon, the hotel staff softened and came to his aid. The banquet was a triumph. It was not only Dean's first paid gig, but he got to cook for all his music heroes. When he got his check, he went back home and immediately bought two new guitars. ACR and the hotel came out winners, too. And it was a groundbreaking moment for chefs everywhere.

We kept on booking big-exposure events. I booked Wolfgang as executive chef for the Grammy Awards dinner at the Biltmore hotel in Los Angeles. It was part of the contract that he got an on-camera appearance. More guilt by association; put Wolf next to Sammy Hagar and it elevates Wolf in the public eye. I booked Dean again, to cook for the Independent Spirit Awards in a hotel in Santa Monica. The money kept getting better, and the excellent exposure transformed their careers.

Also in 1993 I arranged a unique deal to team ACR, Time-Life, and Elektra Entertainment for a video series called *Cooking Is Easy*. We produced a three-videocassette boxed set, the first cooking series of its kind to feature a group of master chefs: Daniel Boulud, Dean Fearing, Emeril Lagasse, Pino Luongo, Michel Richard, and of course Roger Vergé. It was Emeril's first time on camera; he was thirty-four and looked twenty. Cookbooks came with the videos. It all suggested that there was more to food than just eating—that it was bigger than just what was on your plate, it was about lifestyle, too. The spotlight was on our chefs. *They* were featured, not the food. Later I got Sony Records to produce a series of CDs called *Musical Meals*. They combine music and food, matching recipes by chefs with music to eat them by. Like linking Paul Prudhomme with music by Aaron Neville for a Sunday picnic of Cajun food. A CD that came with a recipe book by Emeril featured twelve songs by Buckwheat Zydeco. We sold CDs at all the chefs' live appearances.

Another huge breakthrough came in 1993 when Reese Schonfeld, one of the founders of CNN, launched the Food Network. Oddly, he was very vocal about the fact that he did not like chefs and did not like the culinary arts. His wife, who was the head of production, wasn't too crazy about chefs, either. Now, I had been friendly with Reese before this, and I knew the Food Network was the answer for turning my chefs into celebrities. When I read that Reese was struggling to get it off the ground, I saw my opening. I knew paying the on-air talent was a big expense. If we offered them talent for free, they would not be able to resist. I met with Reese and made him the offer. All I asked in return was one free commercial per program for my clients' products. He jumped at it.

The results were *Emeril Live!* and *Too Hot Tamales,* featuring the Border Grill's Mary Sue Milliken and Sue Feniger. With Mary Sue and Sue, the free commercial was for their dried chili peppers. With Emeril, his now-famous "Emeril's Essence" spices.

Both shows were very successful. The Food Network was on cable and the audiences were small. Still, it helped get across the idea of chefs as celebrities.

I saw supermarkets as another untapped income stream for chefs. If you walked into any shopping mall, almost every store was a chain outlet run by national buyers who shipped product to their locations. Foot Locker, Radio Shack, JCPenney—in every one, celebrities were driving the products. Cheryl Ladd's line of clothes in JCPenney, Michael Jordan's Nikes in Foot Locker, and so on. In the music store there were big posters and cutout figures of the bands to help move their records. In the bookstore, authors made live appearances to sell and sign their books.

In supermarkets, the only celebrities with products to promote were Chef Boyardee, Mrs. Butterworth, and Aunt Jemima. I met with some supermarket people and asked where their biggest profit margin was. They told me it was in prepared foods. "We can sell an uncooked chicken for three dollars a pound," one guy told me, "but if we cook it, we can sell it for seven dollars a pound."

I said, "Would there be any interest in selling Emeril's barbecue chickens, using his spices? But I'll only do it if you display his spices next to the chickens." A supermarket chain called Frye's in Phoenix took me up on it, and it worked like a charm. They sold their Emeril's barbecued chickens by the truckload, and moved a lot of Emeril's Essence as well. Bam!

|||||||||||||||||||||||

With the exception of Vergé and to an increasing extent Emeril, the chefs on my Alive Culinary Resources list were business relationships. We liked each other, but we weren't neighbors, I hadn't gone to college with them; they were clients. In Hawaii, meanwhile, my group of friends included a lot of chefs. We cooked together a lot, I ate at their restaurants, they came to my house. Although they never sat me down and said it, I knew that a lot of them were a little hurt that I wasn't representing them, too.

Like everything else in my life, a confluence of things made that happen. One was that Joe Gannon, my closest friend by that point, whom I'd worked with for years, was living in my house with his wife, Beverly. Joe was a bit at loose ends. Moving to Hawaii had taken him too far away from his Broadway and touring shows business. Beverly was a caterer; they had met on a Liza Minnelli tour. She was a wonderful cook and made some fabulous meals at my house. After maybe six months in my house we were having dinner one night with a few friends and neighbors and got to talking about how Joe and Bev could make a living in Hawaii (and move to a place of their own). She was such a good cook that three of us agreed right there at the dinner table to put up the money for her and Joe to start a restaurant. Dick Donner, a great movie director—the first *Superman,* all four *Lethal Weapon* films—who lived near me on Maui, and a friend from Las Vegas named Jennifer Josephs, and I put up something like fifty thousand dollars each. We would take no piece of the profits, just asked them to try and pay us back when they could.

We found a location way, way upcountry, on a pineapple plantation called Hali'imaile. An old general store for the workers was empty. We rented it for maybe two hundred dollars a month, got a set designer to make it look good for cheap, and called it Hali'imaile General Store. Beverly was a complete unknown as a chef, and Hali'imaile was way out in the country, a forty-five-minute drive from the nearest hotel. We had to make it a destination. I started driving my celebrity friends up there to eat—Stallone, Schwarzenegger, Willie Nelson, Alice—more guilt by association.

Meanwhile, whenever I was around my Hawaiian chef pals we kept dancing around the subject of ACR. They didn't want to ask me how the agency was doing because they didn't want to hear it, and I didn't want to tell them because I didn't want to make them jealous. Finally it occurred to me that this was an opportunity for another win-win. I proposed that we start a Hawaiian regional cuisine movement. A few of them were agitated that it would include Beverly, a newcomer in every way, but I said she was part of the deal, or no deal. My idea was that if we could make this movement work we'd make Beverly and Hali'imaile famous and successful quick, and get us all our money back.

We began meeting at my house: Roger Dikon, Sam Choy, Mark Ellman, Peter Merriman, Roy Yamaguchi, Jean-Marie Josselin, Alan Wong, Philippe Padovani, Gary Strehl, George Mavro, Amy Ferguson, and Bev. I had chef jackets made up for all of them, with HALI'IMAILE GENERAL STORE on them, because that was what I wanted to promote. I got Dean Fearing, as a founder of southwestern cuisine, and Roger Vergé, as a founder of nouvelle cuisine, to come talk to us about how to make a regional movement work. They both told us the same thing: Regional cuisine is dependent on local farmers. But if you go to your local farmer and say, "I want you to grow arugula for my restaurant," he will take out his shotgun and chase you off his property. Why? Because ten years ago some hotel chef came to him and asked him the same thing. The farmer grew a bunch of arugula, and nine months later brought his boxes of arugula to the chef. And the chef said, "Oh, thanks, but we've moved on and arugula isn't on the menu anymore." So you have to find a way to *guarantee* the farmers that they will be paid for what they grow for you. Then you can have your regional cuisine.

We had another meeting on the Big Island, at the hotel where Peter Merriman cooked. Peter brought local farmers and a representative from the state's department of agriculture, and we talked it out. Within a few months the department of agriculture agreed that if we couldn't pay the farmers for what they grew for us, the state would. They saw that promoting a new Hawaiian cuisine movement could be great for the state's tourism industry.

So the Hawaiian regional cuisine movement (HRC) was born. Now I had to go to work and make people understand why it was important. The way to do that was to get all the Hawaiian papers writing front-page stories about it, then all the papers in the world. As I was thinking about all this, sitting in my Jacuzzi smoking a joint one day, I got an invitation from Arnold Schwarzenegger to come to his new restaurant in Santa Monica, Schatzi on Main. I thought, Hmm, maybe there's a play here.

And I did what I do. I got the Hawaiian tourism department to pay for my chefs to fly to the mainland. I got Arnold to agree to introduce Hawaiian regional cuisine at Schatzi. I got Vergé to come and cook with them, to get HRC some international attention. And I got as many celebrities as I could possibly get to come to the event.

It was the hottest ticket in L.A. The crème of Hollywood was there—Michael and Alice and Stallone, James Cameron and Linda Hamilton, I think Luther came, even Sam Shepard, who never went to anything. I put them all in leis and chef's jackets that said MAUI VISITORS BUREAU, because they paid for them. Hawaiian tourism sent Miss Hawaii to do the hula. It was a great night, and win-win in all directions: for Arnold, for HRC, for Hawaii and Maui, for Vergé, for all of us.

Over a few years, just as nouvelle cuisine and southwestern cuisine spread around the world, so did Hawaiian regional cuisine. In restaurants everywhere now you see seared ahi tuna or mahimahi in Thai sauce on the menu. Both started out as signature HRC dishes.

|||||||||||||||||||||

I was still thinking of ways to create new income streams for chefs. No matter how great a meal they cooked, the bill was always going to be eighty, a hundred dollars. How could we increase the perceived value of what they did? I was managing performers who made a quarter of a million dollars in one night. Maybe we could make what chefs did more of a performance. But there was a hitch. When Alice went to a city to perform, there was a stadium or arena there ready for him. When chefs went on tour, there was no such facility. If Wolfgang wanted to come to Maui, he couldn't just take over somebody else's restaurant.

But there were hotels. Hotels often had chefs come and cook for special events. They did it for free, which I thought was nuts. When Vergé did his Master Wine Class, for example, people paid $2,500 to attend, and the hotel paid him nothing. It seemed to me there must be a way to take that to another level and make it a win for everybody—the customers, the hotel, *and* the chef.

All my chefs had large local followings in their own cities. These were people who liked and could afford to travel. What if we targeted a chef's hometown fans and offered them an opportunity to come to Maui with him? We could package their rooms, meals, cooking classes, entertainment, beach time. All I had to prove was that a celebrity chef could draw the people. If the hotel booked the event during one of their normally slow periods, they'd fill rooms that were usually empty and maximize their annual profits.

I knew Chuck Sweeney, owner of a beautiful hotel in Maui called the Kea Lani, right on the beach. But next door were a Four Seasons and a Grand Hyatt, brands known internationally, with huge ad budgets. He had asked me, "Can you think of anything I can do to differentiate us from these guys and compete with them?" There were probably a lot of hotels in that position. If I could prove it worked for Chuck, I'd have a model program I could use to build a circuit. I could have these guys traveling around the world. If we could fill fifty hotel rooms for four nights, that'd be $100,000 the hotel made. The chef could take a percentage and be making real money instead of being treated like an indentured servant.

Chuck liked it. I went to American Express and Hawaiian Airlines and they liked it. So we became what we call in Hawaii a *hui,* a group or association. Chuck and I had a beautiful outdoor kitchen built, so you could sit outside, leave your table, and come watch while the chefs were cooking. We brought in all the great chefs—Vergé one time, Charlie Trotter another, Nobu, Emeril, Alice Waters, etc.—and paired each with an HRC chef and music. Willie Nelson and Leon Russell were our first guest artists. We had 150 people at a time, and they loved it, and it was a wildly successful kickoff. Again, a win for everybody. Over the next three or four years, we did it in Hawaii, in California, and even in India (I'll come back to that), and it worked beautifully every time. We got the chefs two first-class airline tickets, a luxury car, the best rooms in the hotel, and maybe $2,500 for the weekend. All the perks and benefits they had never gotten before.

I also got involved in some restaurant chains in Hawaii. After the success of Carlos'n Charlie's in L.A., I invested in a couple more in the San Francisco area, so I had some experience in franchising. When I moved to Maui there were one or two Maui Tacos locations, owned by chef Mark Ellman. We built that into a national chain of something like thirty-two locations, including a great one in Newark International Airport, then sold it to Blimpie.

I'm particularly proud of another one of those projects. One day Chuck Sweeney told me he'd just bought a shopping center in Honolulu, the Aloha Tower Marketplace, in a beautiful location right on the water. He thought it would be a great location for me to do a restaurant. At first I thought about putting a Trader Vic's there. Then I had a better idea.

Outside of Hawaii, I guess Don Ho is remembered only as the guy who did "Tiny Bubbles," which was a pretty inescapable hit record in the mid-1960s. But in Hawaii, Don Ho was the Man. I mean *the Man*. I had only met him peripherally, but I thought what could be better in Honolulu than a Don Ho version of Arnold's Schatzi? It was a no-brainer. I went and met with him, and we got along really well. He was one of the most amazing human beings I've ever met in my life. Funny, loyal, solid. I can't say enough good things about him.

The result was Don Ho's Island Grill. I felt we needed to start it with a really nice statement to the local community, so on opening day we fed the homeless, with celebrity waiters: Alice Cooper and Albert Finney, who were staying at my house, and my Maui neighbors Willie Nelson and Magic Johnson. As we were flying over, we all started telling our favorite Don Ho stories. In Hawaii, everybody has a Don Ho story. Everybody. Either they first made love to Don Ho's music, or they were conceived to it, or he proposed to her at a Don Ho concert, something. So we all told our Don Ho stories—except Albert.

When we arrived at the Grill, Don ran over and gave Albert a huge hug. I didn't even know they knew each other.

Don said, "Albert, you never told them the story?"

Albert looked sheepish, so Don told it for him. When *Tom Jones* came out in 1963, it was Albert's first starring role, and it made him a matinee idol around the world. The fame started to get to him, so he went to Honolulu to get away from it for a while, and got friendly with Don. Don put him up at his home and set him up with a woman he knew. One night Albert went to the woman's home with her, and they were in bed when her husband came home. Albert jumped out the bedroom window, naked. The only other person he knew in Honolulu was Don, and Don was giving a show that night. So Albert Finney walked naked into Don Ho's show. *That* was his Don Ho story.

I loved Don. As I write this it's been eight years since he died, and I miss him a lot. He was as solid a partner as I've ever had in my life. Never said no, always with a smile. Loved food, loved life. Just a great, great guy. I don't think I ever saw him in a pair of long pants. Only shorts.

20

ONE DAY IN THE MID-1990S I walked into a restaurant in Phoenix with Roger Vergé and ran into Joan Bickson, mother of my friend Raymond, the general manager of the Mark who was so gracious to His Holiness the Dalai Lama. Joan lives in Honolulu and is like family to me. She was sitting with a man from India named Ratan Tata. In introducing us, Joan told him that one of the things I do is ask my clients what their dreams are, then try to make them happen.

"I have a dream," Tata said instantly. He spoke about the Nuclear Non-Proliferation Treaty, an international pact to ban the spread of nuclear weapons that started in the 1960s. Over the years, nearly two hundred nations signed on, including the United States. But India, Israel, and Pakistan, all of which have nukes, never signed. India refused because it said the treaty created "nuclear haves and have-nots." Tata believed that the disagreement over the treaty had prevented the United States and India from enjoying the type of relationship they should have. As the two biggest democracies in the world, we needed to be closer.

"So my dream," he concluded, "is to build a bridge between India and America again."

"That's way beyond my pay grade," I said with a smile. But it did give me an idea. I had just read that for the first time, culinary tourism in Italy was larger than culture and history tourism. Maybe one small piece of his bridge could have to do with promoting India as a destination for American foodies.

He got very interested. It turned out he had something to do with hotels, but it wasn't clear to me at that point what that was.

"Come to India," he urged me. "Help me build a bridge."

I had no idea at that moment what an amazing opportunity he was presenting to me, so we left it there.

A morning or two later, I was in New York, staying at the Mark, and got a call from the front desk.

"There's a very nice Indian fellow in the lobby. He's come here to take you to India."

What?

I went down to the lobby, where this man was waiting for me.

"My boss, Mr. Tata, said to bring you to India."

"No," I said, "I can't go to India."

"You just met him. Mr. Tata."

"Yes," I said, "but I'm sorry, I can't go to India."

We batted it back and forth a little longer, then he gave me his business card and left. I went back to my life and forgot all about it.

A year later I was having dinner with my friend Tom Pollock of Universal Pictures. He said he was on his way to India because they had targeted someone there who was a potential source of financing: Ratan Tata.

"That's so funny," I said. "I actually met him in a restaurant in Phoenix about a year ago. He wanted me to come to India." And I told him the story.

Tom said, "You didn't go? Are you out of your mind? Do you have any idea who this guy is? Ratan Tata is the number-one industrialist on the planet. *And* one of the world's biggest philanthropists."

No, I hadn't known that. I just thought he was a nice man with a lofty vision who was somehow in the hotel business. I researched him, and holy cow. Ratan Tata was the chairman of the Tata Group (he has since retired), a vast global conglomeration headquartered in Mumbai. It had huge interests in all sorts of economic sectors. It was, for instance, the largest employer in England, owner of Jaguar, Land Rover, Tetley tea, and British Steel. It owned Tata American Express in India, Tata Starbucks in India, Tata Swatch. It had subsidiaries in energy, engineering, chemicals, communications, banking. And it owned the Taj Group of luxury hotels and resorts, something like 150 locations, mostly in India but also around the world. In all, the Tata Group accounted for something like 6 percent of the gross national product of India. It was also one of the largest philanthropic entities in the world, putting an incredible two-thirds of its enormous annual profits into various charities and nonprofits, millions and millions of dollars for hospitals, the arts, scientific research, and so forth.

Thanks to Joan, I had first met the man who ran all this. Thanks to Tom, I now began to understand *why* I met him.

My wheels started turning. This was a very, very powerful man, but also a man with a vision I could get behind, and what looked like limitless resources to try to achieve it. I was a little Jew from New York, but I saw a small role I could play. We got back in touch and talked more about culinary tourism.

"The first hurdle we have to jump," I told him, "is that when I talk to Americans who could afford to come to India and stay in your hotel, within thirty seconds they say, 'I'm not going there. You get sick from the food.' It's that common a perception in America. We have to break that perception."

"How do we do that?"

"You get the greatest chefs in the world to come to India. Take advantage of this culinary movement around the world. If I'm an American and I hear that Jean-Georges Vongerichten or Nobu has opened a restaurant in a hotel in Mumbai, I think, Oh, maybe now I can go to India. There's at least one place I can eat."

We also talked about the idea of Vergé creating an Indian fusion cuisine. Could you take Indian food and combine it with French techniques and come up with something really exciting that would bring in Western culinary tourists? Maybe Tata could send me and Vergé around to his hotels in India; Vergé could meet his chefs, give lessons, exchange ideas.

"Yes, yes, yes," Tata said. "Come to India. We'll work it all out."

So I went to India with Vergé. Tata treated us exquisitely. We stayed in huge, gorgeous suites at the five-star Taj Mahal Palace, the Mumbai hotel that would be made famous around the world in 2008 when it was attacked by Pakistani terrorists. But in the 1990s it was perfectly safe, rated one of the top five hotels in the world. Everyone stayed there: Beatles, Jackie Onassis, the Clintons, the Obamas, royalty, Oprah, and now Shep and Vergé.

We had our first meeting in a library on one floor of the hotel. Sitting with Tata was Krishna Kumar, who ran the hotels, and the corporate chef, Hemant Oberoi. It started off horribly when it became clear that Kumar had no idea who Vergé was. Not a clue. Ten minutes into it, and we were already heading in the wrong direction. I looked at the shelves of books behind Vergé, and a title leapt out at me: *The Great Chefs of France*. I had never seen this book before, but I took a chance.

"Before we go any farther . . ." I said. I stood, took the book off the shelf, flipped it open. Of course Vergé was all over it. I showed it to them, and that turned the meeting around, luckily. It was just the first step in a years-long journey. I'll give you a few of the highlights.

First, Vergé and I went on a tour of seven or eight of the Taj hotels around India. He met with the chefs, while I met with farmers to make sure we could get produce. Eventually we started some organic farms. I realized early on that we couldn't pair wines with dishes the way Vergé would at the Moulin. Most Indians don't drink alcohol, so wine with meals just was not in the culture. Even though we wanted to create a French-Indian fusion to appeal to Western tourists, wine would be inappropriate and inauthentic. Indians do drink a lot of tea, however, and Tata is the largest producer of tea and coffee in the world. Why not match teas instead of wine with dishes on the menu? I convinced Kumar to let me bring in a tea sommelier. The concept was very new. It was nonexistent in India, and there was only one tea sommelier in America: James Labe. We hired him away from a chic restaurant in New York to come work for the Taj chain in India.

To give them a sense of what a great restaurant could be like, I got Kumar to come to France and eat at the Moulin, the first time for him. I wanted him not just to taste the brilliant food, but to experience the truly great and gracious hospitality. He was tremendously impressed, the way everyone is.

Then I said, "And now, maybe the most important part of the lesson. I'm going to take you to a hotel nearby that's widely considered the greatest hospitality facility in the world. One of the most beautiful, elegant, luxurious places in the world. And you're going to see how you can have all the best resources in the world, and screw it all up."

I took him to have tea with Monsieur Arondel, the general manager at the Hotel du Cap, knowing that he would put his foot in his mouth within three seconds. And he did. He told stories like the time, just for fun, he threw Brad Pitt out of the hotel. "I did not like the color of his shirt, I lock him out. It is my hotel." And more, bragging about how he abused his clientele.

Kumar's jaw was on the floor by the time it was over. He walked out aghast. And I said, "Mr. Kumar, with all due respect, when I stayed in your hotels with Mr. Vergé we weren't treated much better. More polite on the surface, yes, but still with that same attitude. You need to get the greatest hospitality guy you can find to come in and be under you, or you could end up with a Mr. Arundel. There's no point spending a lot of time and money creating a place to attract Americans and Westerners if your people have that attitude. You won't win."

He did as I suggested, and it worked beautifully.

The first international cuisine we brought to India was called Wasabi by Morimoto, at the Taj Mahal. Morimoto was very famous at the time as the Iron Chef. His was the first sushi restaurant in India, and I'm told it still has the highest per-person check. (It was also where the terrorists holed up when they took over the Taj Mahal in 2008, and was completely destroyed.) Then we did an organic vegetarian restaurant called Pure, in the Taj Lands End hotel in Mumbai. It was created by Michel Nischan, who had created Heartbeat, the first heart-healthy restaurant in New York. Pure was the first organic restaurant in India, which was very difficult to do. Besides a chicken farmer we found in Delhi, there were no organic farms, so we had to create them. But getting the great Michel Nischan to do a restaurant in India went straight to the heart of what we were trying to do, trying to get Westerners not to think of vomiting when they thought of traveling there.

For the next part of building the bridge, I turned to Jean-Georges Vongerichten. To me he was the epitome of the highly respected chef in New York City. He had a Thai restaurant, a French restaurant—he seemed able to do anything. I told him I had money from these Indian guys if he had any interest in opening another restaurant. As it happened, he and his partner Phil Suarez had just taken a lease on a space in the Meatpacking District, around Fourteenth Street in Greenwich Village, which was originally where wholesale butchers were concentrated, then became a zone of gay clubs in the 1970s and was now entering a new phase as an area of upscale boutiques and new restaurants. After a very good conversation with Jean-Georges, I asked Tata if he could provide a plane for Jean-Georges to fly around Southeast Asia researching all the different street foods. Jean-Georges asked if he could take Gray Kunz, the brilliant chef at Lespinasse, along with him. Getting the two of them involved was beyond my wildest dreams. Gray was one of the highest-rated chefs in the world. We flew to India, then the two of them went on to Singapore, Cambodia, and Thailand. The result was Spice Market, which they opened in 2004. It was another way to combat the American prejudice against Southeast Asian food; if Jean-Georges and Gray Kunz approved, it must be all right. Spice Market is still doing very well more than a decade later.

At the same time, the Taj Group was seeking to take on a prestige hotel in New York. The management contract for the landmark Pierre on Fifth Avenue was available. The Pierre is a mix of hotel rooms and condominiums. The condo owners' association decided who'd get the management contract, and for whatever reason they would not consider an Indian management group.

Now, I knew that many Pierre condo owners were huge supporters of Citymeals on Wheels, the nonprofit started by James Beard and food critic Gael Greene to bring meals to the elderly. One of the biggest food festivals in New York City is the annual

Chefs' Tribute at Rockefeller Center Plaza, when the best chefs in the city donate their time and skills to raise hundreds of thousands of dollars for Citymeals. I told Tata and Raymond that if the Taj Group became a sponsor of the Tribute, at the same time that the new Spice Market was getting great reviews, at the same time that we were opening the first organic and sushi restaurants in India . . . then we'd have a real story to tell. So they did that, and I had very elegant invitations sent to all the Pierre condo owners. I can't say for *sure* that we swayed them—but shortly after the Tribute, they voted to accept the Taj Group as the new management.

As I said, this all took place over a number of years. We must have had an impact, because American tourists are visiting India in record numbers. Maybe it's even helping to build Tata's U.S.–India bridge. I certainly hope so. For me, besides the satisfaction of high-fiving myself in the mirror for having conceived it all and pulled it off, the greatest benefit of my involvement has been meeting and becoming friends with Ratan Tata, as beautiful a human being in his own way as Roger Vergé and His Holiness are in theirs. He's an enormously wealthy man but lives in a two-bedroom apartment. He never married—he was always too busy running his global empire, serving on the boards of numerous charities and corporations, jetting from meeting to meeting to meeting. For him, money clearly is only as valuable as the good he can do with it in the world. A number of cancer hospitals in India are funded by the Tata Group and serve their patients for free. He's revered in India—people bow as he walks by. He could be their prime minister, but he's done more good being himself. He's one of the most powerful and influential men in the world, yet very humble, quiet, and unassuming. When he stayed with me in Maui, he walked around in bare feet and shorts like all the rest of us. A beautiful, beautiful individual. I'm so thankful I got to know him. One of my great joys was introducing him to Clint Eastwood, one of his heroes. They bonded over a mutual love of flying helicopters and continue to stay in touch.

||||||||||||||||||

Of all the American chefs I worked with, one of my favorites is Emeril. From that first time we grinned at each other in the busy kitchen of Commander's Palace, there's always been something naturally simpatico between us. He has a big coupon with me. The best coupon is not always a simple quid pro quo. Sometimes it's exchanging something more intangible, like honor or loyalty. Emeril Lagasse proved to me more than once that he is a loyal and honorable person.

When he and I started packaging and marketing his spices, we were fifty-fifty partners. As usual, there was no paperwork on it; we shook hands. For honorable people that's enough. I found us a hundred-year-old family company in Arizona to handle all the aspects of packaging, warehousing, and shipping. They were a tiny mom-and-pop company, but they held up their end. Emeril and I each made maybe $150,000 a year from it.

As Emeril's career took off, so did the orders for his spices. William Morris became his agency. They wanted him to drop the family, whom we liked and enjoyed working with, and switch to B&G, the second-biggest spice company in America. They wanted him not only to leave the family behind, but me as well.

His agent called me. "What're you willing to take?"

I said, "Willing to take? We're fifty-fifty."

"Do you have that on paper?"

"No."

"Too bad. Well, look, we'll get you a finder's fee or do something else. I know you brought the client. We'll take care of you."

"Yeah, you're taking good care of me. I got it."

I called Emeril. "Do you know what's going on?"

"Do *you* know what's going on?" he said. "I got a memo telling me how I should fuck you. How you don't deserve to be my fifty-fifty partner. And how giving you a small piece of something big is more than fair. What do you think about it, Shep?"

"We shook hands. We're fifty-fifty partners. You do what you want to do. You want to cut me out, cut me out. I'm not going to sue you. You do what you gotta do. You gotta live with yourself."

"They're telling me I'm being fair to Shep Gordon. 'We do these kind of deals all the time.' Is this done all the time?"

I said, "Yeah. The industry is full of cocksuckers."

He thought it over. And told them, "Screw yourselves. Shep's my partner." And having seen how they operated, he added, "And I want *that* on paper."

That's a supermensch. That's someone with honor.

|||||||||||||||||||

I know my strengths and my weaknesses. I'm not a great organizational guy. I don't have a great attention span. I'm a very poor administrator, and I'm a horrible executive. But I'm *fantastic* at launching the rocket ship. It's what I do best. I sit and smoke a joint and think, Wouldn't it be amazing if . . . ? And then I start figuring out how to pull it off.

After several years of working my butt off for the chefs, I was ready to step away and let them fly the rocket themselves. I felt I'd done what I'd set out to do for them. Most of them were rich and famous now, which is what I do for you. In some ways I might have done my job too well. Most of my HRC chefs had grown to where they owned multiple restaurants on many of the same islands, so they were becoming competitors. Other chefs wanted in, but the group didn't want to expand. Nerves got raw, and there were petty disagreements about what to do next and how. I was not interested in playing the negotiator. I stepped away, and the organization died.

But look at what we accomplished. Just as I had done for Alice and Teddy and others, I hadn't sat around waiting for the culture to create opportunities for us. I created a culture in which chefs are celebrities and cooking is cool. A lot of what we did that was cutting-edge then is standard practice today. Now everyone takes it as a matter of course that great chefs are celebrities. Today, hotels everywhere bring in top chefs for culinary tourism packages. Culinary travel shows and chefs like my friend Anthony Bourdain are all over TV. Everybody is a foodie to some extent now. People clamor to get into a new restaurant the way they do for a big box-office movie on opening weekend.

It's easy to forget that this phenomenon is only twenty-some years old. Twenty-five years ago, Americans didn't know a single chef's name besides Boyardee, and their favorite restaurants were McDonald's and KFC.

I've given a lot of thought to what it was that made this food culture take off the way it did. Was it really just that we made the chefs celebrities? Or is it something about food itself? Food isn't just food, after all. Food *is* culture, food is art, food is recreation, food is a trophy in your house, food is a way to have a social life. Music is a luxury. Food is the core of life. It's more than something you shove in your mouth three times a day. I think that's something Americans had forgotten. Europeans understand it. Go to Italy, to France, and good food is a daily preoccupation. It's integral to their cultures and their lives. I think we brought some of that to Americans.

21

IN THE MIDDLE OF ALL MY RUNNING AROUND FOR THE CHEFS, I had the first big health scare of my life. I'd always been pretty casual about my health. I had lived the high life, done a lot of drugs, didn't always eat right, and was a bit overweight. I didn't have a doctor and never went for check-ups. Then again, I was going on fifty and had never had a major problem.

In the early 1990s the artist Peter Max, a really good friend of mine going back maybe a quarter of a century at that point, told me that he had just had this diagnostic procedure, a full-body scan. The machine was brand-new at the time. He encouraged me to do it. I said sure, then forgot about it.

A few years went by. Meanwhile the machines were popping up in hospitals everywhere. One day I was in Phoenix with nothing planned, and in my usual way I decided that what I'd do that day was go get scanned. The next day, on my way to play golf, I stopped in to get the results.

The doctor said, "You're going into bypass surgery right now. It's amazing you're alive. You have ninety-nine percent blockage in the arteries going to your heart."

I had been on my way to play golf. I felt fantastic. Now suddenly I was on death's door? My reaction was nothing like I would have expected. For years, when trying to comfort someone who was confronting their own or a loved one's mortality, I had a set speech I always said. It went something like this:

I happen to believe that the universe is not here by chance. I believe somebody created it—call him God, call him Allah, call him a mad scientist, anything you want. And there are only two things he guarantees to everyone in our species: you're born, and you die. In between it's completely random, and no two people are alike. You could be black, white, yellow. You could be tall, you could be short, you could be a guy, you could be a girl. Billions of us on the planet, and out of them all, you are absolutely unique.

Now, if there is a creator, why would he go to all that trouble to make each and every one of us unique, and to give us everything that happens to us between birth and death? Is he a scumbag? Or is it all a gift? Birth, death, and everything that happens to you in between? Accept it. Embrace the miracle.

I really believe that. But now *I* was the one who was dying, and my philosophy didn't do me any good at all. I fell apart. I went into a complete, terrified panic. Holy fuck, I'm going to die. Some gift. I felt faint, I broke out in a sweat, I was angry, I was scared, I was filled with self-pity, everything.

The doctor wasn't kidding around. He had me undressed and in a hospital gown in no time. In my panic I found the presence of mind to think, There must be someone else I can talk to before I let this guy cut me open.

I remembered a man I'd met on a plane. I had been in New York talking to American Express about getting involved with ACR. My flight to L.A. was on the runway when a flight attendant got on the speaker and asked if there was a doctor on board. The guy seated next to me got up and went forward. An ambulance rolled out to the runway and they took somebody off. While this was going on, I glanced at the book the man had been leafing through. It was called *Week by Week to a Strong Heart.*

When the man sat back down I asked him what had happened. He said, "I think he had a little heart attack."

"You're a doctor?"

"Yeah, I'm a cardiologist in fact. I teach at Yale and have a private practice."

It turned out he was Dr. Marvin Moser, the coauthor of *Week by Week;* he had been leafing through it to bone up for a TV interview.

I had one of my moments when things just clicked in my head. I told him who I was, that I represented all the great chefs in America, and wouldn't it be great if he collaborated with them on a heart-healthy cookbook? He said he'd already written a dozen books on hypertension and didn't think he had anything new to say on the subject, but I was on a roll. Wouldn't it be good to clarify some of the myths and misconceptions about diet? Antioxidants, garlic, food additives, heart disease, cholesterol? But at the same time demonstrate how people could remain on a low-fat, low-cholesterol diet and still enjoy recipes put together by America's leading chefs?

He started to warm to the idea. I grabbed the phone in front of me—they still had phones on planes then, before the age of cell phones—and started calling some of my chefs. By the time we landed in L.A. I had gotten agreements from Larry Forgione, Alice Waters, and Jimmy Schmidt, and found us a publisher. *Heart-Healthy Cooking for All Seasons* came out in 1996.

So now, sitting there in my hospital gown facing death, I called Dr. Moser. They got him out of class to speak to me. I explained my situation.

He said, "Do you have any pain?"

"No."

"Have you had any in the last few weeks?"

"No."

"Okay," he said. "I want you to listen to me really carefully, Shep. You are not going to die in the next day or two. Do you understand me? *You are not going to die.* Calm down. You're more likely to die from sheer nervousness. I can hear it in your voice. Now, you're going to go to the doctor and tell him that you're not having the surgery. You're going to go get dressed, then book a flight to New York. You're going to *calmly* fly to New York. I guarantee you're not gonna die on the plane. And you're going to go see my partner at his office in Connecticut."

So I flew there to see Marvin's partner, who looked at me, looked at the results, gave me a stress test, and said, "Yes, it's true you have very high cholesterol. There will come a time when you will probably have to do something about it, but you're not at risk now. You should do no procedures whatsoever. I know one great cardiologist in Hawaii, Irwin Schatz. He's retired from private practice and teaching at the University of Hawaii, but maybe he'll see you."

He hooked me up with Dr. Schatz. Every six months I would fly over to Honolulu and he would check me out. After six or seven years he said, "Now you're at risk. Your blockage is getting serious." We called up Dr. Moser, who arranged for me to fly to Mount Sinai Hospital in New York, where they put in three stents. Dr. Moser had made sure the top doctors there did the procedure, and it went beautifully. A couple of years later I went back to have two more put in.

After that I got lucky again and came under the care of Dr. Robert Huizenga, who blew the whistle on steroids in the

NFL after being the team physician for the then–Los Angeles Raiders, and whose work on obesity led to the TV show *The Biggest Loser*. A couple of years ago he advised me to get a stent put in my carotid artery. There's a small chance of stroke, like a 3 percent chance, if the carotid gets blocked. I said, "I have a fairly large estate. If I put you in my will, will you kill me if I have a stroke? Because I wouldn't want to live after a stroke."

I've seen what a stroke can do. Vergé had a stroke a few years ago. At first he was in a wheelchair—there it is again—but able to converse and feed himself. But his condition deteriorated gradually, until he couldn't speak anymore, never left his room, and I don't think he knew I was there when I visited. It was very sad to see him, and almost a relief when he passed away in June 2015. Wherever he went on to, it had to be a better place.

I'd rather they kill me.

Or at least I say that now.

||||||||||||||||||

In the early 2000s I woke up one morning in L.A. and decided it was time to retire. It wasn't something I'd been thinking about or planning for at all. It was never a goal. Like so much else in my life, I just woke up and there it was. What am I doing today? I'm retiring.

I hear myself say "retire" now, which is interesting, because that word wasn't actually in my brain at the time. I was still managing all these artists and chefs. I was still using drugs. I was not in a relationship. I was starting to feel the lack of a biological child in my life, as much as I love my kids. I had to do a couple of things for clients that day that I didn't want to do. I had to say no to some people, and I never liked that part of my job. I realized that my income had hit a plateau, because I was never really good at running a business. I had twenty-five people in my office for whom I was making tons of money, while my income stayed exactly where it was.

What was it all for? What's it all about, Alfie? I had no idea. I felt like I had spent my life living other people's lives. I didn't know if I had no personal life because I had been so very busy for so many years, or if keeping busy was just an excuse not to develop a personal life. Now I really wanted to figure that out, and the only way to do that was to get rid of any excuses. Given my health scares, who knew how much longer I had to find out?

I called Alice.

"Where are you?"

"In L.A."

"You got anything going for lunch?"

"No."

"Will you do me a favor? I've decided to call everybody this morning and resign. Will you come get me and take me to lunch so I can get really drunk when I'm done?"

I told Alice that I'd still manage him. That was a given.

I spent all morning calling other clients, explaining that it had nothing to do with them, only with me. I gave each of them the option of leaving the company or staying with the person in my office who was best able to continue handling them. I had no contracts with anyone that had to be broken, so that part was easy. I reached maybe half of them that morning. Almost all of them sounded happy for me.

Then I went back to Maui, ready to begin this "retirement" and figure out who I was. . . .

And discovered that I was the same person I'd always been. No big revelation, no Zen satori. I wasn't happier than I'd been, but I wasn't unhappy about it, either. You are who you are, I guess.

And anyway, people wouldn't let me quit. When I decided I was sort of retiring, my friend Sammy Hagar decided I was *not* retiring. And Sammy can be very persistent. When I convinced him that I wasn't managing artists anymore, he talked me into going to see Cabo Wabo Cantina, the restaurant in Cabo San Lucas, Mexico, he opened in 1990. So I go, and in the restaurant there was a wooden barrel on the counter, which Sammy said held tequila that a local family had been making for him since 1996. I tasted it and it was fantastic, which gave me an idea.

"I really don't want to do any more restaurants," I said to him. "But if you want to have some fun, Jimmy Buffett has already laid out the highway for us. You know how he branded his Margaritaville tequila and distributes it all over the world? We could do that with Cabo Wabo tequila."

Even as I was saying it a voice in my head was saying, *Holy shit, now I'm going to have to work at this.* And it was just me at this point. I didn't have a staff anymore, didn't have an office, nothing. But now I'm committed, so I need to figure out how to make this easy, fun, and, of course, win-win.

We spent the next six or eight months distilling the tequila, tasting it, refining it, designing the bottle and the label—a lot of steps. When we were ready I decided we should test-market it in Hawaii. I had one thousand cases shipped. By the time the tequila arrived, the Rolling Stones were coming to Hawaii to play a Pepsi convention on the big island. Ron Wood and I have been good friends for years and years, from back before he joined the Stones. He slept on my couch many a night. I piggybacked a couple of Rolling Stones concerts at Aloha Stadium onto the Pepsi convention. And I gave the band some Cabo Wabo Tequila, and they liked it. They were flying home in a private 747. I couldn't resist asking Ronny if they'd agree to be photographed going up the stairs into the plane carrying bottles of Cabo Wabo. If the press asked, they were to say they really liked it, and it was only available in Hawaii, so they were taking some home with them. Ronny and the guys were very gracious and did it, and it made all the Hawaiian papers. We sold out one thousand cases in a heartbeat.

Now it just so happens a guy from Wilson Daniels, the high-quality wine and spirits distributor in Napa Valley, was in Hawaii. I knew him a little through the chefs, and took him out to dinner. We made a deal right there at dinner for the prestigious Wilson Daniels company to be our national distributor. And we set it up so that Sammy and I took no financial exposure on it at all. Wilson Daniels would order, say, five thousand cases from us, at say $40 a case. (I'm making these numbers up because I honestly don't remember the actual figures. But these are close.) They would give us a promissory note for $200,000. We'd take that to the bank. Then we'd order the five thousand cases from our Mexican distiller, who charged us $20 a case. The bank paid the distiller the $100,000. When the five thousand cases arrived at Wilson Daniels's warehouse, they had ten days to pay us the $200,000. We'd use half of that to repay the bank, plus a small handling fee they charged us, and pocket the rest.

It was beautiful. Sammy and I were making money hand over fist, and never laying out a dime of our own cash. We had no office, not one employee, no overhead. I did it all from home. I even designed the ads myself. By the time I sold out my interest to Sammy, we were billing $30 million a year.

〰〰〰〰〰〰〰〰〰

A few years into my "retirement" I got a call from a friend who wanted me to think about managing this new young raw food chef, Renée Loux. I said my usual piece about how I was retired, wasn't managing chefs anymore, and on top of that didn't particularly like the raw food diet, which emphasizes a lot of fruit and uncooked or barely cooked vegetables. Then I agreed to meet her anyway.

When I answered the door a few days later this beautiful reddish-blond vision was standing there. For me it was love at first sight. I was still thinking about getting married again and having children. I was also still my usual fumbling self around a beautiful woman, but I invited her to stay in my guesthouse and she accepted. Despite roughly thirty years' difference in our ages we found we had a lot in common—she was even from New York— and had a wonderful time the next five days, walking and talking on the beach in the days, cooking together at night. I learned to like raw food, which my friend Tom Arnold says is when he knew I was in love. The fifth night we moved the relationship to a more intimate place, and on the sixth day she moved in.

Two years later we got married on the lawn, the sun setting behind us, sixty-five friends there to cheer us on. I was three days shy of turning sixty, and she had just turned thirty. I had joked, "We only have a small window of opportunity here. Let's get married when there's only twenty-nine years between us." For our honeymoon, Fiji Water offered an extremely exclusive resort on a tiny, remote island. Usually there's only one couple staying there, but this time there was one other guest. One day Renée's laptop stopped working. I called the desk to ask for help. A few minutes later the computer repairman was at our door. It was Apple founder Steve Jobs, who was the other guest on the island. He got Renée's laptop working, and she made him dinner for the next few nights. It turned out he was already into raw food.

When we returned to Maui I got to work managing Renée's career. I got her a book deal and a television show. Meanwhile, I still really wanted children. We worked at it, but it didn't happen. I thought we should seek medical advice; she felt that pregnancy should occur naturally or not at all. That and other issues gradually pushed us apart. After four years we split up. Like so many of the other women I've been with, we couldn't stay together, but we've stayed friends.

22

I PICKED UP GOLF AGAIN WHEN I MOVED TO MAUI. I hadn't played since freshman year of college. Soon I was playing four or five days a week. I never really took it seriously enough to get very good at it. For me it's like it was with my dad, a way of bonding with friends. Michael Douglas and I have been on some epic golf trips.

I started taking Chase golfing with me when he was six, and he grew up to be a much better golfer than I am. Alice and I have golfed together a lot, too. A lot of ex-alcoholics and ex-druggies play golf because it's a great way to be addicted to something safe. Golf is extremely addictive. If you have an addictive personality, you're probably never going to get rid of that part of your personality. It's integral, chemical, hardwired in you. Rather than try to cut off that part of who you are, I think it's better to embrace it and just shift the addiction from dangerous things like drugs and alcohol to something good, safe, and fun like golf. Why torture yourself every day, denying who you are? Embrace the fact that you're an addict, and use it. Don't run from it, don't get depressed by it, don't get eaten up by it. Use it. Say to yourself, I'm *lucky* to be an addict. If I wasn't, I wouldn't be such a good golfer! It's another miracle.

One morning in January 2012 I drove out to the Kapalua golf course with Chase and Alice. Kapalua is about a forty-five-minute drive from my house, which is farther than we usually go, but the Hyundai pro golf Tournament of Champions had just been there and we wanted to go play while the course was still in tournament condition. For years I'd had a history of gas and irregular movements. This day I hadn't gone to the bathroom in a couple of days, so it wasn't abnormal for my stomach to hurt. I just thought it was gas. It had hurt a little the night before; I woke up in the morning and it was still there. By the fourth or fifth hole I was getting really uncomfortable. I put my feet up on the front of the golf cart while we were driving, to try to release the tension. At the ninth hole I said, "I think I'm gonna go home, guys." They didn't think anything of it. I rarely play eighteen holes.

On the way home I stopped at a pharmacy and bought some Gas-X. By the time I got home, my guts were starting to hurt a little more than normal, but still not so much that I thought it was anything but gas. Still, something must have shown on my face, because Nancy, my assistant, asked if I was okay. I made a couple of phone calls and then got in the Jacuzzi, hoping the heat would bring out the gas. After fifteen or twenty minutes in the Jacuzzi I realized this wasn't going away; in fact, the pain was getting worse. This wasn't just gas. It was sharp pains and dull ones, every kind of pain, rumbling all over my guts, getting more intense by the minute. I called the office on my cell, but Nancy had gone home by then, so I texted Chase, who had just come back.

"I think I need to go to the hospital," I groaned, "and I don't think I have time to wait for an ambulance."

Chase helped me to the car and started driving to the hospital, which is in Kahului, near the airport. Normally it's about a thirty-minute drive, but he was driving really fast. The pain was now so intense I was stomping my foot and punching the door and dashboard, which really worried Chase. He knew me as such a placid guy. Through gritted teeth I told him not to drive so fast, because if we were pulled over I was really fucked. But he was really concerned now and we pulled up outside the emergency room in twenty minutes. He jumped out and helped me inside.

I had asked Chase to text Nancy, so she was there waiting for us. We rushed past the other people in the waiting area and went straight to the admitting desk. I remember her asking me for my ID and my insurance card, and that's pretty much it. I have a vague scrap of memory of lying on an examination table and looking up to see Nancy, Chase, and a nurse, a friend of Nancy's who was running the emergency room. And that's all I remember until I woke up in a hospital room days later.

Afterward I learned what heroic efforts Nancy had made while I was unconscious. For two days she was on the phone 24/7 with all my doctors in L.A., all my friends. They sent a plane over to get me, because half my friends and half the doctors said I needed to be brought to Los Angeles right away. The other half said no, I needed to be operated on right away, I'd die on the plane. Nancy had to make that decision. A tough decision to make for your boss. I would not have wanted the pressure. Meanwhile, I was lying there, blissfully unaware that I was dying.

Nancy finally said, "Do it." So they operated on me in Maui. It was touch-and-go. I flatlined twice. Died on the table. I had suffered an intestinal infarction, colloquially known as "a heart attack of the intestines." Just as the arteries to the heart can get blocked, so can the ones to the bowels. The lack of blood flow causes the lower intestines and colon to stop functioning. The doctors told

Nancy that about a foot of my small intestine had died and had to be removed. I was extremely lucky. I'm told that four out of five people don't survive.

I woke up in a blank white hospital room. Nancy's was the first face I saw. I felt this incredible sense of peace and ease. I had no pain—I was still on a drip, of course—and no idea of all the drama that had just ensued. I was feeling really blissful. And it occurred to me that I would have been just as happy if I hadn't woken up.

The next day, I was beginning to feel pretty low and sorry for myself. It struck me as a bit sad that the first face I saw when I woke up was Nancy's. She talks about this in the movie, because it struck her as well. I don't mean that I was sad that it was Nancy, but sad that it wasn't a wife or family standing there. It was an employee. And now even she wasn't there. I was sixty-six years old, I was alone in my hospital room . . . *and* it was Friday the thirteenth.

That's when Mike Myers called.

"Ready to say yes now?"

‖‖‖‖‖‖‖‖‖‖‖‖

I really liked Mike. We had met on the set of *Wayne's World* in 1991, at an important point in Alice's life and career. The early 1980s had pretty much been one long lost weekend for Alice. In addition to the drinking he started smoking crack. The quality of his albums deteriorated. For a while he was so bad I couldn't stand the heartache of being around him. He was terrifyingly malnourished and emaciated, sick in other ways, and always zonked out of his mind. I couldn't pull him out of it. Nobody could—not me, not Sheryl, not his poor parents—until he decided to do it himself. Finally, he agreed to go back into rehab.

He called me from a hospital bed and I agreed to help him try to make a comeback. It was a long, tough climb. For a while I took most any offer that came his way, just to get him started up again. That's how Alice starred in one of the worst movies I have ever seen, a horror picture called *Monster Dog*. I knew the producer, Eduard Sarlui, who ran Trans World Entertainment, a small production and distribution company. They shot it in Spain, with an Italian director and an entirely Spanish cast except for Alice, then dubbed it in English for the U.S. home video market. When they showed it to me and Alice, the voices were completely, wildly out of synch. I mean *way* out of synch—and no one had even noticed until we pointed it out. They just shrugged and released it anyway.

It was all up from there, but slowly. Alice put out a new album in 1986, *Constrictor,* on MCA, and went on tour for the first time in a few years. We billed the tour as "The Nightmare Returns," and he worked really hard on it, staying on the road pretty continuously from the fall of 1986 through the spring of 1987. It worked—his old fans were glad to see him back, and younger fans were glad to see him, period.

In 1991, we got a call that Paramount was making a movie of Mike Myers's "Wayne's World" routine from *Saturday Night Live.* They needed a big rock icon to be in the scene where Wayne and Garth (Dana Carvey) fall to their knees and do their famous "We're not worthy!" Alice was not only one of the biggest rock stars of all time, he could act, so it was an excellent match. They would shoot a bit of Alice onstage, and he'd get one song on the soundtrack.

When I met Mike, he was pretty set on the idea that the song had to be one of Alice's giant hits from the early days, either "I'm Eighteen" or "School's Out." But Alice had a new album coming out, *Hey Stoopid,* and I didn't see any point in his being in the movie if it didn't feature a new song and help promote the album. You know, win-win.

Mike said no.

I was firm but not unreasonable with him. I said, "I happen to know that you start shooting in two weeks. You really don't have a choice. Now, I read the script, and I see the band is only onstage for eight seconds. No one will remember anyway. He's got a great song on the new album, 'Feed My Frankenstein.' Put that one on the soundtrack, and if you put 'School's Out' in the credits, everyone will think that's the song he sang."

The movie came out in 1992, and "Feed My Frankenstein" is on the soundtrack, and it was a great moment in Alice's career. Since then, I have never walked through an airport with him where he didn't get a few dozen people going down on their knees and chanting, "We're not worthy!" And it was the start of a beautiful friendship with Mike. After *Wayne's World* his father died and Mike was struggling with grief. He came to my house for a weekend and ended up staying two months. I cooked for us both. It's what I do. He's the best audience for my stories. He *loves* hearing my stories. After a while he started saying, "You have got to let me get these stories on film. Let me tell your story. The story of a guy who created all this culture."

That day in the hospital I finally agreed.

They sent me home a few days later. Marty Kriegel was living in Taiwan at that point. He flew to Maui to keep an eye on me. He'd gone to med school, done everything except actually get an M.D., so he was great to have around. He changed my bandages and monitored my condition. At one point he noticed some excessive bleeding and got me right back to the hospital to fix a stitch. The first few nights he actually slept in the bed with me, keeping an eye on me. He ended up staying for two months. That's a pretty good friend.

Three or four weeks into my recuperating, when I was feeling much better, I called Mike and asked him to call the movie off.

"Too late," he said. "We already staffed up."

So he made his movie. My agreement with him was that I would not be involved in any way, other than to sit for a few interviews and refer him to some other people who might have something interesting to say. "It's your movie," I told him. "Your story. Tell it the way you see it." I did ask him to show it to me when he had a rough cut done, just in case there was anything in it I really didn't think should go public. I wasn't thinking about covering my own ass. I just wanted to make sure that it would not contain anything that might be hurtful or damaging to others.

It was a labor of love for him. He put a lot of time and some of his own money into it. When he was ready I went to his apartment in Soho in New York City to see it. When I walked in the door his little dog got all yappy and snappy with me. "Oh sorry," he said quickly, and locked it in another room. It's one of the ways I know who my real friends are. They never force me to pretend I like being around their dogs.

It's a very strange feeling to sit and watch a whole movie that's about you. I thought it was great, but it's definitely Mike's movie, his version of my life and who I am. When it ended, he said, "Well?"

"It's your story," I said. "Just do one thing for me."

"Name it."

"Take me to lunch someday with this guy Shep."

EPILOGUE

WHEN I MOVED TO MAUI, I discovered the remote little town of Hana. You can only get there over a very winding road, a difficult, two-to-four-hour drive through dense rain forest, with dozens of hairpin turns and maybe sixty one-lane bridges. You have to want to be in Hana. I fell in love with it the first time I saw it. Hana is largely untouched by man. It's in the tropical jungle, so the air smells like rain all the time. Everywhere you look are long, rolling valleys, dark green pastures dotted with horses, lush mountains shrouded in clouds.

In 1976, I rented the old Lindbergh cottage in Kipahulu, an unspoiled wilderness next town over from Hana. It's a simple A-frame with lava rock walls on a hundred-foot cliff overlooking the Pacific. Charles Lindbergh had it built for him and his wife, Anne Morrow Lindbergh. She wrote her books there; he died there and is buried outside a local church, in a eucalyptus casket. Shirley MacLaine lived and wrote there, too.

At that time I was still the cool guy from Hollywood, running a big office, going a million miles an hour. I loved that Hana was so very different from L.A., so much slower and more relaxed, but I thought I still needed to be able to conduct business when

I was there. The problem was, the telephone in the house was a three-person party line. I worked the phones a lot. A party line just wasn't going to cut it.

I looked up the one phone company in Hana, which turned out to be in a house about a thirty-minute drive away. When I arrived I found a family eating their lunch. An older man, maybe seventy-five, greeted me. I explained to him that I did a huge amount of business by phone, and that I needed four dedicated lines, with a hold button. I was speaking about a million times faster than people in Hana do. He heard me out, looking at me like I was from Mars, then said, "Listen, son. You don't need a hold button. If you don't have time to talk to someone, call them back later."

That's Hana. It's not a place you go to conduct business. There aren't many places to meet except a few restaurants. No malls, no movie theaters, no golf courses, no traffic lights, nobody moving fast. And no hold buttons.

In 2003 I bought a share of a condo there in a small hotel complex. It sits on a long, sloping hill with a postcard view of the ocean pounding a black lava jetty. It has everything I need. There's a little patio where I can sit peacefully smoking a joint and watch humpback whales breach in the ocean, then have dinner by candles and starlight. It has a small kitchen where I can cook my favorite meals with the world's best produce. There's even a small wine cellar.

For me, Hana's a magical place where I can make believe for a little while that I don't have responsibilities to artificial things anymore. There, your only responsibilities are to yourself and the planet.

Even though I'm "retired," I'm as busy as ever. Every year I organize a big New Year's Eve party and concert to raise funds for charity. They started out on my lawn but grew too big over the years. It's a tremendous amount of work and it nearly kills me every year, but what a great time. For 2015 the charity was the Maui Food Bank. Alice and his band played, and Sarah McLachlan and Ray Benson, and my friends and neighbors Steven Tyler, Lily Meola, Pat Simmons, Pat Simmons Jr., Michael McDonald, local hero Willie K, and Weird Al Yankovic. So far we have sponsored 308,000 meals for the people of Maui. Yes!

I still travel extensively at least six months out of the year. When I'm away for long periods, I can't wait to escape back to Hana for brief getaways. I tend to go there when I can string three, four days together. I enjoy coming with special people, and I enjoy coming alone. When I'm alone, I don't talk for three or four days. Only in my head, to myself. Just like when I was a kid.

I think of Hana as a tuning fork. It helps you fine-tune and get yourself back into whatever natural rhythm is most comfortable for you. If you're *un*comfortable with yourself, it's a very hard place to be, because it forces you to deal with your discomfort, too.

Whenever I'm there, I find a miracle in every single moment. There are rainbows every day. There are amazing waterfalls. The beaches are spectacular—black sand, red sand, white sand. Even the roosters crowing all the time next door is miracle stuff to me.

One evening I drifted over to the hotel for a quiet martini. While I was enjoying my drink, a couple of middle-aged hotel employees, native Hawaiians, got on a makeshift stage and started playing and singing songs. No high-tech speakers or amps. No roadies arranging lights or expensive gear. Just one guy on a faded purple ukulele, the other on an old scratched-up guitar. And they seemed thrilled, very happy doing what they liked to do, singing nostalgic, traditional Hawaiian songs to twenty, thirty people.

For me, this was another little miracle. It confirmed for me everything I've learned and said and written about fame, success, and happiness. I realized how incredibly lucky I am just to be alive to experience such wonderful moments.

||||||||||||||||||

Today is May 5. Mia's birthday. If you're reading this, Mia, here's what's happened in the family over the last few years:

Keira and her beautiful daughter Karter are living with Winona and your grandmother Terry. Karter is a piece of work. Like her mom, she eats only mac and cheese. I love her so much.

Amber is an angel in human form. She loves L.A., works in the industry, and has received production credits on a few films. She's my go-to person when I need someone to talk to about real stuff.

Chase has been living in Maui the last four years. Lucky me, a golf buddy. He and beautiful Natasha have two-year-old Zada. She has replaced chicken soup in my life—she cures everything. She's so sweet and Hawaiian.

Monique is doing great. Our relationship was bumpy at first. It must have been tough to have this new person show up when her mom died. I was sadly thinking our relationship was disappearing altogether when she called to tell me she was getting married and asked if I would walk her down the aisle. I cried. I have come to love and respect Mo, her husband. He's a traditional tattoo artist—no, I'm not getting one—and a great cook. He loves Monique and the whole family.

You did well, Mia.

Thank you, thank you.

||||||||||||||||||

There it is again, those two simple words. For the last fifty-five or so years of my life I have said these words first when I wake up and last when I go to sleep, and more times than I can count in between. It still makes me feel good every time I say it.

So:

Thank you to my father . . . It's only recently that I have come to realize how much of my journey, which at times I thought unique, was molded by the love and sacrifice of my father for me and my family. As I tried to understand why I made and continue to make choices in my life, I have come to realize that his love, and his selfless sacrifice in trying to give me a better life than he had, drive everything I do. So lucky to have had him in my life.

Thank you to all my aunts, uncles, cousins, nephews, my brother Ed and his beautiful children and grandchildren!

Thank you to the amazing mentors in my life. . . . They taught me to be thankful and to see the miracle in all things. They have shown me through example that service to others is a true path to happiness. I'm particularly grateful to Chef Roger Vergé. I can't imagine what path my life would have taken without him. As I was writing this book Mr. Vergé passed away, and he is missed every day.

Another mentor who passed is George Greif. He taught me everything about everything . . . and made the best chicken soup!

Thank you to my clients, who allowed me to do my job without creating losers, and to help create culture and history, not wait for it. You believed in me maybe more than I believed in myself. Alice tops the list—first client, last client, and best friend.

Thank you to Mike Myers for your love and belief in me . . . for taking what I always thought of as a random life and giving it some cause and effect. Also for making me realize that maybe there is something in my life journey that can help other people get to where "thank you" has an important place in everything they do. Thanks also to all the people who gave of their time and energy to make *Supermensch*—especially the friends who agreed to be interviewed. Thanks for your time and love.

Mikey D, a scream-out to you. You are always there when I need someone. Thank you.

Thanks to my Alive family: Joe Greenberg, who started it all; Cindy, Donna, Gail, Bob, Joe, Allan, Danny, Noel, Carolyn, Toby, Lionel, Suber, John, and all the rest I left out.

Thanks to my Maui family: Tom and Lynn, Nancy, Joan, Melanie, Dick and Lauren, Jerry and Ani, Steve and Agatha, Owen, Chuck and Gail, Jim F., Mick F., Steven T., Mike K., Pat and Chris, Woody and Laura, Sammy and Kari, Michael and Amy, Mike Meldman and the gang at Makena who have made life on Maui even better!

Thanks to so many friends along the way who have shown me so much love. . . . I can't name you all but you know who you are: Alice and Sheryl, Jake and Ruth, Pat and Chris, Gerry and Heather, Jim, Elizabeth and Robin, Leslie, Peter and Tara, Herb and Julie, Elizabeth and Kim, Kristine, David, Bobs (all of you), Marty. And all my Buffalo colleagues, and the old Jews lunch club: Jerry, Dick, Tom, Larry, Jim, and we all miss Bud. And a big thank-you to all the Hollywood Vampires, wherever you are.

Thanks to all the chefs who shared the journey: Emeril, Daniel, Dean, Mark, Michel, Nobu and the HRC chefs, and all the rest. Congrats, it worked!

Tony, thanks for the opportunity to write this book . . . I think!

And finally, thank you to whoever created this world we live in, for dropping me in a part of the planet where I had the chance to live my dreams. So few humans come out of the womb in a place where they have shelter, food, and safety—where they can grow and be anything they can dream of. Thank you, thank you for this ultimate gift.